Managing Information Technology for Business Value

IT Best Practices Series

IT Best Practices Series

This book is published as a part of the IT Best Practices Series at Intel Press. Books in this series focus on the information technology challenges companies face in today's dynamic, Internet-based, business environment, as well as on the opportunities to improve IT performance and thereby gain a competitive edge. Some of the books explain proven strategies to help business executives and managers develop needed capabilities. Other books show technical professionals exactly how to implement specific solutions. The series overall reflects Intel's Best Practices Program, developed with leading researchers, vendors, and end-users to meet the challenges and opportunities described. These Best Practices recognize that companies must be agile and adaptable in the face of diverse and rapidly changing technologies, and, in particular, must be prepared and able to integrate multivendor, eBusiness tools.

For detailed information about these and other books, as well as announcements of forthcoming books in the series, visit the Intel Press Web site: *www.intel.com/intelpress.*

Managing Information Technology for Business Value

Practical Strategies for IT and Business Managers

Martin Curley

INTEL
PRESS

Publisher, Intel Press
Intel Corporation
2111 ME 25th Avenue JF3-330
Hillsboro, OR 97124-6159
E-mail: intelpress@intel.com

ISBN 0-9717861-7-8

Text printed on recycled paper

1 2 3 4 5 6 7 8 9 10

First printing, January 2004

To Ann.

Contents

5   IT Portfolios and Options   123

9   Putting It All Together   227

Foreword

During the late 1990s, it was conventional wisdom in the business community to expect the Internet to cause a fundamental change in business models and in the basis of competition. Investments in new companies and new information systems were made with little scrutiny. As the Internet boom collapsed, the pendulum of management sentiment swung to the opposite extreme, and many businesses reverted to treating information systems as a regrettable overhead expense.

As with most things in life, neither extreme produces good results.

Information technology continues to be one of the most powerful drivers of productivity in the worldwide economy. Information technology is central to the strategy and tactics of most aggressive enterprises, and it is fundamental to the day-to-day operations of virtually every organization. As a test of these assertions, I often ask managers to perform a thought experiment: simply visualize turning off the information systems that your organization uses today and consider the actions you would need to take to keep the organization functioning without IT solutions. It is eye-opening to estimate the additional people, time, materials, and services required to close the books, design a product, support a customer, ship a product, or even make a sales presentation.

Given the central role that information technology plays in the enterprise, it is critical that we apply systematic management practices as we lead the IT function. Structured management methods for IT are emerging over time in various parts of this complex discipline.

We have made the most progress in managing repetitive processes. Software development processes, for example, have been improving as the Software Engineering Institute's Capability Maturity Model, developed by Carnegie Mellon University, is applied more widely. Service management processes are improving as the Information Technology Infrastructure Library developed by the British Standards Institution becomes a common framework.

However, we have made much less progress in systematizing some of the most important decisions we make as IT leaders. We spend a large fraction of our energy prioritizing areas for investment and taking actions to reduce cost. And yet these are areas where we have had few systematic tools to help us.

Martin Curley tackles the problem of managing the IT function to produce maximum business value. Drawing on the experiences of Intel and other companies, Martin develops a systematic approach to identifying and prioritizing opportunities, reducing cost, and optimizing the business value of IT investments. The methods that Martin describes have been used successfully to improve the quality of discussion with CEOs and CFOs, to improve engagement with line-of-business executives, to improve the internal decision making processes within large IT organizations, and ultimately to deliver improved value from IT. I believe that these approaches can be used at any scale, whether considering the investments needed in a small business or startup or planning the enormous investments of a multinational corporation.

There is a long road between today's practices and a mature discipline of information technology management. *Managing IT for Business Value* is a significant milestone on that journey.

—Doug Busch, Vice-President and CIO, Intel Corporation

Acknowledgments

I would like to acknowledge the wonderful love and support of my wife Ann through the writing of this book and always. Ann held the fort while I wrote and also provided a steady stream of tea and snacks to keep my strength up. I would also like to thank our children Ciana, Clodagh, Aoibhe, and Liam for their constant inspiration and the joy they bring.

I appreciate the friendship and support of my parents, Brendan and Peig; my parents-in-law, Jim and Vera; and my siblings, Chris, Karen, Deirdre, and Aisling.

This book is a collection and synthesis of many ideas, concepts, and practices of a great many people. It is a first attempt to document and organize these practices into a format that can be useful to others who wrestle with trying to create and derive business value from IT. I thank the many business and IT professionals and researchers who have indirectly contributed to the content in this book.

I would like to thank all my colleagues at Intel IT for their ongoing initiatives in driving IT forward and to all whose work is commented on in the book. Despite the many pressures of his job as CIO, Doug Busch continued to generate an ongoing stream of great ideas as to how Intel could get more business value from IT.

Intel's Katie Haas, Craig Haydamack, Jay Hopman, Sandra Morris, Malvina Nisman, Molly Olson, Bryan Pruden, Brian Gorman, and Jimmy Wai deserve special mention for their ongoing work on different links in IT Business Value chain. Thanks to Jack Anderson, Colleen Snyder, and Jim Zurn for their help with assessment tools. I acknowledge colleagues on Intel CIO staff and the IT Innovation team for pushing the envelope.

I gratefully acknowledge researchers at the Massachusetts Institute of Technology's CISR (particularly, Peter Weill and Jeanne Ross), University of California, Irvine's Center for Research on Information Technology and Organizations (CRITO) (Ken Kraemer, *et al.*), Michigan State University (V. Sambamurthy), Carnegie Mellon University, and other universities for their excellent research and willingness to share. John Mooney of Pepperdine University is responsible for introducing me to the topic of IT business value as a part of my masters work at the Graduate School of Business in University College Dublin. I would like to thank Jim Kenneally for his detailed research on real options at Intel Ireland and for contributing content to this section in Chapter 5.

Dan Fineberg and Eric Heerwagen of the solutions marketing group at Intel initially encouraged me to turn my thinking about IT business value into a book. Also, thanks to Bob Allen, Nick Cherrie, Malvina Nisman, Fergus O'Scannlain, Paul Tallon, and Vish Viswanathan for their insightful reviews of early drafts of the book. John Fleming, Chuck House, Bryan Maizlish, and Bob Semple provided important reviews of later drafts.

I thank Rich Bowles, Intel Press publisher, and his team. Acknowledgments to David B. Spencer, Matthew Wangler, and Denise Myers for production, project management, and marketing support, respectively. Technical illustrator Richard Jevons brought order and meaning to the many figures in the book.

I would particularly like to thank David King, PhoebusGroup consultant and content manager for the Intel Press IT Best Practices series. His helpful suggestions and careful editing have helped make this a much better book. I also thank Susan King, the other half of Phoebus-Group, for her help with clarity, wordsmithing, and typesetting. Working productively online with David and Susan eight time zones away really demonstrates the business value of IT.

There are others who must be mentioned. Thanks to Matt McWha at the Working Council of CIOs, Curtis Robb and Brian Leinbach at Delta Technology, Elwood Coslett at Intel IT, Peter Rogers of Westminster City Council, and John Spangenberg at ING for providing solid case studies and examples. I profited from reviews of my financial projections from Helen Keelan and Bryan Pruden at Intel. Intel's David Fleming helped with key graphics.

Lastly, thanks to the man above for the many blessings in my life.

Martin Curley
December 2003

Chapter 1

Introduction

We cannot become what we need to be by remaining what we are.
—Max DePree, Author

Information Technology (IT) is one of those rare business resources that delivers more capability at a lower cost each year, providing the opportunity for businesses to do more with less. Driven for over 25 years by the relentless march of Moore's Law, IT has itself been a driver of growth and innovation, as enterprises have deployed IT solutions to automate processes, better utilize assets, and reduce costs. IT has supported product development and manufacturing and, more recently, has extended the reach of the enterprise to customers and trading partners. Dale Jorgenson (2001) emphasized the importance of Moore's Law when he said, "Despite differences in methodology and data sources, a consensus is building that the remarkable behavior of IT prices provides the key to the surge in economic growth."

IT and Business Value

IT's contribution to business value is becoming the core topic of conversation for business and IT managers. While it is widely recognized that IT can enable businesses to reduce costs and achieve strategic advantage, why is it that many businesses find it difficult to quantify the business value of IT? In a recent survey of over 400 CIOs (CIO Insight 2002), investigators found that 70 percent believed their metrics did not fully capture the value of IT and 46 percent indicated that they were *not at all* or were only *somewhat* confident in the accuracy of their own return on investment (ROI) measurements. Sadly, many business managers view their IT organizations as problem children with ever increasing spending demands and little visibility of real returns.

This lack of clarity about IT and business value is a problem for the industry, as IT organizations at many enterprises are increasingly being asked to partner with their business organizations both to provide uninterrupted service availability at an aggressively low cost and to attain a measurable source of competitive advantage for the company.

Managing IT for Business Value

In this book, I use the phrase *IT Business Value* to mean the business value contributions driven by IT investments. I intend to extend the definition of business value beyond productivity and to address how to quantify business value, choose the best IT investments, build an IT capability for delivering a sustainable competitive advantage, and manage for optimal IT business value.

Managing IT for Business Value introduces a number of important frameworks for managing and deploying IT. These frameworks are based on ongoing academic research and best practices in the field. It is hoped that the frameworks and case studies provided will equip IT organizations and business managers alike with the insight and tools required to optimize the business value of IT and deliver sustainable competitive advantage. The book makes sense of common acronyms such as TCO, ROI and emerging concepts such as BVI, TVO, TCC and explains what really matters in IT investment decision making.

In addition, I shall discuss how to deploy IT, not on an occasional, opportunistic basis, but in a systematic way that delivers an ongoing stream of accumulating value to the business. The systematic approach uses a portfolio management model and requires a mindset of consistently defining, designing, implementing, and measuring IT in business value terms.

One of my key recommendations is that IT managers use both the language of the business and appropriate business practices when managing IT for business value. For example, Delta Technology has adopted the terminology of air carrier practices when discussing their computing infrastructure with Delta Air Lines. Several oil companies are using an IT portfolio management approach developed by their colleagues in the exploration side of the business. Also, at Intel IT, we have adopted some of the techniques and methods developed to run our factories to run our IT utility.

The strategies and methodologies described in this book draw upon a combination of the best academic research and the best-known practices at Intel and other firms. They address the malaise in the IT industry today with respect to understanding and measuring IT's business value.

Enterprises typically lack both methodologies and discipline when analyzing potential and actual benefits delivered from IT. The Internet boom and its attendant increases in IT investment particularly accentuated this phenomenon. Now that economic realism has returned, and IT investment must compete with other types of capital investments, it is imperative that IT organizations improve both their investment decision making and the way their IT investments are managed.

IT Productivity Paradox

In 1987 Robert Solow, professor at MIT Sloan, stated, "I see computers everywhere except in the productivity statistics." This has become one of the most often quoted statements in the context of IT and business value. Numerous studies have addressed what has been called the *IT productivity paradox*, which postulates that despite enormous improvements in the underlying technology, the benefits of IT spending have not been found in the aggregate output statistics. Recent studies using a production function approach, which involves estimating a relationship between firm outputs (*i.e.*, revenue, stock price) and inputs (*i.e.*, capital, labor), have found positive and above average returns on IT investments.

One of the more significant of these studies is that of Brynjolfsson and Hitt (2002), who analyzed the effect of computerization on productivity and output growth. The study was based upon data gathered from 527 large U.S. firms over the years 1987 through 1994. Brynjolfsson and Hitt found that information technology makes a contribution to measured productivity and output growth in the short term. In other words, as shown in Figure 1.1, when examining year-over-year differences, the investigators found that improvements in measures of productivity were proportional to accrued investment in information systems. Brynjolfsson and Hitt also found the productivity and output contributions associated with computerization to be up to five times greater over longer periods of time—that is, when examining 5 to 7 year differences. I believe that

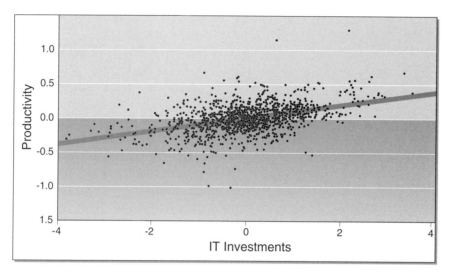

Source: Brynjolfsson (2003)
Figure 1.1 Productivity versus IT Investment

the higher contributions over longer periods of time are probably due to the compounding effect of information technology investments. Over a period of years, new IT investments can take advantage of a range of existing solutions, thus minimizing cost of introduction and time to ROI.

The results of the Brynjolfsson and Hitt study are important on two counts. Not only do they reveal a positive impact of IT spending on longer-term productivity, but the results also indicate that IT is significantly more productive when combined with organizational capital, such as when IT is combined with a work force that is both IT literate and equipped with significant business knowledge and acumen. A corollary to the findings of Brynjolfsson and Hitt is that large and time-consuming inputs are required for IT implementations, and these outputs are often omitted from return-on-investment (ROI) calculations. These costs are important to capture when preparing ROI analyses for new solution development and introduction.

More recently Dedrick, Gurbaxani, and Kraemer (2002) at the University of California, Irvine's Center for Research on Information Technology and Organizations (CRITO) published a comprehensive review of the empirical evidence of economic performance payoff for IT investments. This study concludes that the IT productivity paradox as first formulated has been effectively refuted. This report concludes that at both a firm and a country level, greater investment in IT is associated with greater productivity growth. Dedrick *et al.* also found that business practices around IT have a significant impact on the value extracted from IT investments.

In a study on executive perspectives on IT, Tallon, Kraemer, and Gurbaxani (2000) found that firms that aligned IT with business strategy experienced increased payoff from IT investment and that firms with higher levels of IT investments gained even greater payoff from the alignment. These two findings emphasize the importance of business and IT alignment and lead to a conclusion that firms over-investing in IT compared to their peer groups can achieve higher returns from IT investments.

These recent research studies substantiate the relationship between IT and business value, and they provide encouragement for those of us who manage IT. With the right metrics and methods, we should be able to optimize the return on IT investments. And that is what this book is all about.

Changing Measures of Success

Today, IT organizations are being asked to deliver both substantial cost savings and increasing business value—a difficult challenge, especially when coupled with rapidly increasing IT workloads and business pressure for IT-enabled innovation. In the past, IT organizations gauged success primarily in terms of their services; that is, they viewed higher availability and compliance with service-level agreements as key measures of success. Today, IT organizations are being driven to expand their success metrics to include those related to improving the bottom line. For example, they are reducing time-to-market for new products, increasing revenue, avoiding or minimizing factory capital purchases, and measuring improvements in employee productivity.

The title CIO is increasingly being interpreted by some CEOs as meaning *Chief Innovation Officer*. This is because IT is often seen as a key enabler for business innovation through enhancing and creating new products and services, transforming a business, and perhaps changing the landscape of an industry. However, as one CIO joked, CIO can also stand for *Career Is Over* if this mandate is not executed well. Leading-edge IT organizations are now working to develop IT solutions that systematically manage and harness innovation in business organizations with the promise of much higher yields from innovation-related activities.

However, along with the drive for innovation, CIOs and IT personnel are faced with another challenge: an increasing workload. In an article entitled "Sidestepping the New IT Crisis," Mark Andreesen, developer of the original Mosaic browser and founder of Opsware, captured this point sweetly when he said, "The IT function is the most thankless, cumbersome function faced by Fortune 2000 companies, where your work only gets noticed when things break, you're viewed as a major source of expenses, and your workload has tripled in the past year" (Andreesen 2002).

When the opportunity to innovate is pitted against an increasingly exhausting workload, it is no wonder that CIOs and IT employees are under significant stress. In an uncertain business environment, the CIO, the IT staff, and business managers need to manage IT proactively to avoid their own burnout and failure. Limited resources require more precise allocation processes, and difficult times demand that the business value of IT is optimized.

As shown in Figure 1.2, the challenge that CIOs face is to find the balance point when weighing both investments in innovation and business value against increased workload and attempts to reduce cost. Applying standard metrics and methods for forecasting and measuring actual business value delivered will help. The introduction of such practices will both initially identify previously unrecognized payoffs for IT spending and lay the foundation for delivering increased IT business value.

A strategic partnership between IT managers and business executives is key to realizing business value.

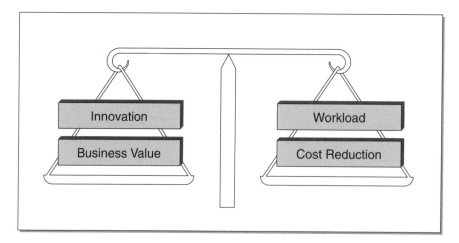

Figure 1.2 The New Challenge

Moore's Law

In 1965, Gordon Moore was director of research and development for Fairchild Semiconductor, a subsidiary of Fairchild Camera and Instrument Corporation. Moore (1965) wrote and presented a paper that contained a memorable observation.

Moore plotted available data—just four annual data points for 1962 through 1965—showing the number of components (*i.e.,* transistors) that could be integrated in a single silicon device. Moore noted that each year's new chip contained roughly twice the capacity of its predecessor.

If this trend were to continue, Moore reasoned, then computing power would rise exponentially over relatively brief periods of time. The trend would enable new devices such as personal computers. The trend that Gordon Moore observed, now known as *Moore's Law,* has continued unabated for nearly 40 years and is still remarkably accurate.

Subsequent revisions of Moore's Law say that computing performance will double every eighteen months or so at less or equal cost than previous capability. Moore's Law has been one of the core drivers of global economic growth over the past few decades.

Business Practices for Optimizing IT Business Value

To help manage these difficult challenges and to optimize the value delivered from information technology I suggest using a four-pronged strategy. IT and business managers must:

- Manage the IT Budget
- Manage for IT Business Value
- Manage the IT Capability
- Manage IT Like a Business

In the following chapters, I introduce capability maturity frameworks that describe a sequence of improvements for each of these four strategies. The simultaneous and sustained adoption of increasingly mature practices can lead to an optimization of sustainable long-term business value from information technology investments.

Capability Maturity Framework

Researchers at the Software Engineering Institute (SEI) at Carnegie Mellon University developed the idea of a capability maturity model as a part of their overall thinking about how to improve the software development process. Stripped of its software development content, the model provides a framework for my thinking about the maturity of nearly any process. Shown in Figure 1.3 are the five levels of maturity that I use: ad hoc, repeatable, defined, managed, and optimized.

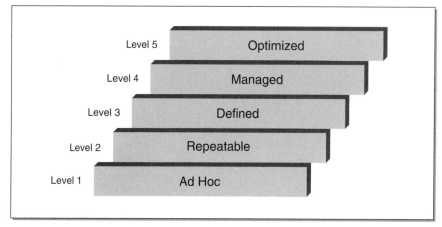

Source: Intel, modified from SEI CMM

Figure 1.3 Generic Capability Maturity Framework

I use capability maturity frameworks (CMFs) for organizing my thinking about IT and business value issues. If I study an IT process and discover that it is undefined and random, I don't aim to optimize it; instead, I think about the next level of maturity: how the process can be made repeatable. I encourage you to identify the current maturity level of your own firm's IT processes using the CMFs that I present and see the CMFs as the steps you must take to provide greater business value for IT investments.

Managing the IT Budget

The old adage that you have to spend money to make money certainly applies to the IT organization. IT organizations must spend money to deliver current and future value. Managing the IT budget is crucial in difficult economic times when there is persistent pressure on IT budgets. In fact, such conditions can be the forcing function for driving a significant industry-wide increase in IT business value practices because in times of economic slowdown, many IT organizations are able to fuel new innovations and solutions only by aggressively reducing the costs of existing operations and services.

Chapter 2 describes a set of practices and tools that can be systematicallty used to manage the IT budget. These practices include approaches such as service-level adjustment, supplier negotiation, and the nurturing of so-called disruptive technologies that can deliver new or equivalent services often at much lower cost than existing products or services. Chapter 2 also explores different approaches for expanding IT funding options.

Managing for IT Business Value

Chapters 3, 4, and 5 describe an integrated approach based on taking a benefits-realization perspective, in which IT investments are viewed and managed, not just as technology projects, but as projects that are expected to deliver overall business benefits. The benefits-realization approach includes adopting core business practices, including basic ROI measures supported by enterprise-wide investment coordination, business case discipline, continuous portfolio management, re-prioritization, and increasingly sophisticated investment performance analyses. In this context, I introduce a basic maturity framework for managing IT business value. This framework organizes the key practices and provides an appropriate sequence for their adoption.

Managing and Measuring the IT Capability

Chapters 6 and 7 explore how to manage the IT organization's capability—that is, what the IT organization and information technology can collectively do for the firm. Managing the IT capability on an ongoing basis is crucial to delivering sustainable competitive advantage from information technology. This effort demands a systematic approach to managing IT assets, the IT value chain that creates business value from IT, and the core competencies that the IT organization requires to deliver IT business value.

An important premise of this book is that sustainable competitive advantage from IT comes not from individual "stove-pipe" solutions, but from an IT capability that is especially effective in delivering new strategic applications and delivering them faster and better than competing companies. This concept is based on original research by Beath and Ross (2001) on achieving sustainable competitive advantage from IT. Chapter 7 addresses the issue of IT capability assessment and measurement. It also provides metrics that have been proven to help an IT organization realize systematic capability improvements.

Managing IT Like a Business

I believe that IT needs to be managed like any other successful business. This concept is covered in Chapter 8. Running IT like a business means that the IT staff must treat their customers professionally, that account managers should make sure that customers get what they want, and that accurate chargeback methods are implemented to manage demand and ensure that customers pay fairly for what they use. Chapter 8 discusses IT governance—that is, specification of decision rights and accountabilities for IT spending and the desirable use of IT in the firm. These governance principles are the same as those used by any successful business.

Note that while I advocate the businesslike management of the IT organization, I do not advocate running IT as a for-profit business. The drive for IT profitability could easily cause a conflict by inappropriately superseding the goal of profitability of the enterprise as a whole. The IT organization and the business organization need to collaborate to optimize IT's contribution to overall business value.

Putting It All Together

Finally, Chapter 9 describes the integrated approach that forms the basis of this book: managing IT to deliver business value. Traditionally, IT business value has been loosely defined as the contribution IT makes to help the business to reach its strategic goals and objectives. However, company executives and shareholders are increasingly asking for more specific evidence that business value improvements have occurred. At the end of the day, IT investments are of value only if they deliver increased business and shareholder value.

Accruing IT Business Value

The value that IT delivers to a firm should be fundamental to everything that the IT organization does. Firms typically realize value from different IT investments, including the following:

- Automating and optimizing existing processes for incremental improvements in productivity, speed, or quality

- Re-engineering core processes for improvements in productivity and efficiency

- Transforming the enterprise with new processes and organizational capabilities to drive new growth

- Embedding IT in products and service offerings to provide a better, higher-value product or service

A study reported by Hartman (2002) provides estimates of the differential magnitude of these investment choices. Based on a survey of 450 companies, Hartman found that investments in optimizing existing processes returned 10 to 15 percent in cost savings. Investments aimed at improving core processes resulted in 2 percent to 3 percent improvement in operating margins. Projects that transformed the enterprise with new capabilities typically returned 10 times the IT investment.

Hartman's research did not report on the returns from embedding more IT into the enterprise's core products and services. This was done by Otis Elevators, for example, to enable proactive maintenance through their information systems. Otis embedded IT in each of their elevators, so that service engineers are automatically dispatched with the right spare parts when elevators report emerging problems.

Companies that embed IT in their offerings, as Otis has done, usually have multiple objectives. Commonly-expected returns for this kind of investment include improved quality, more efficient operations, and closer communication with customers.

How IT Creates Value

Crucial to maximizing IT business value is understanding how IT increases value. In fact some analysts claim that IT itself has no intrinsic value, but when it is coupled with organizations and business processes it can have dramatic impact.

John Mooney, Ken Kraemer, and Vijay Gurbaxani of CRITO at UC Irvine have developed a useful model that takes a process view of IT-value generation. Mooney *et al.* (1994) argue that firms achieve business value from IT through its impact on intermediate business processes, which comprise the wide range of activities in the firm's value chain as well as management of information processing, control, coordination, communication, and knowledge.

Mooney et al. define three value creation mechanisms, which they call *effects*, as follows:

■ *Automational effects* refer to the efficiency perspective of value deriving from the role of IT as a capital asset being substituted for labor or capital assets. Within this dimension value results primarily from impacts such as labor savings, productivity improvements, and cost reductions.

■ *Informational effects* emerge primarily from IT's capacity to collect, store, process, and disseminate information. Following these effects, value accrues from improved decision quality, decreased use of resources, enhanced organizational effectiveness, better quality, and employee empowerment.

■ *Transformational effects* refer to the value deriving from IT's ability to facilitate and support process innovation and transformation. The business value associated with these effects may be manifested as improved revenue, improved responsiveness, downsizing, and product enhancement as a result of re-engineered processes and redesigned organizational structures.

Finally, consider that while in a free market the value of a product or service is typically a reflection of the market price, within an enterprise its value may often be a negotiated convention—that is, it might be measured by perception of value delivered and not only or even not at all measured by an ROI analysis. In delivering and quantifying IT business value, firms need to balance both quantitative and qualitative measures to determine the real and the perceived value. Perception is reality!

IT Investment and Shareholder Return

The objective of IT business value research is to relate IT investment to shareholder return. Some of the more progressive users of IT, such as ING, are starting to communicate this kind of information to shareholders in their investor relations communications. As part of an overall business investment strategy, ING strives to yield a sustained positive return from every euro invested in IT. IT is regarded as a value driver rather than a cost. This strategy has two driving forces: one is that IT is ING's second biggest expense category after labor costs; the other, and more important motivation, is that IT is seen as crucial for future revenue growth and profitability in its core business area of financial services.

New empirical data are starting to appear that makes the connection between IT investment and shareholder return.

A recent research project, conducted jointly by IBM and ING and based on a sample of eighty of the world's largest insurance companies, studied the relationship between IT spending and company performance. Researchers looked at measures such as profitability, growth, and capital efficiency. A category populated by just seven companies, called "intelligent growers," delivered the greatest shareholder value over the investment period, which was 1996–2002. The joint IBM and ING team offered the following observations and conclusions:

- The best performing companies had lower cost bases than other companies, but higher spending on IT. Researchers described the companies as having higher "IT intensity."

- The best performing companies had found ways to spend more on IT development and less on IT maintenance.

- The best performing companies were more likely to use outsourcing as a part of their IT deployment strategy.

Other studies have shown that well-managed IT has a positive impact on shareholder value. Interestingly, ING also found similar patterns when applying the same analysis to its internal business units. Higher performing business units generally had higher IT intensity and spent relatively more on IT development and less on IT maintenance. Following ING's policy of providing as much transparency on its operations to stakeholders as possible, this research study was the subject of an article in a May 2003 edition of its shareholders' bulletin.

Key Strategies for Managing IT for Business Value

A few key strategies underpin this book. If IT organizations are to survive and thrive, they must cultivate sustainable economic models. IT strategy must be in precise alignment with overall business strategy. Year-over-year investment creates momentum that is extremely helpful when moving through tougher times. Finally, a steady focus on IT competencies and capabilities is crucial to success.

Sustainable Economic Models for IT Organizations

Businesses and IT organizations alike are looking for new and sustainable economic models for their IT budgets. Some firms are struggling to avoid a *runaway train* scenario in which IT consumption is accelerating rapidly with little obvious business value to show for the increased spending. Unless this supply/demand equilibrium is managed properly, IT organizations can find themselves in what McKinsey consultants have called the *abyss* (*cf.* Dempsey *et al.* 1997). An IT group is in the abyss when all of the IT budget is consumed with maintaining existing applications, leaving no funds available for future investments. This description shows all the facets of an unmanaged situation.

An enterprise needs to have a proactive and explicit strategy for finding a sustainable economic model for its IT products and services. Such a strategy requires a structured multipronged approach that includes precise costing models, continuous cost reduction programs, automation strategies, and the creative exploitation of disruptive technologies.

Along with the pressure to improve IT investment return, there is also strong pressure to reduce costs. Line-of-business managers know about Moore's Law and have witnessed dramatic improvements in computing performance along with reductions in computing hardware cost. They wonder, "Why aren't the cost savings that Moore's Law implies passed on to us?" Of course, IT managers know that the ravenous appetite of organizations for more processing, storage, and communication quickly balances performance improvements and that the cost of managing systems is not regulated by Moore's Law. Thus, total cost of ownership (TCO), which is the sum of direct and indirect costs of IT, continues to be a very important discussion issue for business and IT managers.

Harvard Business School professor Clayton Christensen (1997) coined the term *disruptive technologies* to describe emerging low-cost, low-performance technologies that grow quickly to be low-cost, high-performance alternatives that challenge incumbent suppliers. The nurturing and rapid deployment of disruptive technologies can help bend cost curves to enable a sustainable IT economic model in the face of expanding demand for IT services. Robust processes for assimilating high technology are needed, and adoption timing is particularly crucial when introducing disruptive technologies.

One important strategy for allowing businesses to see where they are spending their IT budget is the use of chargeback models to map financial impacts to an IT customer's IT consumption choices. Providing this visibility can give businesses more control over their IT spending. A costing tool that provides insight into the cost competitiveness of IT products and services is also essential. Like the cobbler's child who has no shoes, some IT organizations are entirely absorbed in automating and adding value to enterprise business processes, while neglecting to use technology to automate and streamline their own IT processes and systems. Thus, it is becoming a crucial tactic to take a systems approach linked with an automation strategy for IT processes and systems.

Benchmarking, the systematic comparison of IT quality and costs among competitors, provides data that enable each business to have a deeper understanding of IT cost and helps to build credibility with IT's customers. Benchmarking also provides a mechanism to implement continuous improvement for the products and services that IT provides. Benchmarking allows businesses and IT organizations make the right trade-offs between performance and cost in achieving a sustainable IT economic model.

The ongoing tracking and reporting of key performance metrics is crucial in establishing credibility with customers and managing for business value. IT dashboards, which incorporate principles from the balanced scorecard, are becoming increasingly prevalent and, when used consistently, can drive key actions for improving value delivered.

Strategic Alignment with the Business

A strategic alignment between IT and the business is a crucial factor in business value generation. Good strategic alignment implies a virtuous circle, that is, a positive bi-directional relationship between IT and business strategy. In today's world, business strategy relies upon a robust IT infrastructure and applications, and IT, in turn, often directly supports the business strategy. Within this context, IT and business alignment should be measured not only by the extent to which IT supports the business, but also by the extent to which business strategy capitalizes on IT capabilities.

The previously mentioned research by Tallon, Kraemer, and Gurbaxani (2000) produced two interesting findings: first, close alignment between IT and business strategy was beneficial and increased the payoff from IT investments. Second, increasing alignment beyond a certain point led to a decrease in payoffs from IT investments, primarily due to a loss in agility and flexibility.

IT innovations must be accompanied by innovation in business and management practices. In a survey of 420 IT professionals reported by

Cosgrove (2001), over 48 percent of those surveyed claimed that their largest IT initiatives were not directly linked with their own organization's business strategy. With IT spending often running between four and eight percent of corporate revenue, this strategic dissonance between business strategy and IT spending can seriously impact the financial performance of the business.

Effective IT management and planning practices can help improve IT and business strategy. A deeper level of alignment can be achieved by repeatedly validating the IT organization's performance against the firm's values.

At the core of managing for business value is an understanding of the key principles of return on investment and investment return. The typical enterprise has many great ideas and existing products and services competing for relatively small IT budgets that are, on average, four percent of company revenues. Firms and IT organizations should use an integrated set of financial measures to help make the best IT investment decisions. A comparison of competing investments should at least include net present value, internal rate of return, and the payback period of each investment.

The Value of Measurement

Andy Grove has said, "If you can't measure it, you can't manage it." The ability to measure business value is key to being able to maximize or optimize business value. Intel has developed a tool called the IT Business Value Dial Map to identify key business variables and the monetary value of an incremental improvement in these values. This best known method (BKM) lowers the barriers to creating ROIs and helps with the quantification process. Subsequent chapters discuss such methods to help measure both tangible and intangible benefits and costs. This is important, as many of the benefits from IT are intangible benefits.

Associated with a lack of understanding of financial metrics for IT investments is another—perhaps even more fundamental—issue: discipline. As corporate revenues were growing in the early nineties, so did IT budgets; in fact, in many cases it was the increased IT spending that was fueling the growth. However, during the Internet boom in the late nineties, many firms abandoned all discipline and accelerated IT spending without rigorous financial justification. A "battle for eyeballs" ensued until industry in general realized that winning eyeballs alone does not directly translate into increased revenue and net profits.

A 2003 survey referenced by the Working Council of Chief Financial Officers found that 85 percent of companies had a formal ROI process.

However, most companies admitted to "just going through the motions," with 88 percent reporting infrequent or inconsistent usage of the formal ROI process. Increasing pressure on firms to perform will undoubtedly change this dysfunctional pattern. Firms that are actively and consistently managing IT's ROI will be more likely to achieve advantage.

Chapter 3 introduces basic techniques followed by successively more sophisticated practices that help to maximize ongoing IT business value. These practices include TCO monitoring, firm-wide investment coordination, and continuous portfolio management and re-prioritization. It also introduces an investment justification continuum that begins with managing IT options, proceeds to calculating ROIs, and ends with realized benefits through active benefits realization management.

Analyzing the IT Investment

Because of the vastly superior price and performance improvements in IT relative to other assets in the business environment, many opportunities exist to deploy IT to solve business problems. However, along with the opportunities are some constraints or limits, such as the amount of available capital, the number IT staff and their expertise, and the amount of management attention available to IT initiatives.

Another constraint that is often forgotten is the organization's capacity to assimilate change. When justifying new IT investments, an inertia must be overcome: the cost of maintaining the existing IT application portfolio and infrastructure. The technology that runs the business on a daily basis also consumes the lion's share of most organizations' IT budgets. Typically, only a small budget is reserved for new strategic innovations, but, paradoxically, innovation can occur where the biggest opportunity lies, as it is often the implementation of new strategic ideas that delivers the biggest benefit to a business.

What I call investment inertia, Delta Air Lines calls the *IT Operating Tail.* IT managers at Delta have observed that the cost of designing and implementing a system is significantly less than the cost of actually operating and maintaining the system. Figure A.1 shows Delta's view of this effect.) The IT operating tail raises the barriers for investment in innovation and implementation of new IT systems even higher. Expenses tied to the IT operating tail can be attacked with continuous cost reduction projects and well-disciplined decommissioning of older applications and infrastructure. Bringing obsolete technology to its end of life is critical to freeing up money for new investments, especially in a business environment where IT budgets are often tied to a percentage of business revenue.

The ability to choose and rapidly realize the right IT investments is becoming increasingly important. Evaluating competing IT investments is a difficult process, and few firms have robust methods to deal with this process. Unfortunately, decisions are often made on the basis of "he or she who shouts loudest." Because new IT investments are the lifeblood of future competitive advantage and growth, it is becoming increasingly important to use a data-driven approach to make the right investment decisions. Assessing investment alignment with business strategy and analyzing a portfolio inventory of IT activities are activities requiring explicit methods. Also needed are tools that create flexible prioritizations of IT opportunities and help de-politicize IT decision making.

Managing IT Options

IT investments have characteristics that are similar to financial options. The low initial cost of a financial option allows investors to defer making a larger investment decision until more information is available. In a similar fashion, IT investors can make a number of relatively small IT investments and reevaluate them as more business and technical information becomes available. The IT organization and the business as a whole can win by behaving like a venture capitalist who bets that one or two winners will pay for all the losers and then some.

A recent empirical study at Intel Ireland found strong support for the intuition that IT projects include considerable optional value. Chapter 5 explains how to take an options approach that improves the value of managerial flexibility.

Intel IT's Business Value Index Methodology

Another example of an options approach is the *business value index* (BVI) methodology that Intel IT developed to facilitate the process of assessing the potential value of future investments and to allow a comparison of relative potential values for a collection of potential investments. The methodology assesses the attractiveness of an investment along three vectors: business value, IT efficiency, and financial attractiveness. The BVI introduces a common language and vocabulary for discussing investments as well as a mechanism to prioritize investments based on the current business environment.

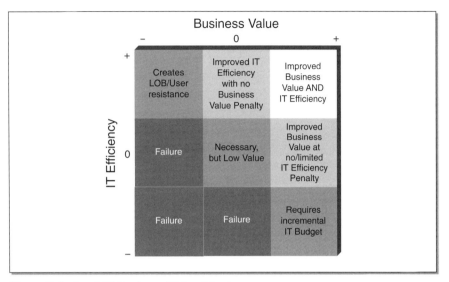

Figure 1.4 Intel IT Business Value Matrix

Figure 1.4 shows two of the BVI dimensions in a 3 by 3 table contrasting business value and IT efficiency. *Business value* measures the corporate impact of a project on Intel's business strategy and priorities; *IT efficiency* measures how well the investment will utilize or enhance the existing infrastructure. This framework was introduced by Intel's CIO Doug Busch in 2001 to help drive a new mindset in IT investment decision making at Intel. A third dimension, not shown in Figure 1.4, is financial attractiveness, a criterion that measures the level of investment and net present value of a project.

The BVI produces an output that provides key decision support to the investment process and enables an ongoing winnowing-out process. In this scheme, an IT solution typically moves through a standard pipeline with various stages such as concept, requirements, prototyping, development, and so on. The pipeline is "stage-gated," that is, the IT investment is funded in incremental stages, with subsequent funding contingent upon meeting designated critical success factors for each stage. As the IT investment moves through the pipeline, its BVI is tracked to allow acceleration, deceleration, and continuance or discontinuance of a particular investment.

Tools such as the BVI become increasingly important as the business value of IT comes under more and more scrutiny. In tough economic times, business leaps of faith in IT investment without analysis and supporting data will become increasingly rare.

IT Competency and Capabilities

While there is much debate about whether IT can provide sustainable competitive advantage, few would argue against the competitive necessity of continuous IT investment and innovation. From a resource-based view, what enhances competitiveness is an IT organization's capability to develop and deploy IT *solutions* that address business problems—not just the organization's ability to field new *applications*. A firm's IT customer care or inventory management applications are potentially reproducible at competing firms and may even share the same packaged software foundation. The IT organization's capability to field IT solutions strategically can be inimitable. Thus, businesses gain competitive advantage when they invent and implement strategic applications more quickly, with better functionality, and with greater cost effectiveness than their competitors.

A great deal of research evidence relates the structure and business practices of firms to the payoff from IT investments. For example, Weill (1992) found that the quality of a firm's management and its commitment to IT enhances the contribution of IT investments to firm performance.

The Business of IT

As IT organizations evolve—with their motivation for deploying IT shifting from cost savings and automation, on to productivity and end user empowerment, and now to business value creation—they need to ask how all of the resources of the IT organization can be marshaled to deliver maximum business value.

I have synthesized and adapted original work by Ross, Beath, Goodhue and Sambamurthy to produce a model of the Business of IT, which is shown in Figure 1.5. This model can be very useful in developing strategies for focusing resources to maximize IT value. Figure 1.5 shows an IT value chain is the set of interrelated processes that are necessary to create IT business value through solutions delivery. At a macro view, the IT value chain could be described as having three core processes and competencies: *innovation, solutions delivery,* and *product and services provisioning.* Innovation is about dreaming up the solution, and solutions delivery means building the solution. Product and services provisioning refers to delivering and supporting the solution.

IT organizations need to proactively manage the IT value chain to deliver value, as shown in Figure 1.5. Building and tuning IT organizational competencies in these areas should result in an improved capability to deploy IT strategically.

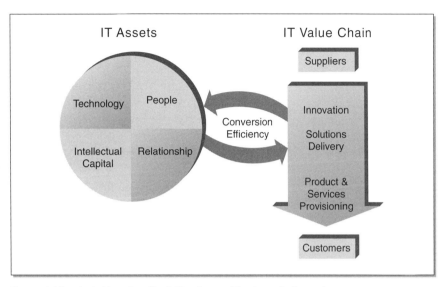

Source: Intel—adapted from Ross/Beath/Goodhue and Sambamurthy/Agawarl

Figure 1.5 The Business of IT

The business of IT is to provide the products and services that directly support business processes, customers, and suppliers. In the process of business value creation, IT assets are leveraged on an ongoing basis by the key processes in the value chain. The primary assets of an IT organization are its people, technology, intellectual capital, customers, and its relationship to the company's business. These assets need to be developed, sized, and scaled to enable the organization to anticipate, respond, and meet future business requirements.

■ A well developed *people asset* consists of a motivated skilled staff that provide and service world class infrastructure and solutions and consistently solve business problems and capitalize on business opportunities using IT.

■ The *technology asset* is the suite of sharable technical platforms and databases that enable system and application integration and make IT applications cost-effective. A technology architecture specifies the primary components for the firm's infrastructure and applications and establishes standards that limit the range of technologies that the IT staff must support. Increasingly, computing components can be integrated appropriately to provide the required level of service at the right cost.

∎ The *intellectual capital asset* is the collection of applications, solutions, data, information, and knowledge supported by the infrastructure, within which core business processes, know-how, and information flows are embodied. As a firm matures and grows further tacit knowledge and unstructured business processes are codified, structured, and hardwired into the firm's applications suite, databases, and information flows.

∎ The *customer relationship asset* is a measure of the strength of the relationship between IT and its customers, who are primarily other members of the firm. Does the IT staff have high level of trust and joint accountability for delivering business value from IT investments? Does the IT organization have credibility with the business and does it know enough about the business opportunities and requirements to match emerging technologies to these areas? Top management must be involved in establishing IT priorities, the IT posture and business value objectives that set the tone for a cooperative IT–business relationship.

Chapter 6 identifies in greater detail the strategies and approaches for managing these assets and the IT value chain to optimize business value. For example, deployment of new solutions to thousands of globally distributed employees requires an efficient, cohesive process. Few productivity breakthroughs or enhancements are more immediately apparent than a timely and efficient hardware or solution deployment. In contrast, a poorly executed deployment significantly impacts business value through increased downtime, productivity impacts, lags, and so on.

IT Organizing Logic

As CIOs wrestle with the tensions of increasing cost reduction pressure and increased organizational workload, they are also expected to provide leadership in forming business strategy and generating business value. The conventional logic of IT organization design is limiting, because positions IT as an effective internal services provider and not as a strategic differentiator. As businesses position their IT organization as a platform for agility and business innovation, new IT organizational logic and models are emerging. While no single correct IT organizational design exists, I provide guidelines for organizing to optimize for business value. In this context, IT organizations also need to act as generators of strategic options for the business as a whole.

The process of transforming an IT organization to meet the challenges of the new business environment is non-trivial and requires top IT and business management commitment and clear strategy and tactics. For example, speed and agility are increasingly desired characteristics of IT organizations. However, the definition of speed is changing; once defined as time-to-project-delivery, speed is now defined as time-to-benefits-capture.

A number of different approaches can be used systematically to improve the capability of an IT organization to apply IT strategically. Such systematic improvement requires an explicit proactive strategy, including using generic principles and tools for high performing organizations and using IT industry-specific best known methods. Chapter 9 describes approaches that help transform IT organizations to adopt a business value posture. Key tactics include inculcating IT business value management into IT culture and ensuring that core IT processes are singular, understood, consistent, and scalable.

Finally, a new organizational form for IT is emerging, which CSC research services call *fusion*, where the IT organization is fused with an operational function, and the CIO has both IT and business operating responsibility. For example, Microsoft's CIO Rick Devenuti has responsibility for both IT and business operations at Microsoft, and the CIO of First Active, a national bank in Ireland, has responsibility for both IT and business operations.

IT Governance

Few would argue that IT organizations would benefit from taking a more businesslike perspective, adapting and adopting standard business practices to improve performance, effectiveness, and efficiency. Chapter 8 describes an approach and best known methods for doing this.

Perhaps the most pivotal business practice than can be adopted is that of governance, which can be defined as the accountability framework and decision rights for the deployment and use of IT in a firm. Long-term IT business value needs to be examined in the context of IT governance, and decisions about IT governance have a strong impact on the stream of value delivered to a firm through IT.

IT governance, as defined by Peter Weill (2002), of MIT Sloan Center for Information Systems Research (CISR), includes the following areas:

■ Principles—What is the primary role of IT in the firm?

■ Infrastructure—What IT resources are shared and what ought the sequence of further investments be?

- Architecture—Does a uniform IT architecture exist and at what level of maturity?

- Business application needs—What applications are required and what are their priorities?

- Investment and prioritization—How much should the IT organization spend and when?

The approach taken to each of these governance areas will have a pivotal impact on an IT organization's ability to deliver future business value. For example, when firm-wide shared infrastructure is a high priority, that infrastructure can often provide a stable platform for launching new strategic IT initiatives more quickly and with smaller investments. It is also critical to recognize that investments in IT must be coupled with investments in organizational assets through practices such as process redesign, training, and employee empowerment.

Ground-breaking research by Weill and Woodham (2002) at MIT CISR found that an effective IT governance structure is the single most important predictor of getting value from IT. Weill and Woodham hypothesized that firms achieving returns above the industry average from IT investments must be making consistently better IT-related decisions.

To understand effective IT governance, Weill and Woodham studied the use of IT in 40 large multi-business-unit firms in the USA and Europe and then analyzed the relationship between IT governance and financial performance of 24 of those firms using both interviews and questionnaires. They found that the governance patterns of the top-performing firms were linked to the performance measure on which the firm excelled (*e.g.,* return on assets (ROA) growth, market capitalization growth), in contrast with the typical firm where IT governance followed generally accepted guidelines for corporate governance. Designing an effective IT governance structure, however, is not trivial; it requires a clear understanding of the firm's core strategic intent and the harmonizing of many competing forces in a large organization.

Many successful IT organizations are adapting business processes that are used to manage product development, manufacturing, and even sales functions. They are also adopting newer standard business practices to help with managing the IT function. For example, the growing use of balanced score cards and CIO dashboards as mechanisms for ongoing performance management leads to more focused discussions of IT business value and to a more aggressive emphasis on continuous improvement.

■ Summary

In this introductory chapter, I have provided an overview of this book and identified from research the real opportunities to use IT for competitive advantage. I also lamented the lack of business practices and discipline that hinder IT organizations and business organizations alike from optimizing business value. In subsequent chapters, I explain how four strategies can optimize business value driven by careful IT investments. Those four strategies are:

- Manage for IT business value to maximize benefits such as corporate profitability and growth with existing and future IT investments

- Manage the IT budget to enable continuous cost reduction and the flexibility to shift budgeted funds from low-yield investments to investments that will deliver competitive advantage

- Manage the IT capability to enable sustainable competitive advantage to be delivered from IT

- Manage IT like a business so that winning business practices enable IT organizations to succeed in their missions.

Chapter 2

Managing the IT Budget

*Management without leadership leads to mediocrity;
leadership without management leads to catastrophe.*
—Anonymous

One of the greatest challenges facing businesses and IT organizations is the management of the IT budget. In some cases, containment is a more accurate term than management, as IT's leadership struggles to meet increasing demand for information services. In the extreme, some firms are struggling to avoid a runaway train scenario where IT consumption increases rapidly, and yet they see little obvious business value to be gained from the increased spending. Unless the supply-and-demand equilibrium is managed properly, IT organizations can find themselves in what McKinsey consultants (Dempsey *et al.,* 1997) called the abyss. When all of the IT budget is consumed to maintain existing applications and no budget is available for future investments, the enterprise has gone into the abyss.

Enterprises need to have a proactive and explicit strategy for finding a sustainable economic model for IT products and services. This strategy must include an aggressive unit cost reduction component, perhaps a set of consumption reporting controls, a method for identifying rapidly maturing low-cost technologies (*i.e.,* disruptive technologies), and a mechanism for shifting saved money into investment budgets.

Inertia, often an unmentioned or overlooked part of IT investment justifications, is the root source of many budgetary problems. If we examine the typical enterprise IT budget today, we would likely find that the majority of the budget is spent on keeping the business running with existing applications and infrastructure. Only a small portion of the budget can be appropriated for new strategic ideas. But, ironically, the biggest opportunities are found when putting new ideas into action.

Moreover, the IT budget in a firm can either exhibit the strengths of a virtuous circle or the symptoms of a vicious circle.

- A vicious circle emerges when IT organizations do not invest in developing future IT solutions. The steadily increasing demand for IT services will lead to a scenario where the entire IT budget is consumed by what I call a "keep the business running" mentality.

- A virtuous circle exists when an IT organization successfully develops new solutions that deliver new capabilities at a lower cost. Cost-saving success reinforces itself by providing more funding that can be diverted to further investment in new solutions.

The vicious circle must be avoided. New strategic ideas that will drive the biggest benefit for the business going forward cannot be the investments that receive the lowest amount of funding. If firms do not invest in future-based IT solutions, they are likely to lose competitive advantage. How can IT organizations overcome the inertia that requires the budget to keep existing products and services operational? I believe that firms need to reduce costs aggressively while allotting more of their IT budgets for investment in new IT solutions—solutions that are far more likely to produce strategic value. In other words, firms must strive to develop a virtuous circle.

IT Budgets

IT budgets expand or contract as a percentage of a firm's revenue and they also depend upon the general business environment, the dynamics of a particular industry, and the business objectives of the individual firm. Figure 2.1 shows fluctuations in IT spend as a percentage of revenue over the years 1997 to 2003. These data were collected by the META Group (2003) in 33 countries and 24 industry sectors. META Group sampled companies considered to be technology leaders. Companies in the sample included IBM, HP, Lucent, Dell, Microsoft, Alcoa,

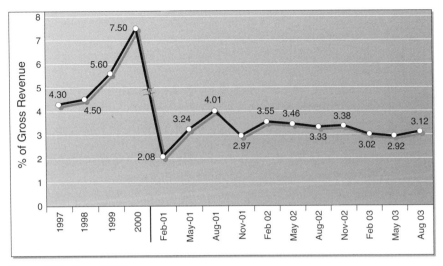

Source: META Group (2003)

Figure 2.1 IT Spend as a Percentage of Revenue

American Express, Cadence, and Cathay Pacific. IT spending for these companies reached a high of 7.5 percent of gross revenue in 1999 as companies invested heavily in new web-related technologies and plunged to a low of 2 percent in February of 2001 as the dot-com bubble burst. As a rule of thumb, firms with progressive IT agendas spend 4 to 5 percent of their revenue on IT.

The significant over-investment in IT in 1999 and 2000 was influenced by two events. First, many companies decided to replace legacy systems and solutions to mitigate Y2K risks. Second, the irrational exuberance of the Internet revolution led companies to near panic buying of servers and systems to quickly web-enable businesses. By late 2000, organizations found it difficult to absorb additional technology. The dip in spending in the following two years was driven by the need for enterprises to assimilate the major IT systems in which they had invested. Finally, worsening global economic conditions contributed to a curtailing of IT spending.

The increase in IT spend in 1999/2000 is not unlike a similar spike in spending when the IBM PC reached the market in 1981. Waves of spend are often followed by troughs of retrenchment. Disruptive technology breakthroughs are often the cause of these irregularities and it is not easy for IT managers to navigate the waves and troughs.

Technology Hype Cycle

Waves and troughs are known in the IT industry as the *technology hype cycle*. As described by the Gartner Group, when a new technology or solution emerges, unrealistic expectations are set by a mixture of marketing hyperbole and high user expectations for a new solution to an existing problem. Typically, aggressive initial spending is driven by the hyperbole and high user expectations. In most cases, however, the first-to-market products are immature and users become disappointed or disillusioned. The trough of disillusionment follows and spending typically declines in proportion to user disappointment. Finally, a plateau of productivity is reached when the technology matures and products begin to deliver real value, meet user needs, and are offered at sensible price points.

A great example of technology hype cycle is eLearning. Online training offerings flourished in the late 90s as the Internet and rich media technology together promised to be a panacea for learning. While the technology did offered a new and richer platform, many developers of eLearning solutions really did not understand how to utilize the new IT-enabled pedagogical improvements. As a result, many eLearning applications were simply web versions of existing textbooks. A significant decline in eLearning revenues resulted when users came to realize what was available. Today, the eLearning industry is beginning to emerge from the trough of disillusionment as customers begin to understand how eLearning fits as part of an overall blended learning strategy and as eLearning suppliers take advantage of maturing technology to deliver better elearning solutions.

Firm Revenue and IT Budget and Demand

As Intel's CIO, Doug Busch, struggled to make sense of Intel IT's own budget after the Internet crash, he began to wonder if there was a pattern for IT budgets related to a firm's business cycle. Figure 2.2 is the diagram he first drew on his white board to show the relationship among firm revenue, IT budget, and demand for IT services for three different business scenarios. This graph provided insights as we struggled to make sense of Intel's IT budget and an ever-increasing demand for IT services. Since then we have validated the graph through discussions with many CIOs and IT Directors who recognize the same business performance, budget and demand trends in their own organizations. Figure 2.2 shows that, irrespective of the firm's revenue trend, IT demand continues to increase.

- In times of revenue growth, IT budgets will likely expand but probably not at the same rate as revenue growth unless IT is understood to be a direct driver of increased revenue.

- In a flat revenue scenario, IT is often used as a tool to help reduce spending and improve operational efficiencies to improve or maintain profit margins. In such a scenario the IT budget is likely to be held flat or decline slightly.

- In revenue down cycles, IT may be primarily used to reduce fixed and variable costs. As revenue declines IT budgets are likely decline more steeply than the revenue decline, as IT is sometime perceived as having high variable cost that is easy to turn on or off.

Notice that demand for IT services continues to grow in each of these business scenarios. I believe that IT is used as a tool for different business objectives depending on the business scenario. The IT demand trend means that when growth is flat or negative, IT organizations will be under severe pressure to meet increasing demand while attempting to reduce costs.

IT organizations themselves need to take advantage of IT to help manage through such scenarios. Namely, the efficiencies that IT has provided to line-of-business functions needs to be deployed within the IT organization. Providing more IT services with a smaller IT budget is increasingly common. In fact, many CIOs and IT directors consider this mode of operation to be business as usual.

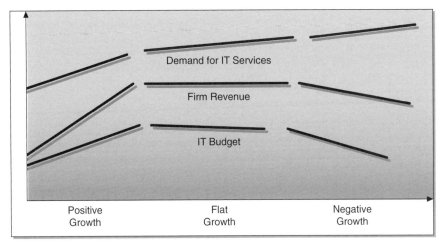

Figure 2.2 Firm Revenue, IT Demand, and IT Budget: Three Scenarios

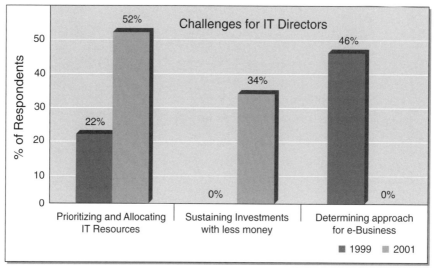

Source: Forrester Research (2001)

Figure 2.3 Priority Shift for IT Directors

The potential for rapidly changing priorities for IT is well reflected in Figure 2.3, which shows some historical results of a Forrester Research survey of IT priorities in 1999 and 2001. Forrester spoke with 50 senior IT executives of Fortune 1000 companies. In 2001 Forrester found that *prioritizing and allocating IT resources* was the highest ranked challenge. *Sustaining investments with less money*, which was not an issue in 1999, emerged as an important issue for 34 percent of the respondents. *Determining an approach for e-Business*, the top-ranked concern in 1999, plunged in importance to zero percent in 2001. These findings should stand as a stark reminder of how rapidly IT agendas can change. While more recent data from Forrester Research suggest a dampening of the rate of change, the lessons of recent years should not be forgotten.

Managing the Rate of Change

Improvements in technology occur far more quickly than the ability of any IT organization to assimilate them. My company, Intel Corporation, ends the year with greater than 90 percent of its technology products having been newly introduced in that same year. At the same time, Intel's leading-edge IT organization has assimilated new IT products and services at a significantly lower rate.

Intel IT budget 2001/2002

Intel IT was challenged during 2001 and 2002 to support the rapidly growing demand for IT services within a budget that was essentially flat. We focused on reducing the unit cost of IT products and services in order to meet this growing demand. We also concentrated on managing demand growth in order to ensure that IT services were used for our business priorities.

Most IT products and services were changed from a per-seat allocation model to a menu of priced choices. This permits individual business unit managers (and in some cases individual users) to select the IT products and services they need and can afford while allowing IT to retain control of standards, engineering, and operations in order to ensure lowest cost, reliability, and security.

In partnership with Intel business units, we reevaluated the priority of each IT product and service, and identified strategies for reducing unnecessary consumption. Some services were converted to a pay-per-use model in order to provide appropriate financial incentives to users.

Thorough cost analysis was performed on the most widely used IT products and services, and numerous changes were made to operations models to reduce unit cost. In most cases, cost reductions were accomplished without reducing service quality or capability. In a few cases, business groups converted to an alternative, lower cost/ lower capability product offering.

During 2002, these changes resulted in a 4 percent reduction in total IT spending, while service consumption grew by almost 18 percent. On a cost-weighted basis, unit costs for IT products and services were reduced by 10.6 percent during 2002.

The important difference is that Intel Corporation delivers discrete products and Intel's IT organization delivers continuous services. Rapidly replacing Intel products with newer and better ones is critical to Intel's continuing success. Providing seamless IT services while continually enhancing the solutions suite in support of business needs is a different, but equally challenging task.

A key IT budgeting challenge is deciding when to retire an aging service offering. Unfortunately, as noted in my discussion of IT inertia, the operating and sustaining costs of existing services consume many IT resources. Furthermore, migrating to new service offerings demands investment. The new service offering is likely to be more cost

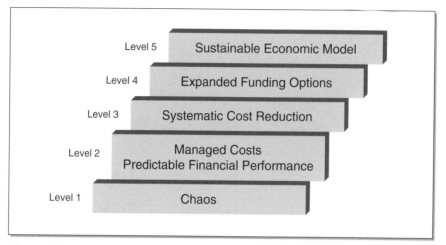

Figure 2.4 CMF for Managing the IT Budget

efficient.Therefore, from a budgeting point of view, increasing the innovation rate in IT organizations depends on liberating funds to drive new projects and will result in a higher return on IT investments.

A Capability Maturity Framework for Managing the IT Budget

Figure 2.4 shows a capability maturity framework that I have created to understand increasing sophistication in managing the IT budget. Here is a synopsis of each of the levels, which will be explored in greater detail subsequently.

■ At level 1, the generic ad hoc level, there is chaos around the budget and erratic financial performance. At this level there is no clear owner for the budget and it is often difficult to determine exactly what is being tracked as part of the IT spend. Even if a budget and plan exists, performance to the budget is often spectacularly erratic.

■ At level 2, IT organizations have a defined budget and performance against the budget is monitored until it is solidly predictable. Achievement of predictable performance against budget is particularly important for firms with proportionally large IT budgets. A variance in IT spending could materially impact the quarterly or annual performance of a firm. Predictable financial performance by the IT organization is one of the key accomplishments in winning the respect of the CFO and earning the right to future new investments.

■ At level 3, IT organizations have introduced systematic cost reduction techniques that focus on reducing the unit cost of IT products and services. Savings realized are to be reinvested in new investments. Disciplined reduction of unit costs using a variety of methodologies and approaches is key to an IT organization—and sometimes the firm—staying in business in an ever changing environment.

■ At level 4, IT organizations have expanded their funding options beyond simply corporate funding and are obtaining funding from a number of different sources, perhaps even internal and external to the firm. Funding options may include pay-per-view usage fees, business unit funding, and external funding from supply chain partners. A characteristic at this level is budget flexibility. At level 4, IT organizations are plowing monies captured from systematic cost savings either directly to the firm's bottom line or to new IT investments.

■ At level 5, IT organizations have achieved sustainable economic models for their budgets with optimized capital expenditures and operational expenditures. The balance between solution development and maintenance/support costs is optimized as well. The ongoing IT budget is appropriate for the firm and the budgeting process helps to maximize the return from IT.

Level 1: Chaos

I will not drill down on level 1 because a description of ad hoc procedures that lead to chaos has no place in a book on IT management. Rather, I shall begin with the first fundamental objective that IT planners should strive to achieve: predictable financial performance.

Level 2: Predictable Financial Performance

Predictable financial performance for an IT organization is fundamentally a factor of understanding the budget of the IT organization and then having the discipline in place to make financial actions happen according to plan. Without an understanding of the budget and visibility and control of the various cash flows around IT services, little progress can be made to achieving predictable financial performance. The Working Council of CIOs has developed a conceptual model called the *Dynamic IT Baseline Budget* model, originally based on a model developed at Harrahs, which provides good insight to the dynamics of the IT budget. Bryan Pruden, Intel's IT controller, has said, "Delivering IT budget financial predictability is absolutely essential before business value and budget expansion discussions can occur with the CFO."

In parallel with a clear understanding of the budget, the IT organization must employ effective controls. Discipline will be needed to execute faithfully against the IT budget. Effective control also means having disciplined suppliers that invoice on time and avoid presenting surprise invoices that create havoc with the budget performance. Effective control also means having accurate asset management systems and a current inventory of services (*i.e.*, a list of server assets and wide area network circuits, respectively).

Dynamic IT Baseline Budget Model

In my opinion, the most critical issue in managing the IT budget and liberating funds for new IT investments is a deep and thorough understanding the makeup of that IT budget.

Organizations that rely primarily on the judgment of the finance department for next year's IT budget are not being proactive. The IT budget ought to use a dynamic baseline model. The Working Council of CIOs details that a dynamic baseline budget model consists of the following elements:

New budget = Initial baseline
+   Impact of previous investments
+   Uncontrollable increases
+   New investments
-   Cost savings
+/- Target for expansion/reduction

- *Initial baseline* is the prior year's budget.
- The *impact of previous investments* will be primarily year-two depreciation of capital assets, operating costs, and maintenance costs.

- *Uncontrollable increases* includes items such as necessary mainte-nance or uncontrollable increases in software license fees, or changes due to regulatory, legal or safety requirements. Higher staff salaries due to skills shortages may contribute as well.

- Proposed *new investments* comprise the startup costs of invest-ments and the first year depreciation of capital assets.

- *Cost savings* is the sum of all cost reduction activities across the IT organization and environment, including recovered costs from retired applications and modified service level agreements.

- Finally, most IT organizations are issued an annual *target for expan-sion or reduction* of the budget by the CFO or CEO.

While CIOs can influence CEOs and CFOs and argue for larger target increases by demonstrating a track record of increasing and accumu-lating business value from their IT investments, the two variables in the dynamic baseline budget equation that are most controllable from a CIO's perspective are proposed new investments and cost savings.

Most IT executives would agree that failing to make some *proposed new investments* each year is the beginning of a death spiral. And, the single biggest lever that the CIO has is the *cost saving* variable. The level of focus and success in achieving costs savings through taking advantage of lower cost technology (*i.e.* the effects of Moore's Law) and other actions directly affects the ability of funds in the IT organizations to make the investments that will sustain IT's future and, indeed, the business's future.

Capital Expenditure versus Operational Expenditure

The balance between capital expenditure and operating expenditure is a key trade-off that CIOs need to make. Too much capital investment may mean overinvestment in IT assets. Overspend builds a backlog of future problems when depreciation eats up a significant share of future opera-tional expenditures. Too little capital investment means IT asset life is over-extended, leading to excessive future maintenance costs and future operational expenditure. Getting the balance in expenditure right and investing predictably according to the plan is important in terms of opti-mizing IT expenditure.

Delta Air Lines identified a phenomenon that they call the *bow wave of deferred expenditure* (*cf.* Figure A.3 on page 251). Deferring planned capital expenditure from one year to the next creates two problems. First, deferring expenditures is likely to increase operational expenditures due to increased maintenance and support costs for older IT assets. Second, deferring necessary expenditures triggers an accumulation of expense that will demand increased capital spending in future years. The budget consequences of deferred IT capital investment set enterprises on a path that is difficult to recover from. The challenge during difficult economic times is to determine what minimum level of capital expenditure is required to refresh computing assets and not create significant budget problems in the future.

Fixed Versus Variable Spending

Any IT budget consists of both fixed and variable spending. Monies budgeted for a three-year network contract with a telecommunication provider would be considered a fixed cost because it is difficult to change such a cost without incurring a penalty. Monies budgeted for short-term contractors are variable costs that can be increased or decreased as business conditions and demand for services change. CIOs and finance managers need to determine the right balance of fixed and variable spending in their budgets to provide the right level of flexibility and responsiveness while also minimizing cost as much as possible.

Level 3: Systematic Cost Reduction

Systematic cost reduction is a key strategy and practice for IT organizations. There are a number of different approaches to achieving cost reduction. One effective method of cost reduction is to apply the Pareto principle. The Pareto principle asserts that a small number of causes is responsible for a large percentage of the effect and the ratio is approximately 20 percent to 80 percent. In an IT context, applying the Pareto principle would mean that 20 percent of IT expenditures contribute to 80 percent of IT's value, while the remaining 80 percent of IT expenditures contributes to 20 percent of value. For effective cost reduction, the Pareto principle advocates identifying the 80 percent of expenditures that offer low returns. A corollary of the Pareto principle would also be that 20 percent of IT's products and services contribute to 80 percent of the costs. Use these two rules of thumb to figure out what cost reductions to target first.

If your IT organization is generally unaware of your costs, you can refer to Chapter 8, where several systematic approaches for identifying and tracking costs are described.

Benchmarking

An alternative and more data-driven approach is to use benchmarking to identify those IT services that are provided at a higher cost when compared to the firm's competitors. Cost cutting should focus on improving the performance of these subset of services.

Benchmarking is an approach where the cost of providing a set of IT services is compared across a number of different companies. The resulting data then allow evaluation as to whether the cost of providing a certain set of products or services in a given company is lower or higher than the median in the set of comparison companies. Traditionally benchmarking has been somewhat one-dimensional with companies really only focusing on the cost of providing services. This approach fails to recognize the quality of a particular service is not independent of cost. Thus, a particular organization may deliver a particular IT service much more cheaply than a comparison company, but deliver it at a vastly inferior quality. A common example of this is the question, "Why is the cost of provisioning email at companies so expensive when individual employees can purchase AOL accounts cheaply or even acquire Hotmail accounts for free?"

At Intel the cost of provisioning email is relatively high but these costs provide for a quality service with 90 percent of large messages delivered within 15 seconds anywhere in the world. This level of service enables truly real-time collaboration. Over 3 million email messages per day are exchanged securely.

To provide a more comprehensive approach Intel IT uses a benchmarking approach which plots costs against quality allowing us to see quickly where we sit compared to peer companies. Benchmarking is an excellent method of communicating to senior business management about the competitiveness of the IT service offerings and can help with arguing against unrealistic IT cost expectations.

Figure 2.5 on page 40 shows the interplay of cost and quality and the desired position is the upper right quadrant. For processes 3 and 10, costs are lowest and the quality is highest. In contrast, process 2 in the lower left quadrant is a poor performer with poor (*i.e.*, high) cost and poor quality. By reviewing cost versus quality charts for the top IT processes and services, business and IT management can quickly identify where cost or quality needs to be improved.

Cost Reduction Strategies

In order to achieve systematic cost reduction, IT organizations need to be aware of the levers available for cost reduction and then to examine each major product or service to see if the use of these levers are appropriate to achieve cost reduction. Accordingly, for each major IT service there are a number of levers or approaches that can possibly be modulated to lower costs. Typical cost reduction levers include the following:

■ Renegotiating or changing suppliers

■ Adjusting service level agreements (SLAs)

■ Increasing automation

■ Re-engineering business processes

■ Tracking consumption with a feedback loop

■ Considering outsourcing alternatives

■ Shifting resources to lower cost locations

■ Substituting lower cost or disruptive technology

■ Managing the IT portfolio—especially replacing and retiring older systems

■ Designing for operations (DFO) to minimize future operations cost while the solution is being designed

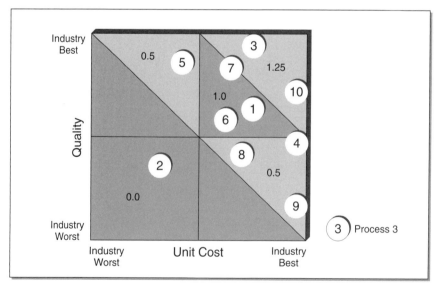

Figure 2.5 Benchmark to Understand Cost Versus Quality

Each IT service should be analyzed to see whether one or more of these cost reduction levels can be applied. Ideally, the best approach is to design low cost solutions and services in the first place. However, most IT organizations are obliged to manage a suite of legacy solutions as well. What follows is a deeper discussion of each of the cost reduction levers with examples as appropriate.

Renegotiating or changing suppliers. On an ongoing basis, firms should negotiate new terms with IT suppliers. The core competency for many IT organizations is the ability to integrate products and services from a number of suppliers in order to deliver internal and external IT services to the firm. Getting the best value for money from suppliers is a crucial part of minimizing cost.

A great example of a cost saving opportunity is the ability to enter into multiyear deals with telecommunication service providers for international private-leased circuits. Telecommunication companies will usually offer significant discounts over multiyear terms. While a firm can lose some flexibility with multiyear deals, the cost saving often justify this risk.

For some companies, it may make sense to consolidate to a fewer number of suppliers. Firms that have had a relatively unmanaged approach to accumulating new WAN capacity, for example, may find that over the years they have accumulated a long list of suppliers. This is particularly likely for global firms that operate in countries or regions with strict regulation of telecommunication services. As the trend toward deregulation continues to unfold in many regions, there is an opportunity for firms to consolidate their telecommunications to one or two vendors.

Consolidation is typically best done by issuing a request for a proposal (RFP). The firm issues a document to suppliers defining the scope of the services required. In response to proposals from suppliers, the RFP may be followed by a request for quotation (RFQ), which typically results in responses from vendors in a position to deliver the services requested. This process can quickly enable a firm to come to a short list of suppliers with whom contracts negotiations can then be commenced.

Adjusting Service Level Agreements. Many IT organizations use service level agreements (SLAs) as a basis for delivering a particular product or service. An SLA defines the boundaries for providing a service to a customer or set of customers. For example, for the IT help desk function, there may be an SLA that specifies the speed with which telephone calls are answered: that is, the average speed of answer (ASA). In specifying an SLA, there is typically a trade-off made between performance or quality and cost. Costs can be cut while sharing control of IT spending with IT's customers when SLAs are renegotiated.

In the case of the IT help desk, there is usually a direct correlation between the number of personnel and the ASA. To reduce cost, a firm may decide that it is acceptable for users of IT systems to wait a few minutes longer for their help calls to be answered. Reducing ASA from 30 seconds to 2 minutes may yield a significant IT head count saving while only minimally impacting users. This trade-off is primarily a business decision.

Another performance measurement for call centers is the percentage of close on first call (%COFC), which is the proportion of problems solved during the first conversation with a user. The %COFC performance is typically related to the competence of the call center staff and the quality of information and knowledge systems maintained within the call center. Investing in call center competence or in better systems for the call center can improve %COFC, which means fewer support calls and hence further cost reduction. Thus, investing in improvements for the call center ultimately can lead to reduced costs due to fewer follow-on support calls.

Increasing Automation. The old saying that the cobbler's children have no shoes often applies to IT organizations. While IT organizations are typically expert at automating the firm's business processes, the use of automation within IT organizations is often lagging. Automation can save significant sums of money by improving performance and productivity and by strengthening budget management in an IT organization.

Opportunities to use IT within IT organizations must be evaluated on equal footing with opportunities to use IT within the business at large. Recent successful automation initiatives include "wired for management" projects that introduce remote control technology to improve the productivity of system administrators through enabling remote PC and server management. Enabling remote management takes the costs associated with travelling out of the equation and dramatically increases the productivity of support engineers. At Intel, most of our worldwide servers are supported from a single worldwide operations support center and this has resulted in significant cost savings for our company.

Many IT organizations use handmade Unix scripts as tools for remote monitoring. However, IT organizations are increasingly using vendor tools for asset and performance management. At a glance, these tools can show the current status and performance history of worldwide computing infrastructure.

The use of computer-aided software engineering (CASE) tools has helped with software development. At the same time, it appears to me that software engineering has some distance to go before it moves from being a craft to an engineering discipline. The reuse of code and automated testing tools have significantly reduced the cost and time spent testing and shortened the time until benefits are realized.

Today's IT organizations often favor the purchase of packaged software rather than taking on the risk of software development. Forecasting costs and schedules for software development projects is known to be risky and often unreliable. A well-tried vendor solution, while perhaps not an exact fit to the firm's specification, can be implemented at a known cost for both implementation and support.

Re-engineer Business Processes. IT-enabled business process re-engineering provides a great opportunity for IT organizations to use IT to transform how the firm's products and services are delivered and supported. As Michael Hammer wrote many years ago in the Harvard Business Review (1990), "Don't automate, obliterate." Hammer's imperative was to rethink business processes before mindlessly automating them with computing systems. Many business processes can be streamlined, or even eliminated. Thus, a business process re-engineering (BPR) analysis is a necessary precursor to looking for automation alternatives.

Intel IT used BPR to significantly reduce the workload associated with delivering laptops to Intel employees and hence to drive down the total cost of ownership (TCO). While Intel IT had a continuous improvement process in place, in 1999 Intel engineers (*i.e.,* the customers for Intel IT) realized that the more stable environment provided by Windows 2000 and future Windows operating systems would allow IT to implement new components more easily than previous operating systems.

Starting in 1995, when Intel IT began monitoring TCO for personal computing resources, estimates at that time showed that it was not cost-effective for Intel staff to be issued notebook computers when compared to desktop systems. Preparing and maintaining a notebook PC for end-user distribution took too long and caused PC delivery to fall behind schedule. A change was needed in the way that notebook PC operating environments were standardized and distributed before TCO was at parity with desktop machines. As notebook technology evolved and new computing guidelines were implemented within Intel, the lower cost and improved value of issuing and supporting notebook computers emerged.

Between 1997 and 2001, the Intel IT department concentrated on streamlining its methodology for building and supporting a common operating environment for notebook PCs. The goal was to reduce the number of operating system images to a single standard. Prior to this consolidation effort, Intel IT had been taxed with configuring each machine to fit a specific job function.

The more stable environment provided by successive Microsoft Windows environments allowed Intel IT to implement new components more easily and enabled the development of a few generic operating environments for each of Intel's functional job groups. On the shoulders of these generic operation environments, a business process re-engineering effort led to a reduction in the number of operating environments at Intel. Supporting fewer operating environments reduced PC TCO because less time and resources were needed to configure and manage individual notebook machines. With a lighter workload, the same number of people could successfully manage many more machines.

Table 2.1 shows our findings. The net result of continuous improvement and IT-enabled change meant that over a six-year period there was nearly a significant decrease in the TCO of a laptop at Intel. The net result of continuous improvement and IT-enabled change meant that over a six-year period there was a significant decrease in the TCO of a laptop and also an increased capability to handle change.

In fact, when the TCO gap between desktop PC and notebook PC had narrowed from over $4000 in 1995 to $800 in 1997, this became an inflection point to drive mobile computing into the mainstream at Intel. Over the following five years our employee PC profile changed from being approximately 80 percent desktop and 20 percent notebook to 20 percent desktop and 80 percent notebook.

Table 2.1   Productivity Improvements in Deploying Notebook Computers

Variable	1997	2001
Build Time	2 hours	1 hour
Development time	8 person weeks	2 person weeks
Testing time	2 person weeks	4 person days
User base	30,000	70,000
Number of platforms	4 per year	5 per quarter

Tracking Consumption with a Feedback Loop.   When a resource is offered for free or perceived to be free then the resource may well be squandered or overused. The implementing of a chargeback system for

IT resources, which is also known as consumption-based tracking, can be a significant incentive for behavior change among IT consumers.

For example, many IT organizations manage the cell/mobile phone programs for enterprise and in some cases users have limited visibility to what the actual cost of the service is. If users have no cost measures available to them, then they cannot manage usage. Users will typically become much more sparing in their use of cell phones when they are presented with a monthly report that shows just how expensive international roaming can be. Introduction of consumption-based billing can be achieved at a low cost and can have significant and immediate impact on company IT spending. Chargeback strategies are discussed in greater detail in Chapter 8.

Consider Outsourcing Alternatives. IT outsourcing is the transfer of an IT function from the firm to an external supplier. This function may be as small as contracting to an outsider to develop some modules of code or outsourcing may engulf the entire IT function. Outsourcing is today's term for subcontracting, often on a large scale.

The decision to outsource is linked to an economic theory postulated by Ronald Coase (1937). In its simplest form, Coase's Law says that a firm will expand the scope of its operations until the firm discovers that it is cheaper to buy a particular product or service in the open market rather than build it within the firm. Coase was observing the nascent automotive industry, wherein initially Ford and General Motors made electrical components, batteries, tires, and other products that are now seen as peripherals to the automobile.

In considering IT outsourcing, a firm needs to take into account the cost of agency. If a firm delegates acquiring a service to an agent, there will be an agency cost because of the inevitable divergence between the goals of the firm and the goals of the agent. Forecasting the impact of agency cost can be difficult. Agency costs can be minimized in outsourcing scenarios that include pay-for-performance clauses in their contracts.

Outsourcers take advantage of economies of scale, that is, they provide the same or similar services to a number of different companies so as to be cost competitive for each firm served. Thus, outsourcing can be an attractive method of cost reduction. As with any alternative source of services, however, firms need to recognize that there might be costs associated with the transition and risks associated with depending upon external suppliers of any kind. Thus. outsourcing agreements are best negotiated over multiyear terms with trusted partners.

When internal IT resources are constrained, firms can use outsourcing as a method of moving their resources up the IT value chain, while outsourcing the utility-like function to an external company. Moving up the value chains means that IT employees who were previously helping deliver utility-like functions can be refocused on higher value-add tasks such as new solutions development. When outsourcing occurs, typically some fraction of the host company's IT organization is retained to manage the out source vendor.

Insourcing is an alternative to outsourcing. Insourcing means contracting a service to a specialist group within the firm. Some firms, including Intel, have created flexible internal workforces that compete with external resources on a project-by-project basis. Insourcing is a strategy that is particularly useful when the external IT labor market is constrained and when external IT resources are expensive.

Shifting Resources to Lower Cost Locations. As firms are under increasing cost pressure, outsourcing and insourcing to lower-cost geographical locations are gaining popularity. However, firms need to look at the total costs and benefits before blindly committing to follow this route. Be sure to include increased travel and communication costs. Consider quality of service and weigh how effective a staff can be when not co-located with other team players. These expenses and risks can quickly eat into benefits delivered through cheaper labor and lower facilities costs in a lower cost geography.

Substituting Disruptive Technologies. Computing infrastructure in an enterprise can be described as an integration of a variety of processing, network, and storage components. IT organizations hope to optimize these components to deliver the best overall performing platform at the lowest cost.

While few empirical studies exist, IT architects certainly try to choose over time the most cost effective mix of IT components that can provide reliable and flexible IT services. The challenge is similar to solving a collection of simultaneous equations on an ongoing basis. IT planners have only limited algorithmic techniques in place with which to estimate the demand and model the suitability of various configurations to meet that demand. While incremental substitution of IT system components can provide modest ongoing cost savings, breakthroughs in cost reduction can be achieved when so-called disruptive technologies are introduced.

According to Clayton Christensen (1997, 2003), disruptive technologies are those technologies that appear in the marketplace as low-cost, low-performance alternatives and grow in capability to displace incumbent technologies. The IBM PC based on an Intel microprocessor is, of course, a prime example. Disruptive technologies cause turmoil in existing markets and effectively change the rules of the game for a class of products and a collection of suppliers. I believe that IT organizations should proactively seek out, identify, and rapidly exploit the opportunities offered by lower cost disruptive technologies. Here are a couple of examples of the use of disruptive technologies at Intel:

■ We switched to the Linux operating system on servers using Intel processors to support Intel's engineering computing (EC) function. Intel EC was faced with rapidly increasing requirements for computing capacity. As hardware purchases increased, so did the cost of engineering design automation (EDA) software. A team of engineers pointed out that if Intel EC were able to use Linux on Intel® processor–based servers, the company would realize a significant cost and performance advantage over the expensive RISC systems that were the main computing engine for Intel's chip design.

Intel EC conducted a successful pilot study, and then decided to make the switch. After a period of several years, Intel architecture-based servers running Linux became the standard at Intel, and we saw a combined savings of $450 million over a 5-year period when we subtracted the actual cost of new systems from the projected spending needed to acquire equivalent RISC-based servers. For details, read the full case study, Linux on IA for Engineering Workloads, in Appendix A.

■ At Intel IT we have used peer-to-peer computing as a disruptive technology for a number of years. Between 1994 and 2001 computing demand grew by an average of 89 percent annually. Users were continually demanding better solutions and performance, and while enterprise systems were highly utilized, we realized that workstations and PCs were often idle. To increase efficiency, we developed a peer-to-peer solution, the Intel Distributed Computing Platform, which enabled us to distribute batch computing jobs onto idle or underused workstations. rapidly. Corporate file sharing at Intel uses each PC as a caching device to allow faster delivery of large files to users while reducing wide area network traffic. This optimizes the enterprise infrastructure to ensure that the best performing corporate computing platform is delivered at the lowest possible cost.

Peer-to-Peer Computing

Peer-to-peer computing is the sharing of computing resources among peers. This is in direct contrast to a client/server architecture where workstation resources are dedicated to each user and servers provide shared resources for larger workloads.

The concept of peer-to-peer computing is not new, but it is only now coming of age. Its recent emergence as a potentially disruptive technology can be attributed to three technical and economic forces:

■ The relentless march of Moore's Law resulting in an abundance of inexpensive spare CPU cycles available on PCs and other computing devices.

■ The emergence of the Internet and seamless IP connectivity that makes connecting PCs and other devices much easier.

■ The enhanced network performance from the explosion of available bandwidth and continuing improvements in transmission bit rates.

Peer-to-peer computing allows better utilization of existing workstations and PCs, with equivalent or better performance at lower cost. It allows enterprises to quickly deploy new capabilities without having to implementing new systems. Information can be stored on PCs instead of on more high-powered computing resources, and network traffic can be shifted from expensive wide area networks (WANs) to local area networks (LANs).

Peer-to-peer computing is emerging as an excellent opportunity to exploit the latent potential in enterprise infrastructure to deliver new capabilities and better performance.

Design for Operations. In 2001, Intel IT set a three-year goal to achieve a 50 percent reduction in the cost of our basic IT products and services. A colleague of mine, Tony Maggi, Director of Global Infrastructure, developed a multiyear strategy he called the *battle against cost*. Maggi's battle-against-cost approach was predicated on this key insight: we can influence costs most prior to deployment of a technology. Once deployed, we are somewhat limited as to the options and the potential impact of any cost reduction strategies.

Figure 2.6 shows the battle-against-cost tactics deployed by Intel IT to drive cost reduction. Figure 2.6 shows which actions are likely to have a higher impact on cost reduction.

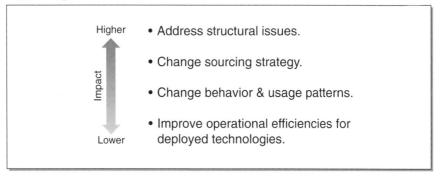

Figure 2.6 Battle Against Cost Tactics

This is what I would call a design-for-operations (DFO) approach that designs solutions to minimize operating costs before the solutions are deployed. The DFO approach is based on more widely-known engineering techniques, particularly design for manufacturing (DFM). The DFM approach encourages engineers to design products so that manufacturing complexity and cost is minimized. Similarly, the DFO approach for IT solutions and infrastructure means that IT architects should aim to minimize maintenance and operational costs at the onset, when designing IT architectures and solutions.

Addressing structural issues is primarily about changing the architecture of the infrastructure and solutions. One example is using wireless LAN instead of wireline LANs in both new and old buildings. Other examples include using the Internet and virtual private network (VPN) technology to offer secure, low-cost wide area networking in place of dial-up access. Within Intel we saved more than $4 million dollars in 2001 by migrating several thousand users from dialup networking to Internet access with VPN security.

At Intel, we learned a key structural cost lesson when we purchased twenty thousand *value PCs* in 1997. After eighteen months, the PCs had to be replaced because they were not powerful enough to handle an operating system upgrade and new versions of applications. Replacing the PCs meant a capital write-off of $40 million dollars—a substantial budget impact. Our after-the-fact analysis showed that we should purchase the second highest performing configuration in the marketplace. Doing so deployed more powerful PCs in the hands of knowledge workers and also minimized total cost of ownership. Not buying the highest configuration avoided paying a premium in the marketplace for the latest technology (*cf.* PC Cost of Ownership over Years, Figure 4.4 on page 96, for more detail).

Another way to reduce structural costs is to increase device densities in data centers. Increased density can be achieved by using blade servers rather than standalone or rack-mounted servers. Greater density reduces facilities costs and can also enable data-center consolidation. The move to high-density began with a migration to rack-mount servers, which is still a common approach. Blade servers are the next step in the evolution of dense rack-mounted processors.

Blade servers take advantage of low-power, low-heat operation to house more than 300 blades into a single rack. Each blade is a typically a complete computer system, with on-board multiple processors, random-access memory, network connections, and associated electronics. A server blade slides in and hooks up, eliminating the need for extensive cabling. Notably, server blades share a storage chassis, redundant power supplies, cooling, and network cabling, but they do not include mass storage (*i.e.*, disk or arrays of disks); mass storage is accessed over a network.

Increasing density in the data center is an excellent example of the design-for-operations approach. When a server blade fails, it can easily be replaced. The reduced need for large facilities space, combined with maintenance and operations savings can add up to significant savings for firms with multiple large data centers. Although experiences will vary, it is reasonable to expect that the repackaging of server farms into blade servers could save an organization between $500,000 and $1 million per rack—and, as I shall continue to emphasize, reducing operations costs allows funds to be diverted to other investment areas.

Tracking Cost Reductions. A useful method for managing and tracking cost reductions is to create a map that contains key IT services ranked by their ongoing cost. An example is shown in Table 2.2.

For each service, cost avoidance and cost savings can be tracked along with the status of actions that might possibly reduce cost. If updated regularly, this map will provide at a glance the current status and opportunities for cost reduction and serve as an invaluable tool for the IT organization to manage cost reduction in a cohesive, holistic fashion. Bill Sayles, Intel IT's global engineering director, has run a cost reduction program based on this approach that has yielded tens of millions of dollars of cost savings and cost avoidance each year for Intel.

Table 2.2 Example of a Cost Reduction Map

Service	Cost Avoidance ($k)	Cost Saving ($k)	Renegotiating or Changing Suppliers?	Adjusting SLAs	Increasing Automation	Re-engineering Business Processes
Data Center Operations	25000	300	Yes	No	Yes	Yes
Global Network Services	200	1,500	No	Yes	Yes	No
PC Help Desk	400	100	No	Yes	Yes	Yes
Inventory Control Systems	0	0	No	No	No	No
...	...	...	...	...	...	...

In addition to the ways I have identified for managing the IT budget, there are other methods that require a longer-term multiyear time frame to drive cost reduction and typically affect structural issues across the business or IT organization. Changes may include redesigning the complete architecture of the IT infrastructure. Often there will be bubble costs (*i.e.*, non-recurring costs) associated with these multiyear projects, and these costs need to be taken into account when considering the short and long term impact of the structural change.

Level 4: Expanding IT Funding Options

Having evolved to the point of getting their budgets under control through systematic cost reduction, the credibility that an IT organization gains through demonstrating systematic cost reduction can be leveraged to find alternative sources to increase the level of IT funding available. Innovative IT organizations will shift their focus at this stage to expanding their options for obtaining funding to increase the business value they deliver to the firm.

Some advanced IT organizations are discussing the creation of capital markets within their firms to provide financing for information technology investments. At the same time, a number of tried and trusted alternative funding mechanisms already exist. Table 2.3 on page 52 offers a list of four internal and four external funding models originally developed by the Gartner Group. I have expanded their list with additional options that should help in minimizing operations support.

Table 2.3 Internal and External Funding Models

Model	Description
Internal	
Corporate funding	The traditional source of funding from the corporate budget
Business unit funding	Funds from the business unit that will benefit from the investment
Pay-per-view funding	Short-term funding from the business with a usage-based fee system (*i.e.,* pay-per-view)
IT funding	Short-term funding from the IT departments using funds on hand
Venture funding	A loan from the finance organization for new investments dependent on level of risk
External	
Vendor or external service provider funding	Cost-sharing or discounts from a contractor motivated by experience gained for future projects
Government grants and incentives	Funds from local jurisdictions that promote job creation and are to be invested in a local economy
Consortium	The pooling of funds with possibly private and public partners to develop a common, shared solution
Revenue creation	Selling IT services or solutions on the market with a margin to create revenue and profit
Leasing	Avoiding capital expenditures by renting equipment
Borrowing	Borrowing externally to finance a risk-based IT investment

Internal Funding Options

Corporate funding is the primary model that exists in most enterprises and it is often tied to an annual budgeting cycle. It is unfortunate, however, that the best ideas often don't occur at the critical periods for annual budgeting; important opportunities might be missed if they have to wait for the next annual cycle for funding.

Funding from the unit that will benefit from the development of the solution can be a more flexible option, whether the project is a significant development or a simple solution. At Intel, we refer to it as *pay-per-view* when a business unit funds IT on an ongoing basis for the duration of development and operation of a particular solution. Another option is for the IT organization to collect a margin on services it delivers to internal customers. The IT organization taps into the accumulated margin to fund new products/services that can then be charged out at a price that covers the development and operating costs as well as a margin for further funds accumulation.

Finally, a venture capital model can be used within the firm to fund risky propositions. An internal venture fund can be created for projects with high potential benefits and high risk. The venture capital model ordinarily provides for funding to be shut off quickly if the promised return is not being delivered (*cf.* Chapter 5 for more detail).

External Funding Options

The first option for external funding is to have an outsource, vendor, or external service provider make an investment in providing a solution in return for a regular payment to provide IT services in support of the solution. During the Internet boom, many vendor finance deals were cut by communication equipment providers to help businesses adopt their technologies earlier and faster. This type of funding can be appropriate when no other source of funding is available for the vendor's solution, but because the obligations associated with the deal are often quite onerous, it is important that the firm and the IT organization are comfortable with the arrangement before proceeding.

Many countries and states offer grants and incentives to support local job creation and local investment, and such opportunities may exist in your area. Intel IT has taken advantage of funding from the Irish Industrial Development Authority to accelerate our IT R&D activity.

Another mechanism for funding is through joining consortia that are either self-funded by member firms or funded through a mechanism such as the European Commission. Intel IT has been part of a number of consortia that have been funded by the European Commission to research a particular area of interest to consortia partners. We also help fund some research centers that are consortia-based, and by contributing, we are able to access to less expensive and better quality research than we could probably do on our own.

Some firms' IT organizations choose to provide services on the outside market. The success of this will likely be determined by the maturity of the IT organization, its business prowess, and the type of market served. With this model there are both success stories and spectacular failures.

Leasing is a form of funding that helps avoid up-front capital investment and allows the expenditure for an IT investment or solution to be more evenly spread over a period of time.

Finally, there is the possibility of actually borrowing the funds for an IT investment from an external source such as a bank. While this option may not be available today, I believe that some banks with a lot of experience in IT projects may actually begin offering such products.

The type of funding that is most appropriate for a particular scenario depends on a number of factors—the scale of the project, the time frame of the investment and the associated benefits realization period, the level of risk, the importance and criticality of the investment, and so on. These factors should all be considered and weighed when firms look to expand funding options beyond the traditional corporate funding model.

Level 5: Sustainable Economic Model

At level 5, IT organizations have achieved a sustainable economic model for their IT budgets. This is measured by having an optimal capital expenditure (CapEx) versus operating expenditure (OpEx) and having an optimal development/maintenance spend. As you will see in the Delta Technology case study (*cf.* Appendix A), having the right level of capital expenditure is crucial to the ongoing operation of the business and IT budgets. Maintaining a regular annual capital spend keeps the infrastructure fresh and ready to support new business initiatives with minimize incremental costs. Reducing a planned capital spend in a year or skipping it all together creates what Delta calls a *bow wave* of investment in the following year.

Reduced CapEX also leads to increased OpEx, compared to the scenario where a planned capital investment was made. This is because computing assets require more maintenance as they age. Warranty agreements that support recently purchased equipment expire, making maintenance even more expensive. In addition, due to the speed of change in the computing industry, computing assets quickly become both difficult and costly to maintain. A case in point is any firm that still depends on Digital VAX computers; those who did not make the investment to upgrade or port applications to newer platforms are paying substantially large fees to support the older ones.

Spending on Development Versus Maintenance

Another characteristic of a level 5 organization is that they are able to optimize their ratio of spending on development versus maintenance. In an ideal world, firms would spend as little as possible on system maintenance and operating costs and invest as much as possible in new solutions that will deliver competitive advantage. As discussed in Chapter 1, several researchers have found that more successful firms are those with higher ratios of IT development to maintenance spending. Unfortunately, in the real world, the operating budget often consumes the lion's share of the IT budget. By using systematic cost reduction techniques and expanding funding options, IT organizations can increase the size of their budget while simultaneously taking cost out of their operating budgets. Those organizations operating at level 5 with respect to managing the IT budget exhibit the agility and predictability required to make IT a strong asset for the overall firm.

Summary

Identifying IT cost savings is imperative to the future health and growth of the IT organization and the business. Whatever the approach, it must be focused and disciplined to be successful. CEOs and CFOs who do not see this kind of disciplined cost management in the IT organization are unlikely to entrust greater funds to the CIO for new investments. Thus, IT budget management and effective cost-reduction are not only necessary to keeping the business running; they are also fundamental to the CIO's ability to invest to deliver future IT business value.

Chapter 3

TCO and ROI

Effective management always means asking the right questions.
—Robert Heller, American editor

Chapters 3, 4, and 5 provide methods and practices that support a capability maturity framework (CMF) for managing IT for business value. In this chapter, I introduce the CMF and explore the methods and practices that comprise level 2 and level 3. In particular, I focus on total cost of ownership (TCO) and return on investment (ROI) and show how these basic calculations inform IT investment decision making and help managers to invest in IT projects that contribute to business value. Later chapters explore investment performance analysis methods, such as portfolio management and options techniques.

Before launching off, I want to look briefly at IT investment trends and explain why I think that focusing on and maximizing the return from IT investments will be increasingly important for firms.

IT Spending Trends

Investment in IT will continue to increase in spite of a sharp retreat in global IT spending beginning in 2000 and ending in 2003. In my view, the wave of irrationally exuberant IT spending in 1999 and 2000 was

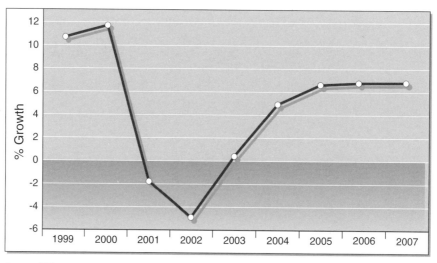

Source: IDC

Figure 3.1 Worldwide IT Spending Growth

followed by a trough of irrationally pessimistic spending. Beginning in 2004, it appears that a more normal pattern of IT spending has emerged.

As Figure 3.1 shows, IDC reported two years of negative growth in IT spend, ending with a forecast of positive growth in 2003 onward. In addition, IDC forecasts single-digit growth hovering around 7 percent through 2007 and not a return to the double-digit growth of the dot-com era.

Not all analyses agree about IT spend as a proportion of firm revenue. In 2000, Gartner issued a forecast that by 2005 investments in eBusiness applications and infrastructure will drive average IT spending in North America beyond 10 percent of a company's revenue. While this forecast has so far proven to be dramatically incorrect, it might lead you to the conclusion that IT spending will ultimately increase. In 1999 the U.S. Department of Commerce reported that IT-related capital expenditure consumed 50 percent of the typical enterprise's capital budget. However, when plant and equipment items, which include some forms of IT, are excluded, and when national communication infrastructure is excluded, a figure of 30 percent emerges as more sensible.

I conclude that a significant proportion of revenue will be allocated to IT investments, many of which are approved with soft-justification business cases. For other categories of investment, more precise justification would be required. And, in the near future, IT investments will be inspected with greater precision. IT strategists should be prepared.

Redefining IT's Mission

Leading-edge firms are redefining their IT organizations' mission and focus beyond merely building, delivering, and supporting systems. New IT mission statements underscore that IT investments must achieve business objectives, which are either revenue gains, cost savings, or both. Therefore, it is becoming more important for IT organizations to identify IT investments that will support key business priorities. Given firm-wide competition for investment capital, IT managers must answer the question, "How can IT and business managers make good cross-functional decisions that lead to the right IT investments?"

Unfortunately, undisciplined investment decisions are driven by the he-who-shouts-loudest criterion, and, most often, investments that keep the business running win out against investments that are earmarked for the future. What is needed is an independent data-driven approach that balances urgent short-term projects with strategic longer-term investments that, while less urgent, may reap greater returns. He-who-shouts-loudest decision making favors short-term goals, and sustained short-term thinking can bankrupt a firm's IT portfolio, jeopardize a firm's competitiveness, and even threaten the firm's future.

The central problem, I believe, is how to evaluate IT investment choices systematically so that all perspectives are included in the analysis. The process should be de-politicized as much as possible. Priorities should be explicitly stated, and the decision-making process should be visible. A prerequisite to enabling rational decision making is a common language and framework for comparing IT investments. How do you compare a major operating system upgrade with a speculative investment in a new and potentially disruptive technology? One answer is that perhaps you shouldn't.

Managing for IT Business Value Maturity Framework

As the IT discipline continues to evolve, I believe that a hierarchical approach to measuring business value is emerging. It appears to me that investment decision making is ripe for the introduction of a maturity framework that describes the key practices that an IT organization and a firm needs to have in place to fine tune processes for delivering increased business value. Figure 3.2 shows my capability maturity framework for managing IT business value. The key practice in use is shown for each level.

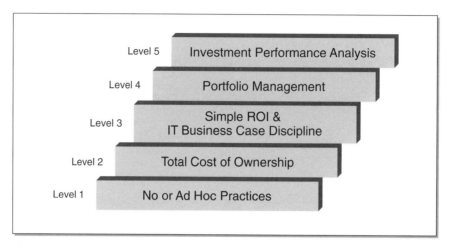

Figure 3.2 Managing IT Business Value CMF

At level 1 in the CMF, the company has no defined or repeatable processes for IT business value management. Typically, at level 1, the loudest shouter gets investments approved. At this maturity level, failure or sub-optimal IT investment decision making is likely unless the decision maker possesses an uncanny intuition for choosing good IT investments. Moreover, level 1 decision-making maturity can be successful only in small firms; the method does not scale to larger and more complex enterprises.

At level 2, IT organizations are focused on the total cost of ownership of IT—that is, the organization is seeking to identify, control, and manage all of the direct and indirect costs of provisioning IT solutions to the business. IT organizations at level 2 are focused on cost and quality of services rather than on the business value that those services bring to the firm. Level 2 IT organizations are also increasingly being challenged by the concept of the total cost of connectivity (TCC), as communication channel services (*e.g.,* wireless LAN, cellular voice and data services) expand.

Organizations that are successfully managing TCO and TCC are ready to move to level 3 and begin to focus on the business value that solutions deliver. Generating business value is achieved when the focus on cost shifts to a focus on return on investment (ROI), and a shift in metrics from TCO to ROI reflects the IT organization's new understanding that business value lies outside of the boundaries of IT. Standard processes at level 3 should include a method and format for developing enterprise business cases as well as a formal investment governance process for making IT investment decisions.

At level 4, organizations take a more sophisticated approach when choosing and managing IT investments, using techniques such as portfolio management, which attempts to optimize a collection of IT investments against certain agreed-upon criteria. Organizations at level 4 also use tools such as a business value index to quantify investment decisions using more than simple financial criteria.

At level 5, organizations begin systematically using investment performance analysis to design, measure, and manage investments for optimal business value. Techniques can include risk-return analyses, real options analyses, and rigorous measurement and tracking of actual and projected benefits. Level 5 techniques are usually based on a strong alignment of business and IT objectives.

I shall now begin exploring the Managing for IT Business Value CMF in depth. As is typical with any CMF, I shall pass over level 1 because level 1 describes an unmanaged situation with no or only ad hoc practices in place. In this chapter, I discuss level 2 and level 3, where organizations employ TCO and ROI, respectively. The remaining maturity levels are discussed in Chapters 4 and 5.

Level 2: Total Cost of Ownership (TCO)

As IT organizations and businesses struggled in the 1980s and early 1990s to better understand IT costs, the concept of total cost of ownership, or TCO, was introduced by the Gartner Group. TCO is a measurement system and approach for managing and reducing costs. The acceptance of TCO by IT organizations was a significant breakthrough and a first step in leading IT organizations to move from a perspective of understanding and managing IT costs to one of understanding the value that IT can deliver. With the help of TCO analyses, the IT organization could now argue effectively for desktop standardization and wired-for-management initiatives. It was TCO that highlighted ongoing maintenance as the largest component of cost in a solution lifecycle. Understanding TCO remains a foundation technique for managing for IT business value.

TCO takes a holistic look at the costs involved in delivering and supporting an IT product or service. Typically, TCO analyses examine the three core areas involved in supporting IT systems: people, process, and technology. Costs are typically broken down into five categories: end-user support, IT support, hardware, software, and miscellaneous.

The importance of TCO is that it recognizes both direct and indirect costs of hardware. Indirect costs are often found outside of the IT organization and include variables such as the time end users must use to spend learning to use new IT systems. Over the years, TCO analyses have shown that labor costs typically far exceed the initial acquisition costs of the software and computing hardware. In fact, one of the most painful truths to emerge from the distributed computing model of the 1990s is that support costs escalated well past anyone's expectations. At one point, it was estimated that end-user time spent on non-job-related PC activities accounted for more than 40 percent of a PC's cost. While maintenance costs are low for supporting a single PC user in an enterprise, the TCO of distributed systems typically escalates as complexity and mission criticality increase.

Remote desktop management and asset management software have greatly contributed to the ability to reduce the TCO of distributed PCs in the past five years. According to studies by Cappuccio, Keyworth, and Kirwin (1996), remote management technology has had the greatest impact. With remote management tools in place, the IT organization, and the firm as a whole, can save over $400 per PC annually. The savings accrue from greater efficiencies in activities such as technical support, system and software administration, and end-user costs. The reduction in support personnel is significant, with typically more than $200 savings per user annually by using remote management instead of local labor to troubleshoot systems and teach users.

I expect further technology development in remote management technology in the near future. My colleague, Dado Vrasolic, vice president of advanced systems development at Intel, is leading a team that is designing semiconductor devices with on-board automated remote systems management and self-healing capabilities. Next-generation processors with this type of automation will help IT managers to realize further operating cost savings.

Accurately identifying and tracking IT costs can be challenging because cost definitions vary, because costs are spread across departmental boundaries, and because some costs, although quite real, are very difficult to track down and quantify. In many cases, accounting mechanisms are not in place to capture indirect costs. Given these challenges, some initial investment is likely to be required to define and deploy cost-tracking mechanisms within your enterprise. Many consulting companies offer services to help firms install TCO programs. I would suggest employing consultants early in a new TCO effort and looking for consultants who have experience with TCO programs at other firms so that you don't have to reinvent the wheel.

Intel IT's Business Case for Laptop Deployment

Intel IT began tracking the TCO of desktops and laptops in the mid-1990s. Typically, the TCO of laptop was significantly higher than that of a desktop. However, due to a combination of Moore's Law and improved processes, by 1997 the difference between desktop and laptop TCO had shrunk to approximately $800. With this information, Intel IT prepared a business case showing that if employees were able to increase productivity by just 30 minutes a week using laptops, a transition to laptops could be justified. The business case presented three scenarios of estimated productivity improvements per employee per week:

- 30 minutes (conservative)

- 45 minutes (moderate)

- 60 minutes (aggressive)

Valuing each employee's time based on annual burden divided by work hours yielded a benefit per hour for improved productivity. However this was divided by a multiplier to reflect the old adage that "work expands to fill the time allotted." Employees in a pilot study were surveyed to estimate the number of additional hours of productivity per week and that estimate was divided by two to ensure a conservative number. Furthermore, the reduced estimate was divided by two again with the assumption of a 50-percent productivity decline when converting available extra hours into productive work.

The pilot group of approximately 100 users received laptops to validate or disprove the business case. The results were impressive. Some people—typically sales professionals—claimed an extra 8 hours of productive time per week. The combination of our business case based on TCO convergence and the pilot study provided a compelling justification to start migrating to laptops. Today, in 2003, approximately 80 percent of Intel knowledge workers have laptops instead of desktops.

Having TCO models and information in place is a key prerequisite to making good investment decisions. For example, because Intel had TCO data regarding laptops and desktops, Intel IT was able to build a business case that advocated moving from an 80:20 ratio of desktop to laptop computers ownership to a 20:80 ratio. This dramatic shift in philosophy and practices fundamentally revolutionized the way that Intel and its employees worked. The shift to laptop computers significantly improved productivity, sped up decision making, and improved work-life flexibility for thousands of Intel employees.

One of the common complaints of TCO is that it fails to examine any return on investment (ROI). This is really a function of the time period when TCO gained favor. The concept of TCO emerged when firms were struggling with escalating operating costs as their distributed systems increased in complexity. Before discussing ROI, however, let's look at an important concept called *value at risk*.

Value at Risk and TCO

Professor Paul Tallon (2002) of Boston College offered a new insight into TCO when he integrated the concept of value at risk (VaR) with TCO. The notion of VaR was originally introduced by the J. P. Morgan financial services company in the 1970s. A VaR analysis is commonly used by fund managers in financial markets to determine the maximum amount of money that stands to be lost in a given scenario of adverse conditions, such as a shift in market valuations (Jorion 2000).

Tallon applied this concept to IT by associating a relationship between VaR of an information system and its associated TCO. Tallon argued that low TCO values can lead to excessively high VaR and excessively high TCO leads to low VaR. Simply put, the greater the business value of a portfolio of IT investments, the greater the value at risk (VaR). The inverse relationship between VaR and TCO is illustrated in Figure 3.3.

Consider, for example, an eBusiness system linking customers and suppliers with a company. A successful eBusiness system delivers significant value to a corporation and thus has a high VaR. Moreover, any interruption in the eBusiness system's availability could stop the entire supply chain and lead to reduced revenues, profits, and even loss of customers. From a pure TCO perspective, the IT organization might be encouraged to find ways to reduce the cost of the eBusiness system. Tallon's observation is that unbridled attempts to minimize TCO lead to a system that puts the enterprise at risk. And, in turn, unbridled attempts to minimize VaR by bolstering the resiliency of the eBusiness system will lead to excessively high TCO.

If VaR is excessively high, hedging strategies can be used to reduce the risk of a loss to a more acceptable level. The inverse relationship between VaR and TCO means that the two metrics can be used to hedge each other. Unacceptably high levels of VaR can be reduced with more reliable and fault-tolerant solutions, and hence a solution with a higher

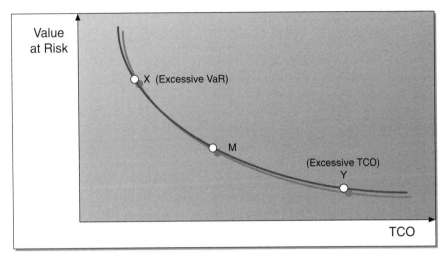

Source: Tallon (2002)

Figure 3.3 Relationship Between VaR and TCO

TCO. Conversely, while excessively high TCO may provide a very low risk of failure for a system, the service level may be unwarranted for the applicable VaR. While I am unaware of empirical data to underpin the trend illustrated by Figure 3.3, I believe that the trend is intuitively correct.

The notion of balancing TCO with VaR suggests that a corporation should spend no more than a dollar (in TCO) to save a dollar (in VaR). This insight is important! The firm might be able to reduce TCO and, while VaR will increase, VaR may still be within management's tolerance limits. For instance, a company might decide to reduce its call center staff, and hence its service levels, causing *average speed to answer* to rise from 30 seconds to 2 minutes. Weighing TCO savings against VaR becomes a business decision. Business managers may well believe that the increase in *average speed to answer* does not seriously compromise the company, and those managers might accept the trade-off.

Understanding the relationship between VaR and TCO is crucial to optimizing business value. Focusing too much on reducing TCO could lower IT expenses, but the potential risk of impact to the business might be too high to make this acceptable. The lesson for CFOs is that driving the IT budget down, typically in times of economic stress, can lead to drastic consequences. CIOs who are forced to make budget cuts that improve TCO may dramatically escalate VaR. This dilemma has kept many CIOs awake at night fearing a catastrophic failure of a key system because they cut costs too aggressively.

Total Cost of Connectivity

An important emerging issue for IT organizations is the total cost of connectivity (TCC). With the ongoing shift to laptop computers in the enterprise, the proliferation of wireless mobile computing devices, and a plethora of new connectivity options, enterprises are seeing an escalation in the costs of communication. While technology improvements and increased competition due to industry deregulation have led to a reduction in the unit cost of communication, an increased demand for anytime, anywhere connectivity is driving an increase in many firms' communications budgets.

Employees with laptops can now be connected through the enterprise's wireless local area network. When traveling, employees can be connected either through a wireless "hot spot," a traditional modem, home broadband, a virtual private network (VPN) using the public Internet, or a wireless wide-area networking solution such as GPRS and 3G. Employees are also using cell phones as well as desk phones, and many have wireless-enabled PDAs and paging devices that allow them to receive email from anywhere, adding service costs to the communications budget.

Unless this situation is managed, it can quickly spiral out of control. At Intel IT, an integrated bill is published specifying the quantity and cost of communications services used by each employee. This information, along with the median cost per employee, is shared with the employee and his manager on a monthly basis. While consumption-based billing helps control costs, it should be part of a greater explicit strategy for managing the firm's total cost of connectivity.

Intel IT was faced with a dilemma. We could "let chaos reign" by allowing individuals or individual businesses to make their own choices regarding communication devices and options, or we could "rein in chaos" by offering standards and corporate-supported services. Intel IT has chosen the latter.

Intel IT decided to make its wireless LAN service a pay-for-use service. General managers for each business unit were asked to decide whether to provide and support their employees with a wireless LAN. The Intel IT organization provided general managers with a standard business case based on a pilot study. The business case helped general managers to decide whether to adopt a wireless LAN and explained that widespread adoption can lower costs because fixed costs can be amortized over more users. I will discuss this business case in more detail in Chapter 4.

The concept of TCC will become increasingly useful in helping enterprises manage their communications costs by enabling them to compare the average cost of connectivity per employee both within the firm and enabling benchmarking across firms. As shown inTable 3.1, TCC is the sum of voice and data communication costs.

Table 3.1 Total Cost of Connectivity

Voice costs	Data costs
Mobile/cell phone	Corporate connectivity
	• Wired LAN
Desk phone	• Wireless LAN
	Home connectivity
Teleconference bridges	• PSTN remote access
	• VPN
Calling cards	• Broadband
Hotel calls	Remote Connectivity
	• Pager
	• Wireless WAN (2.5/3G)
Desk phone	• Wireless hot spots
	• WiMAX (broadband wireless)

TCC itself is a component of TCO and should be included in integrated TCO calculations. TCC is likely to become increasingly important as the number of means of communicating increases.

Visualizing TCO.   I find it useful to draw up TCO projections over the lifecycle of the solution and to confirm that percentage allocation of costs to various categories make sense. Identifying TCC explicitly is increasingly common in my work at Intel.

Dr. Marty Schmidt of Solution Matrix Ltd. uses a similar approach for projecting TCO. Schmidt also advocates looking at the percentages to better understand the sources of future costs.

An example of typical projected costs for a solution is given in Table 3.2 on page 68.

■ The costs are divided into IT categories—user costs, hardware, software, IT personnel, and the total cost of communication.

■ The costs are also divided among stages in the solution lifecycle— initial costs, operation costs, and the cost of upgrades.

Notice that TCC is a category for tracking and allocating cost. Marginal totals and percentages complete the analysis and help us to examine the proportionality of costs across projects with different gross budgets.

Table 3.2 Projected Costs by Category and Lifecycle

Category	Initial Costs	Operation Costs	Upgrade / Scaling	Total	% of Total
User Costs	20	50	15	85	10%
Hardware	50	37.5	20	107.5	13%
Software	40	40	25	105	13%
IT Personnel	70	250	70	390	48%
Total Cost of Communication (TCC)	15	75	10	100	12%
Miscellaneous	5	10	8	23	3%
Total	200	462.5	148	810.5	
% of Total	25%	57%	18%		

When presenting proportional information such as this, I favor pie charts, as shown in Figure 3.4 and Figure 3.5. Pie charts can be quickly scanned for categories of potential concern or to identify problems such as misallocation or over-appropriation of costs.

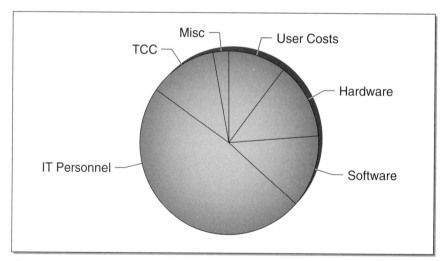

Figure 3.4 Projected Costs by Category

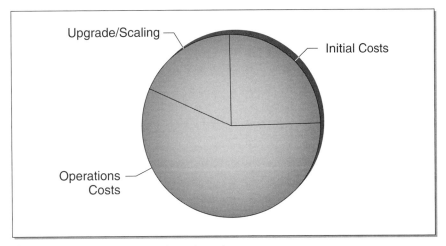

Figure 3.5 Projected Costs by Lifecycle

Interestingly, the percentage allocations in the TCO tables can change dramatically depending on where in the world that the solution is being deployed. In industrialized countries, salaries for IT personnel are very often the highest cost category. Infrastructure for TCC is ordinarily already in place and relatively inexpensive. In emerging countries, hardware, software and TCC costs are often the highest cost categories, while IT personnel salaries are lower. These dynamics make for interesting choices with respect to where solutions get developed and deployed.

IT organizations that have gained mastery of level 2 practices and methodologies such as TCO and TCC are ready to adopt the more value-oriented practices and methods that characterize level 3 of my capability maturity framework.

Level 3: Return on Investment (ROI)

Approval of any IT investments should be based on a business case. The quantitative valuation of that business case is return on investment, or ROI. ROI is widely used as the key tool for IT investment decision making. At its simplest, ROI is simply a measure of the benefit or return received from making an investment. However, the IT industry appears to be a reluctant with respect to researching and calculating the ROI. I believe that this reluctance stems from both a lack of understanding of ROI and a lack of discipline in reviewing ROI estimates when projects are in flight.

Despite this reluctance, ROI is the metric that most companies claim they use to justify IT investments. A 1997 study by Bob Violini published in *Information Week* identified that 92 percent of Fortune 500 companies were using ROI as their financial metric for IT project evaluation.

Why Is an Accurate ROI Important?

ROI is one of the most common acronyms in the vocabulary of IT professionals today, as successive investments come under increasing scrutiny. Still, ROI has several different definitions. I have heard and seen ROI expressed as monetary value, a time duration, and as a percentage. My working definition is as follows:

■ ROI is the ratio of net benefits plus the original investment divided by the initial investment.

Net benefits are total benefits less total expenses over the expected life of the investment. If net benefits are zero over the life of a project, then the ROI is one indicating no return on investment. ROIs greater than one indicate a positive return and fractional ROIs indicate a negative return.

Others define ROI in monetary terms as the total cost subtracted from the total benefits delivered over the projected over the life of an IT project. Yet others talk about ROI as the length of time until the cost of an investment is balanced with its payback, a criteria that I call payback period. ROI is sometimes expressed as a ratio and other times as a percentage. Generally, I suggest that IT organizations adopt the accounting conventions used in the firm at large. ROI's attraction as a financial metric should be its clarity and simplicity.

At a recent major international conference, a fellow speaker indulged in a round of ROI-bashing where he took the ROI claimed by a major global computer manufacturer and services company and in a few seconds eliminated all of the company's credibility. This company had claimed a 1,125 percent return on investment for its human resources intranet. After some simple and correct re-analysis, the ROI was estimated to be approximately 23.5 percent. The audience, which included senior IT and business directors and managers, is likely to treat future ROI claims from this company with suspicion.

ROI Before and After Investments

It is easier to estimate ROI after an investment has been made and the project is complete. Beforehand, there is greater uncertainty with respect to the cash flow, both in and out; after the investment is complete, these benefits and costs generating cash flow are much more apparent. An ROI can easily be prepared on the back of an envelope by estimating the benefits and costs from a solution over the lifetime of the solution. This simple tally can give a first-order approximation of the potential return on a particular investment.

ROI analyses are often relatively straightforward tasks after the benefits of an investment have been delivered, when full visibility of the costs and benefits is available. Vendors can be a source of ROI analyses based on prior installations of their solutions at other companies. Using vendor ROIs as starting points for building a business case within in your own company can be helpful in identifying categories of cost and benefit.

Despite its simplicity, ROI has a number of disadvantages. ROI does not explicitly include the time value of money in its calculation, nor does it easily account for multiple potential outcomes for a project. In addition, ROI does not account for the potential for successive investment opportunities as a result of the original investment. In Chapter 5, I describe real option techniques that address these issues. But for now, let's explore ROI in greater detail.

Lifecycle Costs and Benefits

One challenge when estimating ROI is including the benefits and costs over the full lifecycle of an investment. Many organizations depreciate their physical assets over a four-year period, which is a reasonable length of time for an ROI analysis. Some investments continue to deliver value after all the computing assets have been fully depreciated and the ensuing value beyond this period is often ignored by the business. More commonly, however, ongoing operational expenses aren't tracked carefully. At a StorageTek Forum, Patrick Martin (2003) estimated that for every dollar spent on hardware, 3 dollars is spent on staffing and services. This means it is crucial to look at an investment over the full lifecycle period.

To help communicate the full cost of investing in a solution, Delta Air Lines graphically depicts the initial investment along with all other operating costs. Because the resulting graph looks like the tail of an airplane, Delta calls it their "operating tail." Delta's operating tail has been an important tool for them in communicating and understanding full lifecycle costs. (*cf.* The Delta Technology Operating Tail on page 246 in Appendix A.)

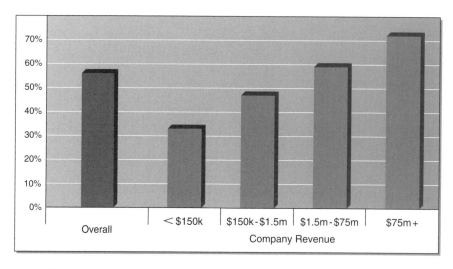

Source: NOP World Technology (2003)

Figure 3.6 Percentage of Firms Estimating ROI after an IT Investment

ROI Usage in Practice

While many firms profess to be using ROI as their financial metric for IT investment analysis, usage research studies paint a different picture. Results of a 2003 NOP World Technology survey of over 1500 firms in Europe and the US that showed that just 56 percent of firms measured ROI *after* the implementation of a major project. This statistic is up from the 44 percent who reported using post-implementation ROI in July of 2002. Figure 3.6 also indicates that the likelihood of using post-implementation ROI increases sharply with the revenue of the firm.

The practice of measuring actual ROI after solution implementation is key to maximizing the business value from IT investments. Ask yourself if you and your firm are paying lip service to ROI and other quantitative analysis of IT investments. If the answer is "Yes," then you are not likely to be optimizing your IT investments.

Avoid One-Dimensional Investment Decision Making

To say that an IT investment returned a million euros sounds great, but what does this really mean? If such a return is against a small initial investment of, say, €100,000, then it might be an excellent return. If, however, the million euro return is from a €30,000,000 investment, then I would consider it a poor investment. Further, how would you distinguish between an investment that delivers €100,000 per year after the first year or an investment that delivers €1 million in benefits after year

10? Looking only at ROI estimates for competing investments does not provide enough information to gain a complete view of an investment decision or to rank or compare a collection of investments.

To acquire a wider financial perspective on an IT investment, I suggest using at least three financial metrics. The three that I recommend are net present value, internal rate of return, and payback period, all within the context of initial outlay required for an investment. Here are definitions for each metric:

- Net present value (NPV) is the net difference between the benefits and costs of an investment in today's money terms. Unlike ROI, NPV benefits and costs are discounted over time to account for the time value of money.

- Internal rate of return (IRR) is the actual rate of return, either projected or realized, of an investment. IRR also takes into account the time value of money

- Payback period is the period of time that it takes the cumulative benefits cash flow to exceed the cumulative costs cash flow. This is also called the break-even point.

Coupled with the level of initial investment, these metrics can really help with the selection of the IT investments with the best profit or benefit potential.

Table 3.3 provides an example of these metrics in use. $14,000 is to be invested over four years. IT strategists have spread the estimated costs and benefits over the solution's four-year expected lifecycle. The discount rate, which is cost of capital for the organization, is estimated to be 15 percent. Estimates in Table 3.3 are shaded; all other numbers are calculated.

- Return on investment, 1.6, is the sum of investment costs and net benefits over the life of the investment divided by the investment costs. As I have argued, this metric taken singularly tells us little. Since the ROI is greater than 1, we have learned that the investment pays back in excess of its costs. And, we have a ratio that could rank a set of investments.

- Net present value, $1362, takes the discount rate into account when calculating the final cumulative benefit. If the discount rate were 0 percent, then NPV would be $3000—that is, the simple cumulative benefits at the end of the investment's life. NPV takes into account the time value of money.

Table 3.3 Calculating Valuation Metrics

	Year 1	Year 2	Year 3	Year 4
Benefits	2000	5000	5000	5000
Investment Costs	5000	0	0	0
Operating Costs	0	3000	3000	3000
Net Annual Benefits	(3000)	2000	2000	2000
Cumulative Benefits	(3000)	(1000)	1000	3000

Valuation Metrics		Discount Rate	15%
Return on Investment (ROI)	1.60		
Net Present Value (NPV)	$1362	Table entries are $	
Internal Rate of Return (IRR)	45%		
Payback Period	2.5 years		

■ The internal rate of return, 45 percent, is the discount rate that would make the net present value of costs over time equal the net present value of benefits over time. CFOs are fond of IRRs that are greater than alternative investments and significantly greater than the cost of capital for the firm.

■ The payback period, 2.5 years, is the period of time until the cumulative benefits value turns from a negative to positive. CFOs are often keenly interested in knowing when this transition occurs and when the investment's benefits overtake its costs.

Time value of money calculations, such as NPV and IRR, contain other assumptions, such as exactly when costs and benefits are paid out and received. For example, I assumed that the initial capital was committed at the start of year 1.

Within your firm, you need to know which of these metrics have the strongest influence in investment decision making. Will your CFO favor an investment with an IRR of 45 percent and a payback period of 6 months over an investment with an IRR of 90 percent and a payback period of 2 years? The business climate and, particularly, the key financial metrics for the firm will have a strong influence on this decision. Companies for which return on assets is a key financial metric may be prepared to wait longer to receive a better return. Companies for which growth is a key financial metric may choose the shorter-term return.

A key problem with generating IT investment financial analyses is that the analyst must estimate project ROI based on historical performance and anticipated changes before the project is selected, executed, and deployed. While tempting, it is generally a bad idea to start with the required ROI and then play with the numbers to produce an acceptable IRR and payback period. Generally, if the investment is a good one for the organization, the numbers will stack up in any event.

I suggest that you also perform sensitivity analyses on the key variables to explore—for example, the impact of a 20 percent change in either expected benefits or costs. Sensitivity analysis of the business case can quickly identify the sources of value and areas of high risk.

The use of different scenarios or different assumptions can be significantly helpful in estimating the likely ROI of a proposed project. While in many cases, investment decisions will be made on the basis of more than just financial metrics, having poor financial metrics is likely to result in setting aside a proposed investment before it has any chance to be examined.

Business value benefits have the potential to make a much more significant impact on the firm's overall financial performance than the benefits of IT efficiency. Business benefits are often described as *above-the-line* benefits while IT efficiency is considered a *below-the-line* benefit.

Above-the-Line   Business Value

Below-the-Line   IT Efficiency

Below-the-line gains in IT efficiency are less significant because the annual IT budget for most companies is a relatively small percentage of annual revenue. According to Gartner (2002), the IT budget average is approximately 4 percent. For example, in 2001 Intel's revenues were approximately $25 billion, while our IT expenditure was about $1.7 billion.

An IT investment yielding a 1 percent increase in revenue would have generated an extra $250 million. Alternately, an IT application yielding a 1 percent reduction in IT costs would save only $17 million. While a $17 million savings in IT costs is significant, it is quickly overshadowed by the benefit of a 1 percent revenue increase.

RyanAir, a leading European low-fare airline, provides another excellent example of this factor at play. RyanAir introduced an online booking web site that significantly improved their revenue and reduced their business operating costs by reducing the number of call center agents. While the investment considerably increased RyanAir's IT costs, their overall reservation costs decreased significantly.

Benefits Realization or Post-Implementation ROI Tracking

Contrary to current practice, there is likely to be more value in measuring ROI during and after implementation than in estimating the ROI prior to investment approval. Post-implementation ROI tracking is a key characteristic of a benefits realization culture. In fact, the key to optimizing IT business value is to expand the value-generation focus from achieving project "end" states to intentionally cultivating and continuously extracting concrete business value from all IT investments. Shared accountability between IT and the business greatly increases the probability that value will be delivered from an IT investment.

An excellent example of a benefits realization approach is that of the Intel IT Business Value program, which was introduced in 2002 to help measure and deliver new business value (Haas 2003). At Intel, we deliberately decided to focus initially on the investments we had in-flight or ones that were completing to both help maximize the return and help quantify and communicate the value of these investments to our business customers. If you are considering implementing such a program at your company, I would recommend that you focus first on in-flight investments, as this is money that is already invested.

The results from the program were significant, with almost $500 million of additional return delivered to Intel over a three-year period with no incremental IT spending. The business value program was also significant as it began to change the mindset of the IT organization to focus more on value rather than just on the reliability and performance of new IT solutions as they were provisioned. At Intel, we created a small business value team composed of analysts who worked with other IT employees to prepare business cases for in-flight investments. The business cases were then reviewed by a cross-IT and finance management review committee that then validated or rejected the return documented for a particular investment. This ongoing business case preparation, validation, and communication of results helped Intel IT to recognize that it is not the delivery of technology, but, rather, the *use* of IT solutions that creates business value.

Intel's IT Business Value Program

At the end of 2001, Intel challenged its IT organization to measure the bottom-line impact of its solutions on their business results. To meet this challenge, an IT Business Value (ITBV) program was set up to assess both the forecast value of an IT project and to track the actual business value that the project delivered. Our CIO set a goal of delivering $100 million in new business value to the company.

Prior to the ITBV program, Intel IT measured success much like many IT shops: higher availability, improved uptime, number of calls answered, and so forth. The ITBV program helped to expand success metrics to include improved time-to-market, increased revenue, factory capital purchase avoidance, and measured improvements in employee productivity, among others. Business units across Intel worked with Intel IT to apply standard metrics and methods for capturing forecast and actual value. The collaborative effort helped quantify IT's impact, provide traceable benefits, and forged a closer partnership between internal business customers and IT.

For 12 months, the ITBV program investigated projects across Intel. The ITBV team successfully documented in excess of $180 million in business value delivered by 16 IT projects. The team uncovered business value in six key categories: head count productivity, hardware and software avoidance, capital equipment avoidance, direct Intel revenue, and other cost avoidance.

The team also learned from the difficulties encountered:

■ Not every IT solution comes with a completed ROI.

■ Business value tools and understanding are often lacking.

■ A common language is needed for business and IT.

■ Productivity-based measurements required extra analysis, data collection, and collaboration to verify business value.

Programs such as the ITBV are changing the corporate attitude toward the value of information technology. IT project owners are now more willing and more equipped to document, measure, and prove the value of their projects in customer terms. The original target of $100 million was exceeded. My colleague, Katie Haas, Intel's ITBV program manager, says "Our success is far from complete. We have measured only a slice of the Intel IT projects. What remains is our endeavor of capturing, measuring, and proving the value and benefit of every IT dollar that Intel spends." Analyzing every IT dollar would indeed be an accomplishment.

The program delivered $498 million of new value to Intel over a 3-year period with no incremental funding, by setting project and operational priorities to focus on delivering maximum value. This result does not reflect a step function improvement in ITBV, but includes a previously unrecognized payoff for IT spending within Intel that is likely to be representative of the situation in many large enterprises. Simply by measuring and adopting rigorous discipline, the value and credibility of IT organizations and investments can be increased significantly.

Relationships among TCO, ROI, and VaR

The simple relationship between ROI and TCO is as follows: the larger the TCO, the lower the ROI. Minimizing TCO results in the highest possible ROI. However, I believe that taking this simple approach can lead to incorrect decision-making because value at risk (VaR) must also be a part of the equation. As shown in Figure 3.3 on page 65, higher TCO ordinarily leads to lower VaR, due to the improvement afforded by greater investment (*e.g.,* affording redundant systems for higher availability). Inversely, lower TCO, in many cases, leads to higher VaR. Solution developers need to find that sweet spot where a new project has an attractive ROI, in part driven by a low TCO solution, while not increasing VaR.

The balance among TCO, ROI, and VaR is particularly important when a new disruptive solution is being introduced. For example, at Intel we evaluated the use of peer-to-peer backup for our PC clients as an alternative to an expensive server and an automated tape library (ATL). The peer-to-peer design was much cheaper than the design using a server and an ATL. Furthermore, PC hard-drive capacity was doubling every year. As a consequence, we forecasted increasingly large untapped storage resources on PCs distributed throughout Intel.

Using PC clients to back up other PC clients was very attractive from a TCO perspective and also promised improved performance when restoring files when compared to a server/ATL solution. The peer-to-peer approach had many of the attributes of a disruptive backup-and-restore technology. Without considering VaR, the decision that Intel develop and adopt peer-to-peer backup system seemed obvious.

However, when we considered VaR, we thought through the consequences of a virus that might be proliferated using the peer-to-peer mechanism. If infections to most or all clients could potentially render all restore possibilities useless, we realized that the reduced TCO would increase business risk and VaR dramatically. We are currently evaluating a hybrid design that uses both server and ATL along with peer-to-peer backup and restore. Perhaps this design will provide improved TCO by utilizing the existing hard-drive capacity on our enterprise PCs while providing disaster recovery backup based on the server and ATL.

The trade-off between VaR and TCO is one that many IT executives may understand intuitively. To see how another team of IT managers thought through this issue, look at the discussion surrounding Figure A.4 on page 251. The semantics are different, but the concern is the same.

No single metric is robust enough to support an important IT decision. Trade-offs abound. The value of including a VaR metric is particularly important because it tracks business risk. VaR is the right complement to metrics like ROI and TCO, which help to maximize value while minimizing cost. And, as disruptive technologies such as peer-to-peer backup and restore mature, the VaR versus TCO trade-offs will change.

Summary

In this chapter, a capability maturity framework for managing for IT business value has been introduced. The chapter has primarily dealt with concepts and metrics such as TCO and ROI and has identified usages and issues with both of these key metrics. I have discussed the importance of post-implementation benefits tracking. I also introduced two new concepts, value at risk and total cost of connectivity. In Chapter 4, I shall go on to discuss how to build high-quality business cases and how to make investment decisions across multiple competing investments.

Chapter 4

Measuring and Managing IT Business Value

This is not Burger King—you may not have IT your way!
—Krista Switzer, past Global Infrastructure Manager, Intel Corporation

One of the most important activities that determines the profitability of a company is the allocation of limited resources among many promising projects. To minimize cost, maximize profit, and remain competitive, all companies need to monitor and adapt to changing industry and market conditions on a continuing basis. Resource allocation for IT investments, in conjunction with the business planning process, is critical to an enterprise's ability to meet its business requirements.

Through an ongoing planning and review cycle, enterprises set and reset strategic IT direction and allocate resources to support their strategic direction by initiating or eliminating projects. Good IT investment management involves an integrated process of selecting and implementing investments that will likely bring the highest value.

In Chapter 3, I explored TCO and ROI and their interrelationship. In this chapter, I discuss in more detail how to build business cases and introduce new ways of looking at IT investments. I also discuss the importance of speaking about IT in the language of the business, using Intel's Value Dials as an example. The Value Dial method reduces the barriers to developing good business cases and improves the quantitative calculation of the value likely to be delivered. I also explain the Intel Business

Value Index (BVI), which is a level 4 capability for the business value CMF. The Business Value Index is a new method of evaluation that supports comparisons among a collection of potential IT investments. The BVI is a hybrid quantitative and qualitative tool for systematically assessing the IT business value and IT efficiency contribution of investments.

Introducing Win-Win Investment Thinking

In 2001, Intel's CIO, Doug Busch, introduced a new way of looking at IT investments at Intel, an IT Business Value Matrix that compared investments from both business value and IT efficiency perspectives. This new framework was intended to drive a new way of looking at and funding investments. The method encouraged those proposing IT investments to seek out *win-win* investments, that is, those investments that delivered both business value and IT efficiency.

Before the IT Business Value Matrix was introduced, we struggled to evaluate a mix of IT investments that had categorically different impacts. For example, a new factory planning system (FPS) system might deliver new value to the business while requiring incremental IT funding on an ongoing basis. Spending for new solutions was often not budgeted beyond the first year of deployment and had to be absorbed into the budgets of subsequent years. Along with the FPS initiative, we also evaluated other IT investments that did not provide new value to the business, but were targeted to improve IT efficiency. One example of an investment in IT efficiency is replacing older servers with newer servers to reduce the total cost of ownership.

The IT Business Value Matrix, shown in Figure 4.1, led to a change in Intel's mindset in discussing and improving IT investment decision making. It is immediately clear that the easiest investment decision to make is one that contributes to business value and improves IT efficiency. Time after time, the Business Value Matrix helped us to make better IT investment decisions. I recommend that you consider this approach to help drive better investment behavior in your company.

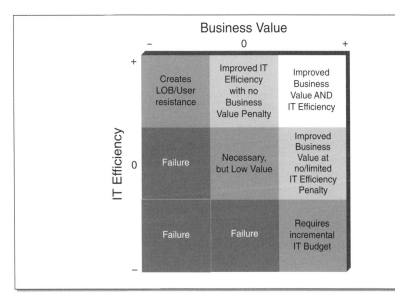

Figure 4.1 Intel's IT Business Value Matrix

Defining a Business Case

A business case is a tool or construct that is used in making decisions where priorities must be applied to a list of choices, financial return is important, and list of choices is limited by constraints (*e.g.,* size of the budget, or the capacity of the organization to absorb change.)

Business cases are increasingly being used in conjunction with portfolio analysis and management—that is, the process of selecting from multiple options a mix of investments that best meets the firm's goals given operating constraints and risk profiles. Portfolio management for IT investments is discussed in detail in Chapter 5.

Business cases typically contain the following four components:

- *Costs*: As discussed in Chapter 3, costs should include the initial investment and ongoing operating expenses over the useful life of the solution. Costs should also include any indirect expenses such as improvements in IT infrastructure and skill training for IT staff. That is, the cost of an investment should be the total cost of ownership.

- *Benefits*: Benefits are typically expressed in monetary terms and generally include tangible benefits as well as quantification of intangible benefit to the extent that this is possible. Business value benefits can be broad-ranging and may include increased revenue, improved productivity, cost savings, and improvements in product and market development.

- *Valuation*: Valuation is a means of evaluating an investment opportunity in monetary terms, usually based on the time sequencing of costs and benefits. Valuation generally includes quantitative techniques such as IRR and NPV, which were introduced in Chapter 3. We discuss other forms of valuation later in this chapter and in Chapter 5.

- *Justification*: Justification is the process of documenting of assumptions and supporting data that lead to a value proposition. The value proposition, which is sometimes called the justification, is the integration of benefits, costs, and valuation considerations and is typically guided by time and priority sequencing criteria.

  It is important to note that a project with a lower valuation may receive a higher priority because of its justification. Some projects are better aligned with company strategy, for example, and other projects satisfy a legal or regulatory requirement.

A business case should address not only quantitative factors, but also the emotional landscape of the organization. The business case for migrating Intel's engineering platform to servers using Intel processors is a good example of a project with significant emotional support. (*cf.* Linux on IA for Engineering Workloads on page 253.) A business case should also strive to depoliticize investment decision making as much as possible by informing the process with clearly stated facts and assumptions.

For any business case, the level of detail and analysis will likely vary with the complexity, risks, and particularly with the size of the investment being considered. Despite these variances, it is important that firms use a standard approach to preparing and reviewing business cases. The quantitative tools used to evaluate costs and benefits will depend upon a number of variables, but two of the most important ones are the complexity of the cash flows and the uncertainty around the cash flows in the business case.

When cash flows are simple and certain, an ROI analysis is usually adequate. As a minimum, calculations of NPV, IRR, and payback period should also be made. When there is more complexity and uncertainty about cash flows, different quantitative analysis techniques may be more appropriate.

Ideally, I recommend where possible to develop and use a one-page summary template for business case documentation; this is a standard practice for leading IT practitioners, such as Deutsche Bank.

It is critically important to document the assumptions around a business case and to have the business managers understand and endorse these assumptions. Small changes in critical variables in a business case can have significant impacts on the potential attractiveness of the investment. Performing a sensitivity analysis, as discussed in Chapter 3, is one way of testing the impact of assumption variances on the strength of the business case.

Business Case Tools

A multitude of tools are available to support building business cases. Some tools are free, while others are available on a pay-per-view basis. Here is a sampling of some choices:

- Total Value of Ownership or TVO is a new approach introduced by Gartner Group to help systematically build better business cases.

- Microsoft offers its Rapid Economic Justification (REJ) tool that assists in estimating the costs and benefits of operating system upgrades.

- Alinean, a company that has a lot of experience in ROI, originally developed the TCO concept that is broadly proliferated by Gartner. Alinean has developed custom ROI calculators based on industry-specific scenarios. Intel has worked closely with Alinean to develop ROI calculators that help customers understand the benefits and returns on investment when upgrading their PCs.

- FAST ROI is a product offered by RMS Inc. FAST ROI is a tool that can be downloaded from the web and enables users to perform ROI calculations.

Generally, these products offer familiar trade-offs. Each has a learning curve, and each makes assumptions about the complexity of the investments being evaluated. In some cases, the sophistication of the tool can be far greater than the complexity of the investment decision.

At Intel IT we use our own homegrown spreadsheet workbooks to document business cases. These workbooks are customized to our environment and contain our standard assumptions. We have also included what we call *value dials,* which I will discuss later in this chapter.

Strategic Business Cases

When an investment is very large or if it will have significant enterprise impact, then it is likely that a one page business case will not be sufficient to contain the justifications and support the decision-making process. At Intel, when we consider a strategic investment such as upgrading our worldwide network our IT analysts prepare a detailed presentation for the executive staff for review. When a large investment is part of a normal business cycle, such as our PC refresh program, then this business case is typically reviewed with the CFO and then is escalated to the CEO, if necessary. In the case of Intel's diffusion intrabay investment, to be introduced shortly, a book-long business case was needed to assimilate the scope and complexity of the investment.

Standard Business Case Templates

It is essential that a standard business case template is used across a firm. This is perhaps the single most important success factor when in selecting the right IT investments. Enforcing IT business case discipline is a key function of IT governance, which is discussed in more detail in Chapter 8. At Intel IT we use a standard business case template which is customized to Intel and is based on internal accounting conventions. You can download a copy of our standard business case template from ITSharenet.org.

Quantifying Business Impacts

You have heard the expression "garbage in, garbage out." This statement certainly applies to the quality and credibility of business cases. In the following sections, We'll discuss practices to overcome some of the common problems and offer solutions associated with building quality IT business cases.

In my experience, one of the difficulties that can emerge in preparing an IT business case is that little financial information is available to analysts about the impact of IT changes to key variables in the business. Key business variables are direct measures of the company's success, such as profitability and productivity. Key business variables such as measures of customer satisfaction are also indirect measures of success.

Studying the relationship between business value indicators and IT investments is valuable in its own right. While identifying key business variables is not difficult, it is often not obvious which business variables will be impacted by an IT investment.

For example, analysis at GE Superabrasives Ireland, a manufacturer of industrial diamond products, has shown that just a couple of key variables impact the output and profitability of the business. New IT-enabled process control systems can improve yield. In addition, automated material stress monitoring can lengthen the life of equipment. Knowing this, IT planners at GE Superabrasives make most of their IT investments in these two key areas.

Intangible Benefits

Companies typically try to justify IT investments with an ROI analysis focused on tangible benefits, such as a quantifiable reduction in costs or an increase in revenues. Tangible benefits are not difficult to determine; in fact, IT vendors can often provides examples of tangible IT benefits from their early-adopting customers. Tangible benefits are especially apparent after a first implementation of a new technology and become even clearer after a series of implementations.

However, there are also important intangible benefits associated with an IT investment. Without taking into account intangible benefits, it is possible that IT projects that should be undertaken are not done because the financial analyses focused only on tangible benefits may not show a high enough return. Even when there is no reduction in costs, significant benefits can be realized in projects that enhance customer loyalty, open up new business opportunities, or increase productivity.

Pat Harker, Dean of the Wharton School, identified what he calls a *subjectivity* gap between what is quantifiable or tangible and what is unknown or intangible. A second gap, identified by Ravi Aron, who is also a professor at the Wharton School, is called the *revenue distance*. Revenue distance is simply the gap between an investment and the revenue, cost or productivity opportunity that the investment supports. The greater the distance from an investment to its consequences, the harder it is to justify the investment. Intermediate measures can sometimes help to bridge these gaps.

For example, investing in IT-based customer care systems should improve customer satisfaction rates, improve customer retention and, in turn, improve a company's bottom line. However, the challenge for IT strategists is to determine just how much gain in the customer satisfaction rate is needed before the return for customer care investment becomes positive. In assessing intangibles, therefore, I encourage you to look at intermediate metrics that can be related either directly or indirectly to key measures of success for the firm. Doing so may require research.

At Intel IT, we believe that including measurements of intangible benefits make our analyses more accurate. Admittedly, quantifying intangible benefits is not as easy as quantifying tangible ones, and translating intangible benefits into monetary amounts can be even more difficult. We continue to improve our methods and discipline ourselves to address intangible benefits head on.

Reduction in business risk is another example of an important intangible benefit that can be difficult to quantify. Here is how Deutsche Bank, a leading global bank, approaches the problem.

Deutsche Bank defines an *event* as any occurrence that has a negative impact on the bank. The estimated risk associated with that event is a product of the likelihood of the event occurring, the likelihood that Deutsche Bank is vulnerable to the event, and the cost of the damage that the event would cause. Risks are estimated and compared both with and without the IT investment. In this manner, the reduction in risk can be included in weighting a decision to, for example, add a third data center. The intangible benefit is the differences in risk with two data centers and the risk with three data centers. In this way, Deutsche Bank is able to monetize this important intangible benefit.

Quantifying Intangible Benefits in Intel Manufacturing

A significant segment of IT activity at Intel is aimed at automating the semiconductor manufacturing process. In 1991, Intel IT developed a business case for introducing a new diffusion intrabay automation system. This business case is a particularly good example of the importance of quantifying intangible benefits.

Diffusion Intrabay Automation

In a nutshell, early in the process of turning silicon into semiconductor devices, wafers are placed in a furnace where heat and a mixture of gases diffuse material into the silicon wafers. This occurs in a "clean room," and, prior to automation, people worked in the diffusion bay (*i.e.*, the area of the fabrication plant dedicated to the diffusion process) carefully moving wafers from cassette carriers to the ovens and back again.

The goal of the diffusion intrabay automation process was to automate the loading, unloading, and tracking of wafers.

The business value of an advanced computer integrated manufacturing system was first evaluated by comparing its performance with the performance of people doing the same job. As we sorted through a comprehensive set of indicators for both tangible and intangible benefits, we began to see that much of the IT business value would be realized from the intangible benefits.

Tangible Benefits

We developed a business case that centered around the tangible benefits of reduced head count, reduced floor space, and equipment cost savings through IT automation. A multiyear projected ROI estimated that we would reach the break-even point after a period of over 5 years, as shown in Figure 4.2. However, in spite of this marginal ROI, the project was approved because its potential to provide the foundation for fully automated fab manufacturing was considered strategically important.

The internal rate of return over this 5-year period was estimated at 16 percent. However, during and after implementation, data were collected, measured, and compared with an equivalent manual manufacturing area in another factory. The data showed a significant intangible benefit that dramatically changed the business case: the introduction of automated processing improved both linearity and consistency of output of the functional area and the entire production area. As Figure 4.3 shows, the

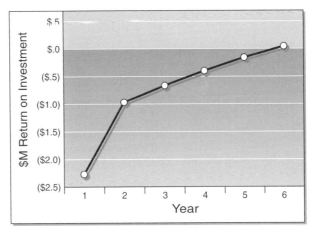

Figure 4.2 Forecast ROI for Diffusion Intrabay Automation Investment

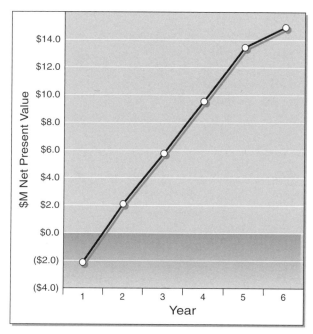

Figure 4.3 Actual ROI for Diffusion Intrabay Automation Investment

value of the increased output of the factory improved the internal ROI to 194 percent, and the project broke even in 6 months.

This example shows the value of including intangibles in ROI and, in particular, the value of using business metrics to track post-implementation results.

Intel's Benefits Visibility Approach

One of Intel's key planning principles is to make benefits visible. To manage for business value, an organization must first create an awareness of the intangibles and then figure out a way to translate these benefits into quantitative terms. Merely defining and designing for business value is not enough; the design needs to be followed through with an implementation and measurement approach that focuses on business value.

The real value of ROI calculation and measurement is in examining all of the costs and benefits—including operations, staffing, new business opportunities—to determine overall business impact. Ideally, all of these aspects of a business's performance should be taken into account to justify project selection, determine break-even dates, and drive business strategy.

The visible benefits approach can be a real challenge when a project is the first of its kind. To be most accurate, ROI must be monitored during the months or sometimes years that it takes to recover project costs. An additional challenge is that project implementation and subsequent changes can alter processes, roles, procedures, tools, customer behavior, and even the original system functions. Many organizations do not quantify recurring benefits and allocate them back to projects, and ROI estimates are often based on current performance assumptions without an understanding of the impact of these changes.

Visible Benefits for the Diffusion Intrabay Automation Project

The diffusion intrabay automation system (DIAS) was deployed at Intel Ireland's fabrication plant (or fab), which is known at Intel as Fab 10. This was Intel's first implementation of an automated materials transport for a functional area. As noted, DIAS was planned as both a strategic investment and as one that would produce an immediate, though relatively modest, positive ROI.

To maximize effectiveness and enhance understanding, business cases and success metrics should embrace the business's terminology. Line managers in process manufacturing talk about and measure output, yield, work in progress (WIP) turns, scrap rates, and equipment utilization. Accordingly, our business case used scenarios targeted and expressed in exactly these terms.

The primary success measures for DIAS were manufacturing output measures—quality, rate, and cost—and overall equipment effectiveness. In Intel's business, equipment cost is the highest proportion of the initial capital cost, and any IT investment that can increase equipment utilization will not only reduce up-front capital expenditures but also reduce ongoing factory operating costs.

Table 4.1 shows the critical metrics for manufacturing production and overall equipment effectiveness improvement for Fab 10 versus a control fab with human operators. A standard measure of functional area productivity in semiconductor manufacturing is overall equipment effectiveness (OEE). OEE is the ratio of actual equipment output to its theoretical maximum. It is defined by Sematech as follows:

$$OEE = Availability \times Performance\ Efficiency \times Rate\ of\ Quality \times 100$$

Table 4.1 shows that Fab 10 demonstrated an OEE of 0.55, which was significantly better than the control fab. Thus, we were able to make the benefit of DIAS visible and we communicated that benefit in terms and metrics familiar to our customer, the fab line manager. (*N.B.* The exact figures in Table 4.1 have been changed slightly to respect confidential Intel data.)

Table 4.1 Improvement in OEE with an Automated IT Solution

Fab	Equipment Availability	Intrabay Human Availability	Total Availability	Performance Efficiency	Rate of Quality	OEE
F10	0.87	0.98	0.86	0.65	1.00	0.56
D2	0.87	0.90	0.78	0.61	0.99	0.48

Intel's IT Value Dials

Intel's benefits monetization process is based on a collection of business variables, which we call *IT value dials*. A value dial is another name for a business variable that can be positively affected by the use of information technology. The IT value dial approach encourages Intel analysts to see how a collection of key business variables are impacted by potential IT investments.

In creating the IT value dial, Intel first translated its key business variables into quantifiable metrics. For example, Intel monitors the number of *days of inventory* on hand. Every additional day that Intel is required to have inventory on hand is a cost to the business and increases the risk of obsolescence. An IT system that enhances just-in-time (JIT) manufacturing, improves the delivery of products, or enables more accurate forecasting of inventory will directly reduce *days of inventory* and indirectly contribute to enterprise profitability. Other examples of value dials include cash cycle variables, such as *days of receivables*, productivity variables, such as *direct labor costs*, and customer service variables, such as *customer satisfaction*.

When developing a business case, Intel analysts identify a baseline value for IT value dials. Once identified and quantified, the baseline can be compared to IT value dials influenced by new IT initiatives. By identifying which value dials should be impacted and by regularly measuring value dial improvements against a baseline, Intel is able to manage IT business value throughout the entire life cycle of the investment.

The ability to tabulate business variables and to identify the monetary value of unit improvements of value dials expedites identification of the total financial impact of IT-driven improvements. The use of IT value dials also provides IT engineers with a reference point as they seek to dream up solutions that will improve business results. Rather than tracking the effect of an IT initiative on a value dial, engineers can begin to think more broadly about how a value dial can be influenced in a positive direction.

As an example, Table 4.2 shows value dials (*i.e.,* quantified benefits) for a new IT application. The new application will improve worker productivity, enabling more orders to be handled per employee, improve the customer interaction process, making it easier for the customer to do business with us, and have a positive impact on market segment share. In addition, by incorporating just-in-time concepts and improved integration with planning and shop floor control systems, the application will enable a reduction in the days of inventory. Finally, because of the productivity improvements, some customer service representatives can be redeployed thus reducing head count.

Table 4.2   IT Value Dial Example

Business Variable	Current State	Desired Future State	Value
Days of inventory	30	28.5	$3M
Daily orders handled by customer service representative	20	35	$500K
Head count	900	850	$5M
Market Segment Share	55%	56%	$33M

Tom Pope, original developer of the IT value dial methodology at Intel, believes that before value dials were introduced, analysts would typically use nonspecific statements to describe projected benefits for a proposed IT project. As with the introduction of any new methodology, Tom had to work hard to introduce, explain and train IT and eBusiness professionals in the use of value dials. It was worth the effort; Sandra Morris, CIO and VP of Intel's eBusiness Group, credits value dials with allowing Intel to define, design, and implement eBusiness systems that deliver business value.

Impact of IT Value Dials at Intel

Today at Intel, those who propose projects are expected to be as specific as possible in defining expected benefits. Loosely described benefits statements (*e.g.,* "This new application will increase flexibility in the supply chain to improve customer relations.") have been replaced with precise language that targets specific business variables (*e.g.,* "This new application will increase supply chain flexibility to achieve 1.5 fewer days finished goods inventory and a 1 percent increase in market segment share.").

Clearly identified business goals are fundamental to the process of benefits realization. Joint ownership and agreement on business goals for both the IT and the business organization significantly enhance the prospects of achieving project goals. The value dials method simplifies the relationship between an IT-enabled improvement and a business variable expressed in monetary terms. Knowing a project's relevant value dials expedites computation of an ROI. IT professionals who might previously have been daunted by the challenge of identifying the monetary value of a project should look to value dials as an intermediate result that restates specific process improvements in financial terms.

Valuing Productivity Improvements

A common problem when preparing business cases is how to appropriately monetize the value of a productivity improvement. At Intel IT we use a productivity framework to help accomplish this. Productivity is a function of *context, key variables,* and *time frame.*

■ The value of employee's time sets the *context* for productivity improvement. For example, an investment that frees up time for a manufacturing technician might directly result in an increase in measurable output. Time savings may be less valued if an investment promises to free up time for a generic knowledge worker who is working with unstructured information in a creative role.

■ *Key variables* are the indicators of productivity appropriate to a context. For a manufacturing technician, productivity might be measured as units produced per hour. For a knowledge worker in a training role, productivity might be measured in student hours. For a knowledge worker in a research role, the metric might be patents per year.

■ *Time frames* for productivity measurement must be established. A baseline measure is needed to compare with future performance. The elapsed time during which productivity may improve must be set with an understanding of the learning curve. It takes time for systems to be assimilated into organizations and their people. Generally, patience is required to allow productivity benefits to emerge.

The productivity of a business process is the ratio of output to input. For IT leaders, labor is often the primary input to this equation. One way to increase productivity is to accelerate the business process. This can either be accomplished with an IT solution that automates the process or by using IT to change the nature of the work being performed.

Andy Grove calls changing the nature of work to improve productivity *leverage*. Leverage is the improvements in output generated by a revised and more efficient work activity. An activity with high leverage will generate high output. For example, leverage is the difference in output from a programmer who writes a program using assembly language when compared to a programmer who writes the same function using a higher level language. Quality and speed are both likely to improve in the latter case.

Assessing Productivity Impacts through Pilots

The best way to assess productivity impacts is to do a controlled pilot study to determine actual benefits and actual costs. Measuring these actual values will allow low cost learning to occur and a more accurate business case to be developed.

We conducted a controlled pilot study to inform our recent decision to upgrade from Pentium® III to Pentium 4 processor-based PCs. While we strive to be on a 3-year upgrade cycle for PCs, we regularly check productivity impacts. In this study, we studied productivity measures with a sample of forty knowledge workers who completed the same set of standard tasks on a new (*i.e.,* Pentium 4/Microsoft Windows XP) and old PC (*i.e.,* Pentium III/Microsoft Windows 2000).

The results were interesting and compelling. On average, users with the new PC completed tasks about 20 percent faster than users on the older PC. Interestingly, we also found that task accuracy was six percentage points higher on the new PC. I believe that accuracy is improving as the speed of the PC gets closer to human processing speed. I think this finding has significant relevancy for firms with extensive keyboard input (*e.g.,* a teller in a bank). We found that faster PCs will lead to fewer data-entry errors, which translates into lower downstream costs incurred by error propagation.

Using the Business Value Trade-off Matrix, we also evaluated this investment from an IT efficiency standpoint. Our historical data, shown in Figure 4.4, indicates that PC cost of ownership starts to rise after year three, driven by increasing hardware failures, extended warranty costs and driver/software issues as new operating systems and applications are introduced. In this instance, the pilot data in conjunction with the historical data provided for a compelling business case that reinforced our ongoing strategic direction to proceed with a three year PC refresh. Intel typically refreshes about a third of our PCs each year.

User Studies.   Another approach to assessing productivity impact of IT is to learn from the users during such a pilot. This learning can take place through tracking activity logs, testing for usability, and conducting formal interviews with users to assess the impact and benefit delivered.

While users can keep activity logs as they work, these logs are better captured automatically. The method you choose will depend on the data you are trying to collect.

■ To help determine whether a business case existed for wireless LANs at Intel, we asked the pilot users to maintain an activity log so that we could understand how wireless LANs affected works and also to estimate time saved.

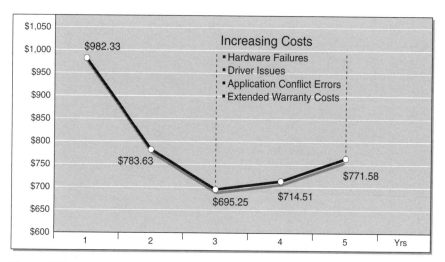

Figure 4.4 PC Cost of Ownership over Years

Time is not always money

Although IT continues to offer opportunities for productivity improvement, many CFOs can be skeptical that all productivity improvement opportunities translate into bottom line earnings increases. They believe that productivity gains don't necessarily cut cost or increase revenue because employees don't necessarily apply freed-up time to work. Ian Campbell, VP of research at Nucleus Research, believes that lower level workers, in contrast to knowledge workers, are more likely to turn extra time into work. This is a consequence of a more repetitive and better defined lower level work environment where output is more easily quantified. Nucleus Research has produced a table that provides a rule of thumb for estimating the percentage of freed-up time that various categories of workers convert into increased output.

Type of Worker	Conversion Efficiency
Assembly line workers	95-100%
Call center support	90-95%
Administrative and support help	70-80%
Engineering (technical)	75%
Engineering (non-technical)	65-75%
General staff within a group (marketing, PR, accounting)	60%

While this chart provides only rough estimates of conversion efficiency, these estimates can be a useful guideline as business cases are prepared.

- ■ In contrast, when we built our business case for developing a peer-to-peer backup solution, IT engineers built a software agent that tracked pilot user activity. The agent monitored the length of time that users were connected to the network, collected a time profile of connectivity, and recorded the speed of the network link.

Usability testing should occur both in the lab and in the real workplace to validate usages models ahead of a pilot. Users should be surveyed and formally interviewed to collect appropriate feedback.

Monetizing Pilot Study Results. In the case of the wireless LAN survey, pilot users were segmented across different user profiles. In monetizing the average reported time saved by each user, we divided the savings reported by users in half and counted half of that again as a monetary benefit through increased productivity delivered. This quantification methodology was approved by the customer finance organizations and the outcome was that if an individual user achieved an extra 11 minutes per week through the use of wireless LAN, then the investment in wireless was justified.

Following the pilot, Intel IT decided to offer investments in wireless LAN to individual business general managers rather than to invest in wireless as a part of corporate infrastructure. Our decision meant that each general manager needed to decide whether to spend on proliferating wireless LANs or spend funds on another business initiative. Because of the compelling business case supported by the pilot study of over 140 users, most general managers at Intel have decided to proliferate wireless LAN technology in their business or division.

Making the Transition to Level 4

As organizations make the transition to level 4 of the IT business value CMF, they have achieved the ability to document and prove the value proposition of an investment with a high-quality business case. Moving to level 4 requires organizations to take an enterprise-wide view of IT investments and to make investment decisions, not on a one-by-one basis, but as part of a comprehensive integrated plan. Level 4 organization can successfully trade off the costs and benefits of different IT investments to make the right decisions for the firm.

Beyond ROI: The Business Value Index

Predicting the ROI of a speculative IT investment is notoriously difficult because there are many factors that will influence the outcome. Factors such as business risk, technical risk, and strategic alignment cannot be precisely stated prior to deployment. Estimates of development, implementation, and sustaining costs can be only approximate. On an ongoing basis, businesses are identifying new opportunities to apply IT for competitive advantage. But with many ideas and projects competing for a limited investment pool and limited up-front information, how should a company identify the best IT investments?

According to research by the Working Council of CIOs, firms that make better IT investment decisions share three characteristics:

- A common vocabulary for describing IT investments
- A comprehensive process to assign value and risk
- An objective scoring method to generate prioritized choices

In line with these characteristics, Intel IT has developed a tool called the IT Business Value Index (BVI) to make more robust our method of prioritizing IT investments. The BVI was developed to work in conjunction with our Business Value Matrix and to allow more formal investment analysis based on the investment philosophy behind the matrix. The BVI is an investment decision support tool which, when combined with a portfolio management approach, helps us to be proactive in maintaining a project portfolio that aligns tightly with corporate strategy. The BVI provides a common vocabulary and methodology, which allows disparate investments to be compared. In addition to evaluating IT investments along the vectors of business value, IT efficiency, and financial attractiveness, the BVI also weights factors impacting the likely value and success of an IT investment based on the ongoing business strategy and business environment.

As shown in Figure 4.5, the IT BVI assesses and values IT investments using three vectors: *business value* (the X axis), *IT efficiency* (the Y axis), and *financial attractiveness* (the Z axis).Each vector is a composite index, derived from a series of weighted factors that affect the investment. Business value measures the corporate impact of a project on Intel's business strategy and priorities; IT efficiency value measures how well the investment will use or enhance existing infrastructure; financial attractiveness measures the financial aspects of the investment including level of investment required, cost/benefit ratio, and the net present value of a project. When a project or program is initiated, a management investment committee (MIC) approves its BVI criteria and associated weights, and will ratify subsequent changes.

A crucial aspect of the BVI is how it addresses intangible benefits and strategic alignment. Some of the evaluation criteria for the BVI use Intel value dials to help quantify the projected impact of an IT investment in terms of the monetary value of positive changes to key business variables. Other evaluation criteria include a scoring of customer pull or demand, level of business and technical risk, strategic fit, impact on revenue, level of investment, level of innovation, and level of learning. The BVI tool also allows the tracking of the change in relative value of an IT investment or

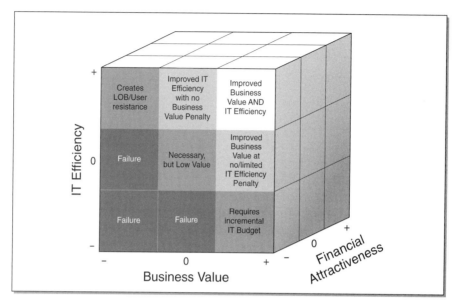

Figure 4.5 Intel IT's Investment Framework

innovation through use of a value curve. A value curve shows the historical trending of BVI scores for a particular group of IT investments. It allows analysis of the relative shifts in assessed value of tracked investments.

The BVI is an effective tool for tracking whether a project or investment is likely to increase or decrease in value. To manage IT investments for optimal business value, the BVI can be used with a *stage-gate* methodology. A stage-gate methodology is a mechanism for funding an investment or project in phases as the project achieves various milestones. With this approach, an investment's performance is regularly reassessed. If specific targets set for a particular phase of a project are met, the project will ordinarily be funded through the next phase; otherwise, the project may be slowed down or even halted.

The BVI can also enable an *options approach* to IT investment. Options in the world of finance represent rights to future investment choices without a current obligation for making a full investment. The holder of an option makes a small investment for the right to decide at a later point whether to actually invest in a financial position. Options buy the investor time, so to speak, until more information is available and the value—or lack or value—of an investment becomes more apparent. IT options investments are difficult to value and assess because there are many unknowns, including likely return, uncertainty, risk, and intangible benefits. While the value of options can be estimated, they are notoriously difficult to predict accurately. The BVI methodology helps measure and track the options value of an IT investment portfolio.

Intel's BVI is an important tool for winnowing down proposed innovations and ideas into a smaller set that is likely to have the highest value. It allows continued and proactive alignment of a company's project portfolio with corporate strategy. As data accumulate, the BVI improves the capability for predicting future value of IT investments by bringing together data to correlate estimated business value contributions for investments with ROI and DCF calculations.

The Sweet Spot

A potential investment is assessed along the three vectors shown in Figure 4.5 to ensure that decision makers have a complete and balanced view. Ideally, the investments that are chosen are those that lie in the *sweet spot*—investments that deliver improved business value, increased IT efficiency, and that are the most financially attractive.

Our peer-to-peer technology-based eLearning system is one recent sweet-spot investment at Intel. The system delivers a new business capability by providing employees with up-to-date rich content-based training. At the same time, the eLearning system reduces training costs. Due to its peer-to-peer design, the system significantly decreases IT infrastructure costs by moving large file traffic from our wide area network (WAN) to local area networks (LANs). The combination of business and IT benefits, and the additional fact that this system can be supported by our existing PC infrastructure, makes the financial attractiveness of the investment very high. This is a win-win-win situation.

Not all selected investments will be in the sweet spot. For example, your business may evaluate an investment in a new eBusiness application that will increase business value, but will require additional WAN capacity and possibly have a negative IT efficiency impact. Other investments will sometimes be chosen to increase IT efficiency while not contributing to improvements in business value.

We found no sweet spot when, some time ago, Intel IT evaluated an investment in voice multiplexers for international conference calls. Intel consumed an average twenty-eight million voice-conferencing minutes per month in 2001. The introduction of voice multiplexers would reduce the bandwidth required to carry this traffic and significantly reduce network costs. From a business-value standpoint, we took into consideration that voice quality would be degraded by 10 percent. However, we decided that this was a trade-off that the business was willing to make in order to achieve substantial savings in network costs. While not a win-win-win opportunity, using voice multiplexing technology was still a good idea.

Using the BVI

Assessing a business value index for a proposed IT investment is a relatively straightforward process. An IT investment owner scores his or her IT investment against specific assessment criteria. The range for each assessment criterion is from a score of 1 (low) through 4 (high) to indicate how likely the IT investment is to succeed in satisfying the criterion. Table 4.3 offers an example using three assessment criteria relevant to a new help desk case tracking application.

Table 4.3   Business Value Criteria for a Help Desk Initiative

Criterion	Weight	1	2	3	4
Customer Pull	3	Low	Medium	High	Very High
Business Strategic Fit	3	Low/NA	Medium	High	Very High
End-User Performance Improvement	2	Decrease	None	<10%	>10%

In this example, each assessment criterion is assigned a weight, based on the importance of that particular criterion and dependent on business strategy and business conditions. Customer pull is weighted 3 because surveys of help desk staff indicate high interest in new and better tracking systems. Weight for each criterion is defined for each of the four possible values. If business strategic fit is deemed to be high for this investment, then the BVI score will be 3. If analysts believe that end-user performance can be improved by more than 10 percent, then the BVI score on this criterion will be 4.

Weighting Considerations

A key part of investment analysis is deciding which factors are most important for the business. One process is to review the assessment criteria and assign weightings to criteria based on *gut feelings*. An alternative approach is to collect weightings from key stakeholders and use the mean weighting for prioritizing investments.

Managers evaluating an investment with the BVI assessment criteria will realize that business typically occurs in cycles and that the assessment criteria need also to be weighted with the company's long-term strategy in mind. Maximizing a return on assets or maximizing net profit may drive different investment choices. Investments that have a direct positive impact on revenue generation are likely to be highly weighted in any scenario. In the Internet boom, investments to grow share of market would typically have been weighted highly. In the post September 11 era, investments that improve security and business assurance are likely to be weighted highly.

The products of the criteria weight and the criteria score for a particular investment are summed for all assessment criteria to produce a total score, which is called the BVI for each investment. The ongoing assessment of weighting of BVI criteria allows dynamic portfolio prioritization, which will be discussed in the next chapter.

The BVI Cycle

The weightings attached to the assessment criteria are subsequently reviewed on a periodic basis, as defined by the investment planning cycle. The following is an example of the flow of the BVI cycle:

1. Investment owners identify proposed investments.
2. The management investment committee (MIC) determines criteria weightings based on business strategy and conditions.
3. Investment owners assess and compute BVI values for their proposed investments.
4. Investments are ranked and plotted by their BVI values.
5. The MIC makes investment decisions using BVI ranking and plots as key decision support input.
6. Investments are made and progress is tracked.
7. As investment progresses, BVI values are re-assessed and recomputed on a periodic basis, typically quarterly.
8. Input is fed back to the MIC for evaluation.
9. The MIC makes ongoing investment decisions. The committee may accelerate, maintain, or halt an investment, or even divest the firm of an investment.

Thus, through an ongoing cyclical process, the BVI tool is used to help select the best IT investments and, proactively, to align the IT organization's investments with ongoing business strategies and needs.

Assessment Criteria

An important factor in the selection of IT investments is the alignment of the proposed investment with the existing strategic objectives of the IT organization. For example, selecting an investment that has potentially high business value benefits but requires a new proprietary technology not currently supported by the IT organization may not be a smart thing to do. While the benefits may be attractive, the TCO for such a system may be high in the longer term. Introducing an IT system that is based on a proprietary or closed architecture—as opposed to a standards-based open architecture—can create vendor lock-in, which can lead to both short-term and long-term support and cost problems.

In the following sections, we discuss specific assessment criteria for the three BVI vectors: business value, IT efficiency, and financial attractiveness.

Business Value Vector

Table 4.4 provides a list of sample business value criteria. These criteria are all factors that influence the potential business value of an IT investment. If there is already significant demand or pull from senior executives in the business for an investment, it is likely that there will be both significant commitment and executive sponsorship for the investment (a very important success modulator for IT investments), and it is also likely that they have seen good alignment between the solution the investment could deliver and the business. Many businesses operate using strategic objectives that are reviewed on a periodic basis and provide the basis for making business decisions. If a potential IT investment is strongly aligned with the business's strategic objectives, the investment is likely to generate business value.

The criteria in Table 4.4 must be adjusted and amended for different industries and businesses.

Business Value Example

Important criteria for assessing business value include factors such as the level of demand or pull for a particular solution. For example, a solution being requested by the CEO of the firm will be prioritized higher than a solution being requested by a middle manager for a department. An investment that is well aligned with the firm's strategic objectives should be prioritized higher than an investment that is not aligned with the firm objectives. Similarly, a solution that directly improves firm revenue should be prioritized ahead of one that does not improve firm revenue.

Table 4.4   Business Value Assessment Criteria

Criterion	Explanation
IT customer pull	Extent to which IT's customers are asking for this deliverable—describe volume and strength and influence of the request or demand.
Firm strategic fit/impact	Level of alignment with strategic objectives (SO)—describe which SOs and how impacted.
Firm end-user performance improvement	User productivity, system performance, quality; not limited to only IT users.
New or enhanced capability	Completely new solution to solve a business problem or an enhancement or incremental improvement?
Impact on firm's business risk	Improvement in firm's business continuity, security, stability, and disaster recovery. (Total risk = severity of occurrence × frequency of occurrence.)
Level of innovation and learning for IT customers	New technology approach/tool for customers.
Impact on key business variables	Deliverable addresses one of the value dials from the list that is not covered by any criteria here —identify the specific value dials that are impacted.
Impact on firm's revenue	Directly related to protecting or enhancing the revenue generation environment, but not the magnitude of the impact.
End customer satisfaction and VOC	Impact on IT customer satisfaction, *i.e.* the firm's business units.
Size and level of customer impact (*i.e.*, visibility)	Magnitude of firm's population affected.
Use of firm's own products	Extent to which project showcases use of the firm's own products.
Confidence of success	Degree of confidence, from a business standpoint, that the benefit will be delivered.
Other intangible benefits	Please list additional benefits not captured above.

As IT solutions become more and more embedded in the business processes of companies, end-user performance of information systems becomes a critical factor in determining business value. End-user performance time is often called out as a specific assessment criterion because it is an important modulator of employees' perception of information systems. Improved end-user performance can help speed new system adoption time and hence time-to-benefits. Remember, as well, that Web services have become more pervasive and computer-to-computer transactions are replacing some people-to-computer transactions. This trend should be taken in account when developing evaluation criteria. For these business processes, replacing end-user performance with transaction-time performance may be indicated.

IT Efficiency Vector

IT efficiency is defined as the impact that an investment will have on the existing infrastructure and overall IT capability. While IT efficiency can be quantified in terms of product and service unit costs, IT efficiency in the context of the BVI relates to a broader perspective of IT. While the BVI focusing on IT unit cost reduction, it also includes factors such as alignment with IT strategic objectives. The BVI analysis sets a higher priority on an investment that is aligned with current IT organization objectives and architecture and a correspondingly lower priority on an investment that is not aligned with current IT objectives or uses a platform that is not part of the standard architecture. An investment that increases the IT organization's ability to deploy solutions to customers more quickly or improves IT employees' productivity will be valued in the IT efficiency analysis guided by the BVI.

BVI criteria for assessing IT efficiency are given in Table 4.5.

Table 4.5   IT Efficiency Assessment Criteria

Criterion	Explanation
Internal IT customer demand	Extent to which internal to IT customers are asking for this deliverable. Include the volume and strength of request
IT's strategic fit and impact	Level of alignment with IT strategic objectives
Level of innovation and learning for IT	New technology approach or tool for IT internal usage
Unit cost reduction	Lowers the unit cost of products - documents the products and the type of costs affected
Time to market	Increases the speed at which IT products and services are deployed to customers firm-wide
IT employee satisfaction impact	Level of impact on IT employee well-being, development, and growth
Confidence of success	Measurement of level of confidence to deliver on commitment
Size and level of impact to IT	Magnitude of IT population affected
Impact to IT employee productivity	Improved efficiency, faster project throughput, higher quality solutions

The impact of IT efficiency can be seen when deploying rich media. Compression of a large video file, which previously took twenty minutes on a PC powered by a Pentium II processor, now can be completed in less than two minutes on a PC powered by a Pentium 4 processor. This order-of-magnitude increase is especially relevant when a task must be performed by many thousands of employees on an ongoing basis. Decompressing rich media for viewing on a desktop or laptop is such an example.

Financial Attractiveness Vector

Several approaches can be taken to determine the financial attractiveness of an IT investment, but I recommend that you use the metrics that are prevalent and trusted in your industry and your business. Remember that it is important to speak the language of your business to make the IT organization's viewpoint credible.

Typical financial attractiveness criteria are shown in Table 4.6.

Table 4.6   Financial Attractiveness Criteria

Criterion	Explanation
Net present value (NPV)	NPV is a calculation that weighs an investment against its payback over time. The calculation demands four estimates: payback amount, payback period, a discount rate, and the investment amount. Negative NPVs can and do occur, both when paybacks are simply less than the investment or when paybacks are overridden by the discount factor, which is essentially the cost of money over time.
Payback period	Period between initial investment and recovery of the total investment.
Level of investment	Total investment required - allows an assessment of how many investments can be made against a particular budget. Includes both initial and life cycle costs.
Option Value	Potential future value not reflected in NPV.
Cost/Benefit Ratio	Total costs / total benefits. The cost/benefit ratio does not capture discount rates, but rather provides a simple ratio of all costs divided by all benefits. Smaller numbers are favorable.
ROI	Net benefits plus investment costs/investment costs. Net benefit is benefit less operating costs. The number 1 indicates break-even. Larger numbers are favorable.
Internal Rate of Return (IRR)	The actual rate of return (projected or realized) of the investment, taking into account the time value of money. (The IRR is the discount rate that makes an investment exactly equal to its payback over time).

The financial attractiveness vector should present a complete view of the attractiveness of a financial investment. Different weightings assessed for different criteria will provide a basis for prioritizing investments. This BVI vector aims to deliver a ranked list of the most attractive

IT investments based on a synthesis of the financial drivers. Financial attractiveness ratings should help, for example, to choose between an investment with a reasonable return but very short payback period versus an investment with outstanding return over a longer payback period. The broader BVI viewpoint helps to counterbalance the fact that ROI estimates do not express the uncertainty of outcomes that a particular investment may create.

Visualizing BVI

The output from BVI can be viewed either graphically or in tabular formats. Figure 4.6 shows the typical graphical output from the BVI tool for a sample of 10 investment alternatives. Competing IT investments are plotted against business value and IT efficiency axes, with the size of the bubble reflecting the relative financial attractiveness of the investment. This presentation highlights investments Enterprise Virtual Drive (#1) and MLearning (#3) because they appear high on all three criteria. Inversely, the investment in WList Spec (#4) is unlikely to survive since it is low on all three metrics.

When two competing investments have the same ROI, it may be the case that one choice is directly aligned with the business's strategic objectives while the other is less directly aligned. Without the business value analysis, this distinction could be missed and a poor investment decision could be made.

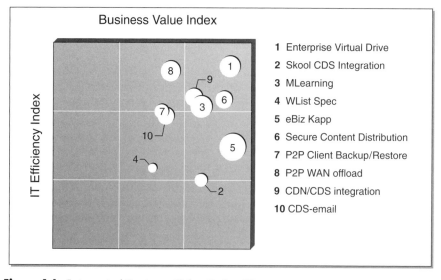

Figure 4.6 Integrated Business Value Index Plot

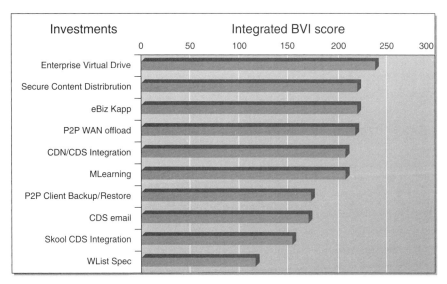

Figure 4.7 Investments Ranked by Integrated BVI Score

To make the best investment decision, the BVI data set should be viewed from several perspectives in both graphical and tabular format. Note that using only financial criteria for decision making would lead to the selection of a different set of investments.

Figure 4.7 shows the investments ranked by composite BVI score. Notice that the Enterprise Virtual Drive investment remains at the top of the list, but MLearning is not in second position, as expected. Eyeballing Figure 4.6 is not as accurate as ranking by the exact composite score.

Figure 4.8 on page 110 ranks the investment opportunities solely by financial attractiveness and eBiz Kapp rises to the top. The Enterprise Virtual Drive project is buried in the middle. That investment is likely to be larger and perhaps riskier.

Figure 4.9 on page 110 shows that the IT efficiency will be enhanced if the Enterprise Virtual Drive project goes ahead. Notice how eBiz Kapp, top rated for financial attractiveness, drops near the bottom when ranked by IT efficiency. There must be a mismatch between current infrastructure and that project's requirements.

Figure 4.10 on page 111 provides a ranking by the business value index. Ranking by BVI brings eBiz Kapp back to the top of the list! Each of these graphs provides a different perspective on the collection of projects.

In these examples, I have purposefully not attempted to explain the substance of the investments so that you can see the methodology most

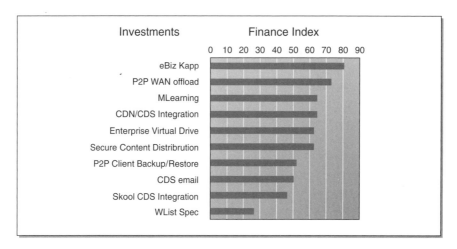

Figure 4.8 Investments Ranked by Financial Attractiveness BVI Score

clearly. Imagine, if you would, how rich this methodology would be when applied to a collection of projects you understood.

A business can gain a holistic view of an investment's financial attractiveness by looking at a variety of financial measures and combining these in a financial index. This approach can help decision making when, for example, one or two large investments that might consume the entire investment budget are competing with many other smaller investments that may have smaller returns but ultimately may be a more attractive route because of their benefit/risk profile.

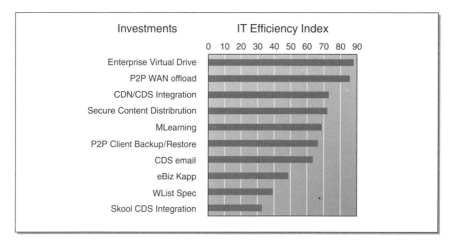

Figure 4.9 Investments Ranked by IT Efficiency BVI Score

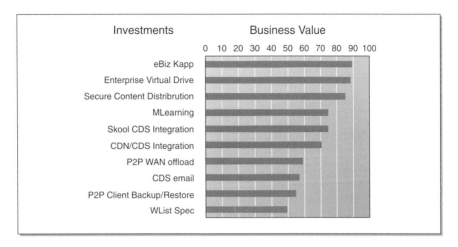

Figure 4.10 Investments Ranked by Business Value BVI Score

Maintaining a Holistic View

A quick BVI scan can provide busy IT directors and business executives with good information to make the right investment decisions. Investment ranking information can also be presented in tabular form and an affordability line drawn to show how many investments the budget can afford.

Ongoing portfolio management requires managers to constantly shift resources from low-return projects to high-return projects. Consistently doing so is key to improving business and financial performance from IT investments. Using a ranked list and drawing an affordability line can be useful as a resource management tool to allocate available resources to the highest potential value investments.

A typical affordability analysis involves reviewing the ranked set of investments, reviewing the available resources, eliminating some investments if there is a resource shortage, or acquiring additional resources to meet original investment list. Using the ranked BVI list means that priority is assigned to IT investments that are forecasted to demonstrate a solid financial return to the company and/or an intangible return in support of corporate objectives and directions.

Table 4.7 on page 112 shows the example projects ranked by the composite BVI index values. The magnitude of the investment is shown for each investment and the cumulative investment is computed. In this example, the total available funds amount to $2.8 million. An affordability line marks the point where available funds are depleted. Investments above the availability line, beginning with the *MLearning* project, will be funded. Investments below the availability line, beginning with *P2P Client Backup/Restore*, will not be funded. Typically, a management review committee would apply judgment to the ranked list before deciding which investments to commit to and which to discard.

Trending BVIs over Time

I recommend preparing trend lines for BVI scores over time, much as you would prepare charts and study trends with stocks. Plotting the scores on a chart allows one to see at a glance how a particular investment or IT option is performing. This allows investment decisions to be based not just on a single assessment but also to include information about the investment's behavior over time. I believe that it is important for firms to invest in IT options—small speculative investments in IT that at worst provide some learning and at best generate real value and potentially differentiating technology or solutions. These small investments behave like options because if results are favorable, then larger investments can quickly follow. In many ways, IT options are like pilot studies.

Table 4.7 Ranked List of Investments with Affordability Line

Investment Project Name	Investment ($K)	Business Value Index	IT Efficiency Index	Financial Attractiveness Index	Total BVI	Cumulative Investment ($K)
Enterprise Virtual Drive	800	88	88	63	239	800
Secure Content Distribution	500	85	72	63	220	1300
eBiz Kapp	550	90	49	80	219	1850
P2P WAN offload	300	59	85	73	217	2150
CDN/CDS integration	100	71	73	64	208	2250
MLearning	400	74	68	64	206	2650
---------------------------------- $2.8 million affordability line ----------------------------------						
P2P Client Backup/Restore	250	54	66	52	172	2900
CDS-email	800	57	63	50	170	3700
Skool CDS Integration	100	74	33	46	153	3800
WList Spec	100	50	39	27	116	3900
Total Investments ($K)	3900					

Intel IT used the BVI methodology with a speculative investment in peer-to-peer technology. The initial speculative investment paid for a quick throwaway demonstration tool. However, the demonstration tool showed potential and, following a second BVI assessment, a subsequent follow-up investment was made to further develop a proof of concept prototype and put it through testing trials. Subsequently a production version of the software was released, but not before several other options from the original investment emerged. A second generation version of the technology is now being used as a building block in several public eLearning solutions. A third generation of the technology is being developed and linked to a future Intel product launch.

For this particular speculative investment the BVI score has continued to grow as greater value accrues. For one of the options spawned, the BVI score has whipsawed when both interest in the solution and business criteria changed.

The BVI is a decision support tool for IT investment decisions. In general, I recommend that BVI should not be used exclusively as the only tool or factor in the investment decision-making process. A thorough IT investment decision should be made based on the BVI results, the business drivers for different initiatives, the dependencies between projects (both within the group and between other groups), the impact on internal and external customers, the amount of investment, and other relevant business or environmental factors.

Two Business Cases

In bringing this chapter to a close, I shall develop, compare, and contrast two business cases. Both cases examine investments in wireless LAN technology. The first case is based on our experience at Intel IT. You may find it interesting because the business case is based entirely on soft benefits. This is not to say that there is not quantitative benefits. More on that shortly. The second business case was developed in the public sector. The wireless LAN is a part of a civic renewal initiative in the City of Westminster. The CEO of the Westminster City Council, Peter Rogers, intends to transform how the city works. Both hard and soft benefits are counted in the Westminster case. I do not consider tax effects in either business case because these effects will differ from country to country.

Wireless LANs for Intel: Valuing Soft Benefits

In October of 2002, Intel prepared a business case to explore the business value of investing in wireless LAN technology. The financial analysis was prepared and justified solely on the basis of soft benefits. This does not mean that our analysis lacked rigor. In fact, quite the opposite is true. Intel's Brian Tucker conducted a pilot study with over 160 users to collect both qualitative and quantitative data. Using the results from this pilot, we were able to translate the productivity gains into dollar benefits that were counted in the ROI analysis.

We set aside the potential hard benefit of wireless LANs, the elimination of the need for cabling for new buildings or retrofitting cables into older buildings. We didn't count the cabling cost savings because we believe that wireless LANs will be complementary technology to our wired LANs. I highlight this assumption because, for many firms, wireless LANs will be a primary network solution and hard cost savings will certainly weigh in favor of a wireless solution.

Before conducting a pilot study, we enumerated the soft benefits that we thought might be delivered by a wireless LAN. Those benefits included the following:

1. Faster decision making because information would be accessible anytime and anywhere.

2. More accurate information as workers capture and share data anytime, anywhere, and in real time.

3. Increased flexibility for staff who would be able to synchronize their work without the need to locate cables and physically connect to the LAN.

We believed that these intermediate benefits should lead to increased productivity. In addition, we thought that we might also measure an increase in employee satisfaction and motivation. Employees should enjoy improved job flexibility and access to latest technology.

To quantify the time saved, we surveyed and monitored a sample drawn from different user segments at Intel—engineering, manufacturing, sales, marketing, and support. Members of the pilot study were provided wireless LAN for a period of three months. Our primary measure was time savings based on self reports of our pilot sample. Average Daily Time Savings per User is shown in column two of Table 4.8. In consideration of a number of factors, including the Hawthorne Effect (*i.e.,* the tendency of a group under study to over-perform), we adjusted Average Daily Time Savings per User by dividing it in half. With the added assumption that not all saved time could be put to use, we divided the time savings by half a second time.

Table 4.8   Results and Analysis of Wireless LAN Pilot Study

User Segment	Average Daily Time Savings per User Reported (hours)	Average Daily Time Savings per User Adjusted #1 (hours)	Average Daily Time Savings per User Adjusted #2 (hours)	Hourly Burden Rate ($)	Productivity Benefit Per Year Per User ($)
Marketing	1.80	0.90	0.45	55	5816
Engineering	1.49	0.75	0.37	60	5252
Support	1.47	0.74	0.37	45	3886
Manufacturing	1.33	0.67	0.33	40	3126
Sales	0.67	0.34	0.17	55	2165

Finally, we multiplied the twice-adjusted time saved per day, the number of work days in a year, and the burden rate for each category of employee to compute an estimate of productivity improvement measured in dollars. Benefit estimates ranged from a high of $5,816 per year for marketing staff to a low of $2,165 per year for members of the sales force. As with any business case, it is important to state and document the scope of the work and the assumptions underpinning estimates.

Two mechanisms may transform these productivity estimates into business value. First, current employees could be more productive, effectively making it appear that there more resources available in the company. Second, business value could be realized by redeploying resources in areas that received the productivity benefits. In practice, IT investments ordinarily lead to a mix of both outcomes. Some managers are satisfied with a workforce that is more productive while other managers aim to redeploy employees because fewer people are needed to do the same amount of work.

With the soft-benefit pilot survey in hand, we can now build a business case for a wireless LAN. The scope of our plan will be deployment and operation of a wireless network using the 802.11b standard to be installed in a large building with four floors, each floor measuring 100,000 square feet. The system would support 800 users. Startup costs will include the purchase and installation of 24 wireless access points per 100,000 square feet of office space.

We made the assumption that the wireless LAN will support 12 to 15 simultaneous users per access point. 802.11a implementations support higher user densities because 802.11a can support up to twelve separate communication channels whereas 802.11b can support only three. Because of its higher speed, 802.11a access points cover a smaller area.

Table 4.9 shows the financial analysis. Based on the pilot survey and our continuing interest in conservative benefit estimates, we assumed the lowest gain estimated by the pilot study, a $2,165 gain for each of 800 users. Total benefits is $1.732 million, as shown on savings (cf. line item 1 in Table 4.9), for Year 2, Year 3, and Year 4. The Year 1 productivity benefit estimate is set to zero to be conservative about ramp-up schedules. We identified cabling and network equipment cost avoidances savings while explicitly setting them to zero as well.

The business plan identified ten categories of costs. We assumed that one full-time network engineer would be required to support every two floors and an additional full time equivalent would be needed at our technical assistance center to support calls for help. Those expenses appear in line item 4. We also estimated that two engineers would required to configure and manage wireless network interface cards (NICs) for the 800 users, and those funds appear in line item 8.

I must pause briefly to note that with the adoption of Intel Centrino™ mobile technology, which occurred subsequent to the preparation of this business case, the cost side of a wireless LAN business case will improve substantially. Eliminating wireless NIC cards eliminates the cost of two engineers managing NIC cards and the cost of maintaining an inventory of spares. The cost of lost NIC cards is eliminated as well. Finally, the capability of a laptop to automatically attach to certified access points will reduce support calls.

The financial analysis results in a NPV of over 2 million dollars and produces an IRR of 255 percent—impressive by any yardstick. IRR was computed using present value cash flow, which takes into account the time value of money. Historical IRR would be calculated from actual cash flow for the project. For simplicity I have assumed that the value to be delivered from the wireless LAN begins in Year 2. In reality this value begins to be delivered immediately to the user. To build a financial analysis assuming value in Year 1 would require quarterly cost and benefit snapshots. The payback period using this approach is 1.4 years.

I hasten to add that while the indicators for this single business case are impressive, the metrics become even more useful when several competing business cases are laid side-by-side.

Table 4.9   Financial Analysis: Wireless LAN for 800 Users at Intel

	Year 1	Year 2	Year 3	Year 4
Benefits				
1. User Productivity Benefits	0	1732	1732	1732
2. Cabling avoidance	0	0	0	0
3. Network equipment avoidance	0	0	0	0
Total Benefits	0	1732	1732	1732
Costs				
1. Capital equipment	(57)	(3)	(3)	(3)
2. Access points	(43)	(3)	(3)	(3)
3. Deploying access points	(96)	(19)	(19)	(19)
4. Ongoing support	0	(450)	(450)	(450)
5. User training	(48)	0	0	0
6. Miscellaneous costs	0	(19)	(19)	(19)
7. User wireless NICs	(72)	0	0	0
8. Install and configure NICs	(140)	(21)	(21)	(21)
9. Spare NICs	0	(11)	(11)	(11)
10. Spare access point equipment	0	(15)	(15)	(15)
Total Cost	(456)	(541)	(541)	(541)
Total Project Cash Flow	(456)	1191	1191	1191
Present Value	(456)	1036	900	784
Cumulative Present Value	(456)	580	1481	2264
Discount Factor	1	0.87	0.76	0.66

Return on Investment (Net Benefits + Investment / Investment)	8.84	Discount rate = 15%
Net Present Value ($K/year, Year 1 - Year 4)	2263	Table entries are $K
Internal Rate of Return (%)	255	
Payback Period (years)	1.4	

Wireless LANs for City of Westminster: Both Hard and Soft Benefits

Westminster is the city at the economic and political heart of metropolitan London and the home to much of the financial community, as well as the Houses of Parliament, Big Ben, and Buckingham Palace. Working together, Peter Rogers, CEO of Westminster City Council (WCC) and Simon Mallet, Leader of the City Council, developed a vision of Westminster as the wireless city of the future.

While technology enabled, the vision is about civic renewal and improved services. Since the arrival of Peter Rogers, WCC has taken an aggressive posture towards IT investments. WCC adopted a customer relationship management (CRM) system for managing relationships with the residents and businesses of Westminster. On the civic renewal agenda was an objective to reduce crime and disorder by deploying closed circuit TV (CCTV). The CCTV investment is expensive with each installation costing £40,000. To improve service provisioning, WCC considered investments that would increase employee mobility. Rogers and Mallett wanted to get city staff out of their offices and to the locations where work needs to be done. They also considered investments in software solutions to help automate workflow and eliminate unnecessary or redundant work. Central to their thinking was the development of a wireless network to support information sharing for mobile workers.

The business case with both hard and soft benefits was prepared by Joe Greene, who is a systems architect at Intel's IT Innovation Centre in Dublin, Ireland. In studying the IT implications of the WCC vision, Joe noted that the cost of CCTV could be reduced by as much as 86 percent by using a digital camera transmitting images over an Internet protocol (IP) network using wireless technology. The significant reduction in cost enabled WCC to consider many more CCTV installations with the same investment. WCC considered digital wireless CCTV to be a hard benefit. Avoiding the cost of office space for WCC employees working from the field or at home was another hard benefit.

The key soft benefit was improved productivity enabled by mobile and wireless networking investments. In preparing the business case, WCC used research conducted by Gartner to estimate the productivity gains.

Table 4.10 shows the financial analysis for WCC's wireless initiative. On an investment of approximately £11.8 million, the NPV is approximately £4.5 million with an internal rate of return of 128 percent. This return is very substantial with the benefits coming from a mixture of hard and soft benefits. The ROI of 1.57 indicates a positive return.

Table 4.10 Financial Analysis: Wireless LAN for the City of Westminster

	2004	2005	2006	2007
Benefits				
1. CCTV capital saved	2423	2423	0	0
2. Office space saving	450	900	900	900
3. Productivity	1313	2625	2625	2625
4. Other	421	1403	1403	1403
Total Benefits	**4607**	**7351**	**4928**	**4928**
Costs				
1. Phase 1	(5982)	0	0	0
2. Phase 2	0	(5859)	0	0
3. Support and maintenance	0	(595)	(1189)	(1189)
Total Cost	**(5982)**	**(6577)**	**(1189)**	**(1189)**
Total Project Cash Flow	**(1375)**	**774**	**3739**	**3739**
Present Value	**(1375)**	**673**	**2827**	**2460**
Cumulative Present Value	**(1375)**	**(702)**	**2125**	**4585**
Discount Factor	**1**	**0.87**	**0.76**	**0.66**
Return on Investment (Net Benefits + Investment / Investment)	**1.57**	Discount rate = 15%		
Net Present Value (£K/year, 2004-2007)	**4584**	Table entries are £K		
Internal Rate of Return (%)	**128**			
Payback Period (years)	**2.16**			

In this case, the hard benefits associated with CCTV installation are likely to be achieved. On their own, the hard benefits would likely be enough to justify implementation of the entire project or, most certainly, the CCTV part of the project. The soft benefits associated with business process and practice changes by WCC employees will be achieved only if changes in work practices can be successfully implemented. The proportion of soft benefits achieved will depend on the quality of employee relations, the way the business case is presented to employees, and the success of the change management process. These perceived risks associated with the soft benefits should be documented and taken into account in the business case.

One approach advocated by Bloor Research (2002) is to multiply the benefits by a figure between 0 and 1 that represents the probability of the benefit being achieved. Other approaches include adjusting the soft productivity numbers downward or increasing the discount rate. Doing either lowers the value of NPV. As always, a small targeted pilot can really help with evaluating how well the business case maps to reality and, in November of 2003, this is indeed what Westminster City Council was planning to do next.

Contrasting the Business Cases

Business cases consist of four essential elements: benefits, costs, justification, and a valuation. Justification for the WCC case was documented in a twenty-page report that accompanied the ROI statement. This document described the opportunities, problems, required high-level business process changes, and expected savings. Depending on the complexity of the value proposition associated with an IT project, more or less information may be required.

The business case for WCC was researched and assembled over a six-week period. After the proposed strategic pilot, the business case will be refreshed and a new assessment made as to whether to proceed with the full implementation. Incidentally, capital spending in the WCC case was spread over two phases and two years to make the project affordable from a capital budget standpoint. The financial scenario shown in Table 4.10 is just the first investment profile considered. Investing all necessary capital in Year 1 is another investment profile. When the spending occurs will depend on the capital budget of WCC and, particularly, on the readiness of the workforce to adopt new practices.

In the Intel case, the value proposition for investing in wireless LAN was compelling and the business case was offered to Intel general managers along with an offer from Intel IT to deploy a wireless LAN on a pay-per-view basis. Informed by this business case, many Intel general managers opted to invest in wireless LAN technology for their business or building. The next step for Intel IT will be deciding when to make wireless LAN technology a part of the corporate infrastructure. The high rate of wireless LAN adoption and the increasing deployment of PCs with Intel Centrino mobile technology are leading us in this direction.

Each business case has to be believable to the people that authorize its implementation. Using a data-driven approach is very helpful in this regard. For Intel, it was crucial to run a pilot study to estimate productivity gains. For WCC, data from Gartner research were used to prepare the case. However, data are often not enough.

A respected champion is also very important for driving the business case into implementation. At WCC, the sponsorship for the business case came from the very top of the organization, the CEO Peter Rogers. Support from the CEO substantially increases the likelihood of a project being successful. At Intel, the champion was our CIO, Doug Busch. The case also gained support from Intel users who were not allowed to provision their own wireless LAN networks. While this community could see the benefits, Intel IT had to rein in rogue wireless LAN deployments to avoid security exposures.

I have two final comments on the Intel business case. First, cost per user for wireless LANs drops as more users are added. Thus the rapid deployment at Intel improved our business case. Second, the business case was also substantially enhanced by the deployment of wireless LAN hotspots in public areas such as hotels and airports. These public hotspots allow a firm's employees to take advantage of wireless connectivity when they are on the road as well as at the office.

Summary

In this chapter I have explored how to build better business cases that include estimating monetary value on productivity and other intangibles. I have discussed Intel's business value framework, a win-win-win investment framework that can drive better IT investment decision making. Finally, I described the Intel business value index as a methodology with metrics that inform better investment decision making.

Chapter 5

IT Portfolios and Options

Strategy is not about the future, but about the future implications
of current decisions and actions.
—Kulatilaka and Venkatraman, 1999

In this chapter, I shall introduce additional level 4 CMF practices for managing for business value. Level 4 practices are distinguished from level 3 practices in that they seek to optimize the return from a set of investments rather than to maximize the return from an individual investment.

Portfolio Management

One of the most important level 4 practices is portfolio management. Portfolio management is an approach combined with a set of tools for identifying, diagnosing, controlling, and increasing the return on aggregate IT investments. The concept is rooted in the management principle that an investment requires careful stewardship and proactive management to maximize value. Such proactive management of IT investments is a key premise of this book, and taking a portfolio management approach helps enable comprehensive stewardship on an enterprise scale.

While portfolio management practices are more commonly applied to real estate or securities management, they can also be applied to IT investments. The goals are the same: maximizing return and business alignment. In the context of IT, portfolio management takes advantage of an integrated set of business processes, techniques, and tools that assist senior decision makers in selecting, executing, and managing an optimal portfolio of investments to minimize risk and maximize value for the organization. Properly executed IT portfolio management also delivers the benefits by helping to balance supply and demand for project resources (*i.e.,* people and funding), to eliminate redundancy, and to enable consolidation of efforts and better alignment of investments with strategic goals.

IT organizations have shown significant interest in the use of portfolio management. However, progress in implementing the concept often encounters a fair amount of resistance. In a report published by researchers from the Kellogg School of Management, Jeffery and Leliveld (2003) found that CIOs and IT organizations were struggling to apply portfolio management principles to their IT investments. The study found that the primary difficulties were reluctant management support, a lack of financial skills necessary to quantify benefits, and the continual shifting of project and enterprise goals. Do these challenges sound familiar?

The good news is that best known practices are now emerging that can help companies benefit from this approach.

Compounding Effect of Interconnectivity of IT Investments

I believe that, by their nature, IT investments are typically more interrelated in a digital, networked environment than in classic commodities such as stocks or real estate. Therefore, portfolio management may have a significant positive compounding effect. For example, previous infrastructure investments can enable a new IT service to be launched at significantly lower incremental cost. For example, because Intel had previously invested in high-power PCs for its employees, we were able to introduce a distributed video-to-the-desktop capability at very low incremental cost. The application runs in a distributed environment using the idle processing power on employee PCs.

IT investment value can be multiplied greatly if a portfolio is sufficiently flexible to adapt to changing business needs and climate. When studying early adopters of IT portfolio management, Mark Jeffery at the Kellogg School of Management found that firms enjoyed both tangible and intangible benefits, including increased credibility with other members of management teams, better guidance when setting spending priorities, improved identification of key gaps in IT spending, and fewer bad investments.

Getting Started on Portfolio Management

Project management techniques can be a good starting point in portfolio management and a competency that should be prevalent in all strong IT organizations. Project management encompasses many of the required techniques for IT portfolio management, including resource allocation and management of the schedule and milestones. Resource limitations in funding, staffing, and hardware determine how many projects or investments can be simultaneously conducted and managed. IT management must study analyses of investment and understand investment dependencies to manage cash flow, reduce risk, improve resource usage, and increase value. IT organizations that have mastered project management techniques should find portfolio management techniques a natural extension of project management skills.

When launching a new portfolio management project, I suggest that you not start from scratch. Instead, consider obtaining some short-term consulting to help establish your portfolio management approach. New software products are emerging that greatly assist automating the process of establishing and managing portfolios. And, remember that portfolio management assists not only in choosing and implementing the right IT investments but also in eliminating unnecessary or low value investments.

The first step to portfolio management is ordinarily a portfolio inventory analysis. According to META Group, the inventory analysis alone can reduce IT spending by 10 to 40 percent. Software to support the inventory process is increasingly available.

Once a baseline inventory is collected, the next step is to analyze and evaluate contents of portfolios from a business value perspective. It is not uncommon to find duplication of services in a first portfolio inventory. The results of this analysis provide an excellent platform for cutting spending and reallocating resources. Thereafter, the portfolios should be adjusted regularly to balance risk, innovation and business value.

Portfolio Management Lenses and Frameworks

I look at a portfolio of IT investments through a number of different lenses. Investments can be judged by cost, value, or volume, for example. Here are additional ways of classifying and analyzing IT portfolios that I have found particularly effective.

Portfolio Management by Management Objectives

I find the strategic investment framework developed by Jeanne Ross and Cynthia Beath (2001) particularly useful. Ross and Beath, researchers at MIT CISR, based their research on a sample of thirty US and European companies. They studied the companies' eBusiness initiatives and the IT investments that supported those initiatives.

The strategic IT investment framework developed by Ross and Beath categorizes IT investments into four types: transformation, renewal, process improvements, and experiments. This classification serves well to form four macro-level portfolios for IT organizations. Here are definitions of the four portfolios, which I have modified slightly from the original definitions provided by Ross and Beath.

■ *Transformation* initiatives create significant long-term infrastructure or solutions that enable major changes in a firm's organizational processes or even lines of business. Intel IT's move from an 80:20 desktop/mobile PC ratio to a 20:80 desktop/mobile PC ratio is an example of a transformation infrastructure investment. This initiative led to significant productivity improvements as well as a change in operating style for the company. Intel's transformation to an eBusiness is an example of a transformation solution. The eBusiness initiative required a large transformational investment but now yields over $500 million per year in savings. The initiative aimed to make all B2B and B2E (business to employee) transactions electronic.

■ *Renewal* initiatives improve the efficiency or effectiveness of existing shared IT platforms. An example of renewal is a program that replaces older PCs with new, more powerful PCs that improve performance and lower TCO.

■ *Process improvement* investments launch business applications or solutions that focus on identifying and developing opportunities afforded by IT. Typically, process improvement investments are aimed at automating new or re-engineered business processes.

Enhancing a CRM system with improving functionality and performance is an example of a process improvement.

■ *Experiments* are initiatives that may improve the performance and effectiveness of IT infrastructure and that improve the agility of the IT organization to respond speedily to shifting business needs or unexpected opportunities. Intel's deployment of peer-to-peer computing is an example of an experimental initiative. The experiment provided a peer-to-peer infrastructure that enabled Intel to quickly deploy video to the desktop when an ROI analysis underscored its business value.

Ross and Beath organize their four categories of IT initiative as shown in Figure 5.1. When considering investments that will strengthen long-term growth, IT planners should look to transformational or experimental initiatives. Investments in shared IT infrastructure, both long and short term, are renewal and experimental. Looking at the categories on the margins (*i.e.,* applications versus infrastructure, short-term profitability versus long-term growth) will further inform IT and business decision makers.

To manage an IT investment budget proactively using this approach, decisions need to be made about how much of the budget is to be invested in each part of the portfolio. The allocation of funds across the different IT investment types will vary from firm to firm, and across industries, depending on factors such as the information intensity of the firm and the competitive landscape of the industry.

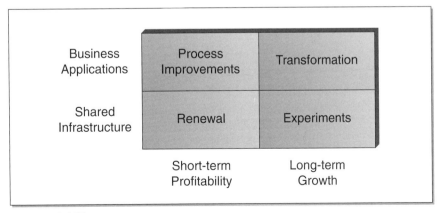

Source: MIT CISR

Figure 5.1 Investment Framework

Figure 5.2 shows an actual portfolio from a Fortune 500 company, illustrating that company's allocation of investments. The portfolio resembles the generic framework presented above, but has been tailored to include a foundation portfolio that includes shared infrastructure across the company.

This IT organization spends 0.5 percent on innovation and would like to double that investment to 1 percent. Currently, the portfolio shows that half of all investment is in foundation initiatives, but the company intends to shift much of this funding into the other portfolio areas and reduce foundation spending to 10 percent. The renewal portfolio includes capital spend on items such as PCs, spend that is cyclically driven.

This company wants to increase spending from 6 percent to 10 percent for quick return projects that are rapidly implemented and deliver rapid realization of results. The most dramatic shift of portfolio weighting for this company is the increase in transformation investments, which rise from 18.5 percent to 39.5 percent. Transformation investments aim to provide breakthrough IT solutions that improve the company's productivity dramatically.

Depending on the type of investment, justification techniques differ. When the focus is on short-term profitability, standard discounted cash flow techniques can be used because of more experience and more certainty with respect to the outcome. For IT investments that are focused on longer term growth, an options-based approach is more appropriate.

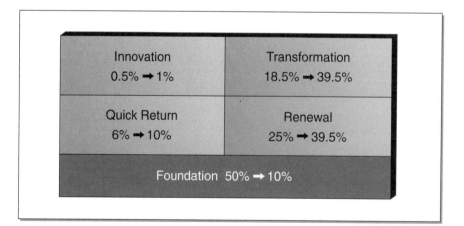

Figure 5.2 IT Investment Portfolios

Portfolio Management by IT Investment Type

Another important approach to portfolio management is the one introduced by Peter Weill of MIT CISR and Marianne Broadbent, now of Gartner Group. This approach is based on allocating investments based on the different management objectives achieved through using IT. According to Weill and Broadbent, firms invest in four types of IT solutions to meet four fundamental management objectives:

- *Strategic* IT investments to gain competitive advantage
- *Informational* IT investments to provide better information to enable better decision making
- *Transactional* IT investments to speed up or cut costs for transactions within the firm or externally with its trading partners
- *Infrastructure* IT investments to provide a foundation of shared IT services for the firm and develop a platform favoring agility in responding to new business needs, challenges, or opportunities

Weill and his associates at MIT CISR have performed extensive research on just what IT investment asset mix leads to the best returns across a variety of industries. Based on a study of 147 firms in 2001–2002, Weill found that the average firm allocates 54 percent of its total IT investment to infrastructure. Of the remaining 46 percent, 13 percent was allocated to transactional investments, another 13 percent to strategic investments, and the final 20 percent to informational investments.

To use his framework for portfolio analysis, Weill recommends classifying planned IT investments into the four asset classes and then analyzing their relative positions compared to the industry average. The allocation of investments in the portfolios depends upon whether the firm's focus is on reducing cost, on increasing agility, or on a balance of both.

Portfolio Analysis by Porter's Value Chain

Using Michael Porter's value chain to analyze where different IT investments are targeted is another approach to portfolio management. Depending on the distribution of investments, you can quickly see whether investments are balanced or prioritized appropriately. For example, a firm competing on its manufacturing capability is likely to have a higher number of its investments targeted at this part of the value chain.

Portfolio Management by Key Business Responsibilities or Objectives

Another lens used for allocating and analyzing IT investment portfolios is is the lens of key business objectives or responsibilities. This method is used at Deutsche Bank, a world-leading financial corporation, where three high-level portfolios are aligned directly to the bank's top-level business objectives and responsibilities.

1. Change the Bank (CTB)—discretionary investments that are used to improve and develop the bank's key products, processes, applications, and infrastructure.

2. Run the Bank (RTB)—nondiscretionary investments that ensure the continued running of the bank's key products, processes, applications, and infrastructure.

3. Mandatory (MAN)—external regulatory, external market, and both internal or external audit-driven investments.

Deutsche Bank has successfully used portfolio management to help measure the value of IT projects. To achieve this they use two key methodologies, investment governance and program governance.

■ Investment governance is the process by which Deutsche Bank manages their portfolio of investments to deliver maximum return on IT investments. Investment governance is used to inculcate a culture of benefits realization across the bank.

■ Program governance is the process by which Deutsche Bank manages individual investments to deliver the desired functionality and benefits. Deutsche Bank believes program governance instills a culture of efficiency.

All proposed investments are allocated to one of these three portfolios. The investment program life cycle for Deutsche Bank includes:

■ Budget
■ Initiation
■ Requirements Analysis
■ Design
■ Development
■ Testing and Review
■ Deployment
■ Support and Maintenance
■ Post Implementation Review
■ Application Decommissioning

Deutsche Bank views its investment and program governance processes as their key processes not only in achieving business and IT alignment, but also in eliminating overlap and achieving synergies among various investments. Deutsche Bank implemented these processes to address a number of different issues. The bank wanted to make sure that necessary global project data were complete, technical/application strategies defined, investments thoughtfully prioritized, benefits well specified, and accountability well understood. Finally, the bank wanted to capture cross-product synergies and avoid duplication of efforts.

Deutsche Bank had two key objectives in implementing investment governance. Firstly, the bank wanted to maximize the return on investment from IT spend and, secondly, the bank wanted to change the culture to focus on maximizing return on investment. As a first step in implementing a portfolio management approach, Deutsche Bank set out to define the various components of its portfolio correctly and globally. Investment, program, and project are the three levels in a Deutsche Bank portfolio.

- Investments form the highest level of aggregation in the project hierarchy. Investments are the major initiatives for a particular year. Typically, a finance person reporting directly to the CIO is assigned to manage each investment. Investments are jointly defined by the business managers and CIO. Investments are composed of a group of programs that support the same strategic or technical deliverable.

- Programs are mid-level in the project hierarchy. A program is a group of projects that together aim to deliver a set of related business or technical services. Each program maps to a single investment.

- Projects form the lowest layer in the portfolio hierarchy. As such, projects are the building blocks for programs and investments. Deutsche Bank defines a project as an undertaking requiring concerted effort that has a defined start and end point, defined deliverables that identify completion.

These clear definitions of components in the portfolio management approach are crucial to a cohesive approach across the company.

To keep the investment governance process simple, Deutsche Bank developed a one-page template that requires a value proposition for every project and program. This template provides a framework for a fully defined ROI calculation with benefit and cost estimates over the lifetime of the investment. The Deutsche Bank template also requires entries indicating the fit with current architecture plans, the expected level of risk, the impact of not doing the project, and, importantly, any business disruptions or shutdowns needed during the project.

Deutsche Bank implemented an investment governance committee to enforce the discipline required to properly govern investments. There is a regularly scheduled meeting with a prior deadline for submission of investment summary forms. Performance of the investment governance committee is measured by progress against a schedule. Regular investment governance meetings help to ensure portfolio management discipline.

For Deutsche Bank, the investment and program governance processes ensure that all investments have sponsors and every investment has well-defined benefits. Deutsche Bank reports improved synergies and substantial benefits realization. The portfolio approach has enabled Deutsche Bank to improve alignment of strategic investments with business value and has also has generated attention on disinvestment opportunities.

Integrated Portfolio Management at Intel

At Intel, a group called IT Business Services (ITBS) is responsible for managing one of our portfolios of IT investments (Haydamack 2003). On a quarterly basis, ITBS compiles a list of new and existing investments. For each proposed or existing investment, ITBS creates or updates two templates.

- The *program overview* is a single-page document that describes the purpose of an investment, its sustaining costs and affordability requirements. The overview also notes other essential information such as a list of affected IT customers, partners, and design organizations. Key program assumptions, project phases and milestones, and resource requirements per quarter are also noted.

  The program overview maps to program governance processes that I discuss in detail in Chapter 6.

- Intel's business value index (BVI) (*cf.* Beyond ROI: The Business Value Index on page 98) analyzes the prospective or current investment in the light of IT business value contribution, IT efficiency impact, and financial attractiveness. The BVI provides a standardized scale with which to compare more than one program.

  Program managers designate the primary investment type (*i.e.,* strategic, transactional, infrastructure, or informational) for each investment.

BVI Analysis

A BVI plot, such as the one in Figure 5.3, is a first step in analyzing which investments potentially fall in a win-win space—that is, in the top right hand quadrant. It is important to note that, while the BVI scores are an important input to investment decision making, management judgment has the biggest influence on which investments are made. Such decisions are influenced by affordability, program phasing, organizational politics (unfortunately), and other factors.

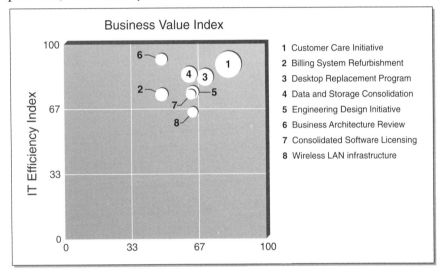

Figure 5.3 Business Values and BVI Scores

Intel also prepares bar charts to see on a linear scale which program is likely to deliver the most value. The chart in Figure 5.4 on page 134 shows BVI scores for all projects. The top two programs, Customer Care Initiative and Billing, contribute the most value and this is because they are programs that contribute value not just across IT but across all Intel groups. Figure 5.4 also reveals that the largest contributions to value are from the IT efficiency category, and this is what is expected. ITBS is offering services primarily targeted at other internal IT organizations.

Portfolio Analysis and Allocation

Analyzing the proposed portfolio by investment type produces the chart in Figure 5.4, which shows the portfolio mix in the current quarter and the proposed portfolio mix by investment type in the next quarter. It's very important not just to take a static look at the portfolio but to know how the portfolio changes over time.

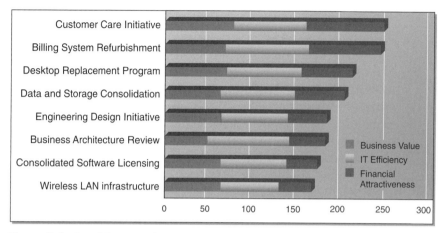

Figure 5.4 Portfolio BVI Showing Component Scores

Figure 5.5 shows that in the current quarter, informational investments were 45 percent of total investments followed by infrastructure at 24 percent, strategic at 21 percent and transactional at 10 percent. When we referenced these weightings to the average weightings for our industry as identified by Peter Weill and associates at CISR, we found that the infrastructure allocation was significantly underweight. As a result, we planned to increase our investments in infrastructure, aiming for it to be 42 percent of the program mix in the next quarter. It is important to note that it is likely that portfolio allocations cannot be instantaneously

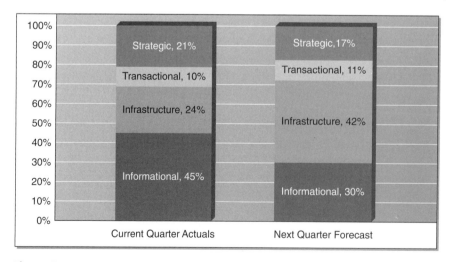

Figure 5.5 Current and Projected Portfolio by Category

fixed but the agility and program and financial responsiveness will determine the agility of the firm in responding to necessary changes.

Pipeline Program Phase Analysis

Another critically important piece of analysis is the phase profile of a particular portfolio. If all the IT investments are in the sustaining phase and none are in the earlier stages of the development pipeline, you may have a scenario that will ultimately bankrupt the portfolio and the value derived from it. On the other hand, if all of the investment is focused on programs that are in the early stage of the program pipeline you may find yourself with a portfolio that is unaffordable without some significant pruning.

Figure 5.6 shows the profile of the ITBS investments by program phase. In the current quarter, 45 percent of the ITBS programs are in the explore, planning or development phase. Given that the total operating costs are likely to be 4 to 5 times the development costs, it is likely that some pruning of this investment portfolio will be required in the future to make it affordable. Ongoing BVI analysis and comparison will be a key driver for the ongoing portfolio optimization and analysis. Also, as the business environment and firm objectives change, the weightings of the various criteria used in the BVI analysis may change, driving different prioritization recommendations, which management can then analyze and act on as appropriate.

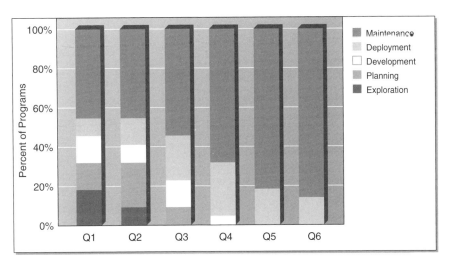

Figure 5.6 Profile of ITBS Investments by Program Phase

Finally, collecting the forward-looking investment requirements of the program is very important to understanding the affordability and ensuring financial predictability of the portfolio. Figure 5.7 shows the projected capital requirements for the ITBS portfolio and identifies a large capital spike required for the portfolio based on the current investment profile.

Having this kind of data available means that investments can be resequenced to smooth the investment profile. Collecting the future resource profile per program also allows a similar analysis showing which resource types will be in under- and over-supply, thus driving forward-looking retraining or redeployment of resources to meet future investment needs.

Yet another perspective on the IT portfolio is business driver analysis. In this view, IT managers inspect the alignment of business objectives and IT investments, The IT portfolio ought to reflect business needs, both in IT's investment priorities as well as in the allocation of resources.

Organizations need to apply integrated portfolio management techniques and processes to managing their IT investment portfolios and creating value. Without this kind of data, firms are flying blind and relying on luck and their ability to do diving catches as they try to maximize the value delivered from IT and make their business successful.

Craig Haydamack, the IT Business Services manager who has driven the development and implementation of the process, says that this approach has significantly helped with managing his organization's investments for maximum value.

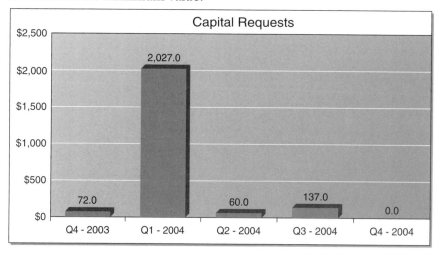

Figure 5.7 Capital Requests

Level 5: Investment Performance Analysis

As firms move to level 5 in the business value capability maturity framework, attention shifts to a methodical consideration of risk. Level 4 provides a necessary foundation, a predictable portfolio of IT investments with known benefits. Using comprehensive risk analysis, firms move on to setting a required rate of return that is higher for investments that have higher risks. Level 5 companies take an options approach to optimize the return on their portfolios of IT investments.

Incorporating Benefits into Future Budgets

As organizations improve in their investment decision making and investment management, they become more able to take accountability for business value by adapting the ensuing years' budgets to take advantage of benefits to be delivered or costs to be saved from a particular project. This accountability significantly ups the ante on the need for the promised business value to be delivered.

Consider, for example, a project that aims to deliver an IT efficiency cost savings and requires a capital investment of $1 million. If successful, the project will increase the number of servers that an engineer can manage and reduce head count by 5 for the ensuing years. In this case, expense budgets are reduced by five times the average burdened cost for a server engineer.

Of course, the IT organizations must deliver the expected efficiency gain. If the project fails, the service might not be delivered as promised or the IT organization will need to overspend. Neither of these are desirable or indeed acceptable outcomes. I believe, however, that increasing accountability increases the likelihood that the promised business value will be delivered. Even where unexpected obstacles are encountered, project teams will be resourceful to try to deliver the committed benefits. "Necessity is the mother of invention."

Federal Express stresses IT accountability in its IT planning process. When a business division signs up for an IT investment, that division states the expected impact explicitly—either in terms of revenue increase or cost savings and these figures are then integrated into both business and IT operating budgets for the ensuing years. This approach puts significant focus on accurately determining up front what the projected impact will be and then managing the investment carefully to ensure that the projected benefits are delivered.

Planning processes that stress accountability work well in an environment where there is a high level of trust (*i.e.,* a strong relationship asset—see Chapter 6) between the business unit and IT. This practice is also an example of how to integrate the managing of the IT budget while managing for increased business value to produce synergies and win-win outcomes.

An Investors' Approach to Risk-related Return

One could argue that as IT organizations are held increasingly accountable for IT efficiency and business value outcomes, the acronym CIO will come to have one of two meanings: "Career Is Over" if business value that is delivered is below expectations or "Chief Investment Officer" if significant business value is delivered. Clearly the CIO needs to pick the right mix of high and low risk investments to deliver an optimal IT business value return.

Most investors are willing to accept a higher level of risk if there is a possibility of increased return, The CIO and business leaders should be not behave differently. What this means in investment terms is that the required rate of return should not be fixed, but rather should across the IT project portfolio. Required rate of return, also known as the hurdle rate, is the level of return that the firm demands given the investment's risk.

Applying the concept of required rate of return to decisions about IT investment means making risky projects more difficult to approve. One mechanism for implementing required rate of return is to make more conservative assumptions for the cost and benefit estimates that affect the NPV calculation which will, in turn, drive NPV down and make an investment less attractive.

Investment Performance

Across the portfolio of investments it is important to track the performance over time. Financial institutions use the term *alpha,* which is a measure of the difference between targeted IRR and actual return, given the investment's level of risk, which is typically called *beta.* ING is an example of a leader who uses this concept to measure the financial performance of their investments.

Figure 5.8 shows the *alpha* coefficient in action, for a given level of *beta*. In this hypothetical example, 12 investments are ranked by their *alpha* values. Sixty-seven percent of the investments have positive *alpha* values, which indicates that 8 of the investments outperformed their IRR target. The remaining third of the investments are underperforming. When prepared on an ongoing basis, charts like Figure 5.8 illustrate both

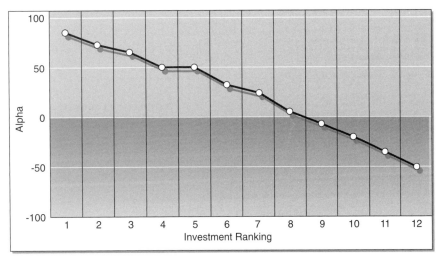

Figure 5.8 Investments Ranked by Alpha

continued value delivery and projects that are in trouble. Plotting *alpha* performance from quarter to quarter produces another view helpful to ongoing investment management.

Taking an Options Approach

Now that we've looked at techniques that manage past and ongoing investments, let's look at techniques that are proactive and forward looking. However intelligent and informed your IT organization and enterprise strategists are, they cannot predict the future accurately. However, by making a number of relatively small information technology investments, you are likely to win no matter how the future turns out. These investments have characteristics that are very similar to financial options. Like options, these investments have a low initial cost and that allows you to defer making the larger investment decision until you have more information about which investments will be winners. Like a venture capitalist, you count on one or two winners to pay for all the losers and then some.

To secure the future of a firm it is necessary to make a series of ongoing speculative investments. As discussed in Chapter 3, assessing the value of these investments is difficult using NPV calculations because NPV does not handle uncertainty or multiple outcomes well. Real options methods, which are used quite extensively in finance industries, hold good promise for use in IT investment decision making.

Jim Kenneally, a researcher in real options, draws an analogy between draw poker and real option models (ROMs). If players had to place their final bets as soon as the first hand were dealt (as standard ROI or NPV calculations do), most would reasonably opt out quickly. But because they know they will have opportunities to refine their hands as they draw additional cards, they can merely put down a small initial stake to stay in the game. Depending on the next card, they pass, match or raise, and so on.

Real Options Reasoning

In applying real options to IT investments there are two levels of engagement; first, real options reasoning and second, real options valuation. The first is straightforward to adopt, and the investment logic is simply that making a modest speculative IT investment creates an option that gives the right, but not the obligation, to invest further. Real options reasoning also involves a recognition of a long-odds structure and a pattern of investing like venture capitalists do. Valuing real options is somewhat more complex, and a topic that is beyond the scope of this book to cover in detail.

Options Modus Operandi

Recent research by Rita Guenther McGrath of Columbia University Business School has distilled some best practices for companies that are achieving growth through learning to innovate systematically. The characteristics of these companies' practices are listed below, and these can be adopted to enhance IT investments.

- *Growth companies emphasize new business development, without ignoring excellence in base business.* This corresponds to earlier recommendations in Chapter 2 about minimizing operational spend to create funding that can be used for new strategic initiatives.

- *Growth companies regard uncertainty as positive, not negative.* It is precisely the uncertainty around the use of information technology and the risk involved that can help add strategic advantage by introducing a solution that, for example, transforms the industry or is difficult to replicate.

- *Growth companies make decisions, even with imperfect information.* Analysis Paralysis is a symptom many firms and IT organizations exhibit—lack of action driven by drowning in data. Tools like the BVI give good but not perfect information and can and should be used for driving actionable plans.

■ *Growth companies make speculative investments* and, while they see many failures, they focus on maximizing the learning rate while containing the cost of failure rather than the rate of failure. This is a subtle but important distinction. Growth firms recognize that in failure there is learning. They take intelligent risks and take a venture-capital approach in investing, recognizing that, while a high percentage of investments may fail, there will be several spectacularly successful ones that will pay for all the failures and more.

■ Finally, *growth companies know when to stop an investment*. IT organizations and business managers need to exhibit this behavior both for early stage developments that indicate that they will not work out and also for solutions that have outlived their useful life and need to be retired.

The same characteristics need to be applied to IT investment. In my own efforts at Intel IT Innovation, the group is making speculative IT investments seeking to find the solutions that will drive dramatic or disruptive changes for Intel. Because the risks and benefits of IT options investments are difficult to predict, we use the Business Value Index as a proxy to measure and track options value. We use the BVI tool on a regular basis to decide whether to proceed with an investment, accelerate an investment, or stop an investment.

Measuring Value Using Real Options

We said earlier that when the complexity of and the uncertainty of cash flows is high and there may be many outcomes from an IT investment, the more traditional valuation mechanisms are not very useful. Yet it is precisely the uncertainty around an IT investment that can lead to the creation of significant value. Expanding the definition of NPV can be very useful in dealing with uncertainty.

Expanded NPV = Passive NPV + Option Value

Passive NPV is the value of the investment in today's dollars without considering the flexibility or options the investment may bestow. The concept of *option value* is that management has the flexibility to change aspects of investment decisions—rate, focus, value derivation, and so on—as more information becomes available. IT Investments can be accelerated, refocused, stopped, or several permutations of these can be used. In other words, management has the ability to capitalize on an investment's upside potential as well as the ability to limit the impact of an investment's downside losses.

Like all valuation, option value is a function of three fundamental factors: cash, timing, and risk. As time moves on and more information is available, risk assessment becomes more accurate.

The ability to start, modify, or stop an IT investment at some point in the future is different from the ability to take advantage of it now. A decision to invest can be made when a particular uncertainty is resolved or when the option to make an investment has expired. In addition, option value is iterative because making one investment can lead to several other investment opportunities, each of which, if taken, can lead to subsequent further options.

As an example, a small speculative investment in a peer-to-peer prototype at Intel IT that was initially deployed to move large rich media files seamlessly throughout Intel resulted in the creation of new options such as peer-to-peer backup and the ability to move an IT product into the marketplace. A third generation of the initial prototype—Intel® Content Distribution Software (CDS)—is now the subject of a technology transfer to external eLearning solution providers, providing revenue to the Intel IT organization and also enabling more Intel processor sales in the eLearning industry.

Evidence of the Option Value of IT

To investigate the option value of IT projects, Jim Kenneally of the University College Dublin Graduate Business School conducted a study on a diverse portfolio of historical and current IT investments at Intel Ireland, one of Intel's largest manufacturing facilities. Seventeen project managers were interviewed regarding 31 IT projects, 14 of which were ongoing and 17 of which were completed. The newest project in the portfolio was in the definition phase, and the oldest project had been completed 18 months before the interview.

Kenneally used Porter's (1985) value chain to classify the investments before analyzing them for option value. As can be seen from Table 5.1, the 31 projects reviewed were spread throughout the value chain with a concentration in operations/technology development, which is what we expected for a large manufacturing facility.

Table 5.1 Number of Projects for Value Chain Classes

	Inbound logistics	Operations	Outbound logistics	Sales and Marketing	Service
Corporate Infrastructure	9				
Human Resources Management	1	2			
Technology Development	3	8	1	2	3
Procurement	2				

Kenneally's team looked at three types of options that affect the level of investment in a capital IT project: reduction options, expansion options, and deferral options.

Reduction Options

A reduction option is defined as the ability to scale down the initial investment should either internal or external conditions prove unfavorable. Twelve projects were identified as having reduction options. Reasons given for why a reduction could be necessary were both internal and external. External reasons offered by project managers were mainly changes in market demand and regulatory compliance. Internal reasons given were related to internal political risk, budget overrun, technical risk, limited resources, and project management difficulties. While the internal reasons were more varied than external ones, external reasons were cited for eight out of the twelve cases of reduction options identified.

Expansion Options

An expansion option is defined as the ability to make any additional investment that becomes beneficial as a direct result of the initial project investment. Most of the 30 expansion options identified come from the ability to increase the number of users, add additional functionality that will provide benefits for relatively small cost, implement the original application in other sites, or apply it to other processes. A critical finding was that expansion returns appeared to be much larger than those of the original projects. This makes sense, as expansion capitalizes on the development work already completed and is a function of the compounding effects of IT investments. The reasons for expansion options are presented in Table 5.2.

Table 5.2   Reasons for Expansion Options

Reasons	Percent
Additional functionality	27.3
Capacity expansion	12.3
Application in other business units	2.8
Increase the number of users on the system	3.3
Implementation at other sites	1.4
External commercialization	0.1

Deferral Options

A deferral option is defined as the opportunity to postpone the irreversible action of making the original investment in the project. All deferred projects were considered to be potentially beneficial because of the opportunity to reduce investment costs during the deferral period. Deferral options, which accounted for only 5 of the 47 options identified, were rejected by many project managers due to both contractual obligations with vendors and Intel's culture of being first to market. Some managers also reported that it is difficult to be critical of your own project. Where deferral options existed, they were primarily viewed as an opportunity to reduce project costs during the deferral period, and not as an opportunity to expand the project if newly arriving information was favorable.

Option Value Results

A full comparison between portfolio value and option value is not possible because detailed data were not available for all projects. However, comparisons are possible between projects and scale-up options because their costs and benefits are conceptually similar. In particular, the portfolio's total cost was about $30 million—that is, the cost of the original projects was $15.5 million, and the expansion cost of the scale-up options was $14.5 million, or about 49 percent of the portfolio cost.

For 20 projects, data about expansion benefits were available for both project and scale-ups—28 options on 20 projects. The total benefit of the portfolio of original projects was about $102 million, a handsome return. The total benefit of the scale-up options for these projects was about $273 million, or 269 percent of the original portfolio benefit. This correlates to a 30:70 split of where the benefits are realized between the original investments and the expansion options they possessed.

These simple comparisons demonstrate that not only are there many options, but also their costs and values are considerably more valuable compared to the original investment. This can mean that for many organizations the true value of their investments may never be fully realized unless they appraise IT investments as real options. The compounding effects of IT investments was also a significant source of increased value.

In conclusion, this research study showed that strong evidence exists for the premise that IT projects include considerable option value and should be managed using a lens of real options reasoning. The options studied resulted mainly from the flexibility of information systems (*e.g.,* adding functionality to systems), from leveraging infrastructure (*e.g.,* deploying training on an existing intranet infrastructure) and from strategic aspects of the systems (*e.g.,* allowing for spare manufacturing capacity).

More detailed discussion of the research and results can be found in Kenneally and Lichtenstein (2001).

Dealing with Uncertainty

The benefits from IT investments are dependent upon both the capabilities that are actually achieved and on prevailing economic conditions. This involves two types of risk: project-related risk and market-related risk. Project-related risk is determined by how the firm chooses to design, implement, and manage the project. For example, when integrating two IT systems, the technology may not turn out to deliver on all of its promises. Market-related risk is based on customer acceptance, competitor actions, and other factors that affect market demand for the firm's products and services. Even when a project is deemed successful—the technology works and the processes run smoothly— competitive conditions can prevent the firm from realizing the planned gain in market share. By staging the investment and making follow-on decisions contingent upon the realization of market and project uncertainty, the firm will be able to protect itself from some of the most undesirable outcomes.

Exercising Options Optimally

As with a financial call option, the option to make a capital investment is valuable in part because it is impossible to know the future value of the asset obtained by investing. As long as there are some probability that the investment would result in a loss, the opportunity to delay the decision—and thus keep the option alive—has value. The question then becomes when to exercise the option?

When a company exercises its option by making an irreversible investment, it effectively kills the option. In other words, by deciding to go ahead with expenditure, the firm gives up the right to wait for new information that might affect the desirability or timing of the investment; it cannot divest should market conditions change adversely. The lost option value is an opportunity cost that must be included as part of the cost of the investment. Thus, the present value of the expected stream of cash from the project must exceed the cost of keeping the project by an amount equal to the value of keeping the investment option alive. IT managers should be motivated to hold options under conditions of high uncertainty, and they should be motivated to strike (or exercise) options under low uncertainty.

When is Managerial Flexibility Valuable?

Real option reasoning and valuation is most important in situations of high uncertainty where management can adapt to new information. When there is high uncertainty about the future (*i.e.,* the project is very likely to receive new information over time), flexibility will have value if management can act on this new information.

IT investments derive a substantial part of their value from managerial flexibility. In contrast to NPV analysis, the higher uncertainty around the potential benefits from the striking of future options is not punished, but it is recognized that a higher uncertainty leads to higher potential benefits while, due to a given flexibility, possible unfavorable developments do not entail losses.

Summary

In this chapter we have defined IT portfolio management, defined different portfolio lenses, and looked at examples of portfolio management in action. By performing portfolio management over a multiyear time period, more value can be accumulated as well ensuring affordability of investments. We then looked at characteristics of successful growth companies as applied to IT investments and discussed the application of real options reasoning to IT investment. We concluded with analysis of the option value of IT projects and cited a research study that found significantly more value was created from exercising the follow-on options, even though these entailed less expenditure than the original IT investments. The lesson: Take advantage of the compounding and option value of IT investments.

Chapter **6**

Managing the IT Capability

In terms of gambling, first there is horse racing,
then there is poker, and then comes software development.
—John Spangenberg, IT Investment Director, ING

This chapter is about managing the IT capability, which I define as what the IT organization can do for the enterprise collectively. IT capability includes the knowledge, skills, tools, processes, abilities, and motivation present and available in the IT organization to support or perform enterprise business activities. When IT capability matures, it is well understood by enterprise executives, becomes a differentiator for the enterprise, and is woven into overall enterprise business strategy.

Unfortunately, some CEOs view the IT function as a cost center, or simply as a nuisance that ought to be outsourced. When this is the case, there are no simple, guaranteed steps that will lift IT capability into enterprise business strategy. Delivering a steady stream of valuable IT solutions to the firm over time is the best path to maturity. There is no alternative to demonstrating the latent potential of IT capability except to climb the learning curve and earn the respect of enterprise business executives.

In this chapter, I introduce a maturity framework for IT capability that should help enable systematic improvement. I advocate a two-prong approach for improving the IT organization's capability: (1) focusing on strategies and actions, and (2) applying assessment instruments to identify and improve decisions and actions.

Competing on IT Capability

In 2003, Nicholas Carr published an article in *Harvard Business Review* entitled "IT Doesn't Matter." It is Carr's contention that IT is now a utility, and investments in IT will not deliver competitive advantage. Carr's article spawned a debate on this topic, and most of the articles that appeared in response attempted to refute his hypothesis. Responders argued that early adopters of IT and first-to-market companies with unique new IT solutions often find significant success in the marketplace.

I support the view that Alex Mayall of CSC Research Services sets forth: improvements in IT capability in recent years have far outstripped our ability to conceive of their use. This situation is very different from when IT organizations first emerged in businesses. In the early years, the limitations of IT were a main constraint. Do you remember punch cards?

Figure 6.1 illustrates that at some point IT's ability to meet business opportunities crossed over from lagging behind business needs to leaping ahead of business needs. Looking at this graph, you might challenge that claim by arguing that IT today is still cumbersome, expensive, and inappropriate for the needs of the firm. If so, you are confusing the technology itself with the capability of the IT function. IT capability might be bogged down by legacy systems and outdated skills, which can create significant barriers to IT exploitation and cause IT delivery to lag behind business demand.

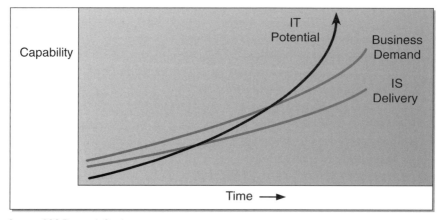

Source: CSC Research Services

Figure 6.1 IT Potential Outstrips Business Demand and IS Delivery

Improving IT Capability

IT capability is measured by the business value that the IT organization, and IT itself, can deliver for a company. This capability includes the role of IT as a strategic options generator, enabling the company to act quickly on new business opportunities and to respond with IT solutions. In different industries and in different firms, IT capability will exist at different levels of maturity. In the package delivery industry, for example, early adoption of new IT offerings has frequently given companies such as Federal Express a significant competitive advantage. At Federal Express, where routing, scheduling, and tracking packages is the core business, IT is absolutely essential to making that core business run efficiently. For Federal Express, IT capability is a key strategic asset.

Not every company chooses to elevate its IT capability to be a part of corporate strategy. In more traditional industries such as the steel industry, companies may be able to survive without advanced IT capability. However, even in traditional industries, players must realize that one company may develop a portfolio of IT solutions that quickly becomes a competitive necessity. When yield management systems were first deployed in the airline industry, for example, all players suddenly needed to develop equivalent systems or perish.

The Five-level CMF for IT Capability

The IT Capability CMF is a five-stage model describing the levels of maturity associated with the IT capability. These levels have been evolved from my work at Intel, which is focused on maturing our IT capability. The five maturity levels for IT capability are shown in Figure 6.2.

For companies at level 1, there is no formal IT presence. Users themselves typically purchase and try to maintain computer systems for their own use. Various departments may have business users with computer aptitude, but interconnectivity is limited and computer solutions exist in islands.

At level 2, IT is viewed as an external supplier or a utility provider that has little or no strategic input to the business. These IT organizations, like power or telecommunication utilities, exist merely to provide standard services to the business. The IT employees may be treated with little respect, and the IT organization is usually viewed purely as a cost center. When the IT organization is able to provide utility services with high availability in support of the core business, the IT organization is maturing and earns more respect.

By the time an IT organization matures to level 3, the organization has developed a track record of providing quality services, has delivered some new solutions, and has gained a reputation of being an organization of technology experts. Business managers would rather seek out an IT expert than attempt an ad hoc solution. Level 3 IT organizations are perceived as reliable IT suppliers who negotiate and keep their service level agreements (SLAs). Systems are highly available, and performance levels are sufficient to meet user needs.

At level 4, the IT organization is recognized as a strategic business partner to the enterprise at large. IT leaders are frequently or permanently invited to the business table to discuss and help set strategic direction. Level 4 IT organizations have often developed solutions that give the firm a competitive advantage in some key business area. IT leaders understand and anticipate business needs and proactively work to provide solutions to these needs. At level 4, key IT personnel may be invited to lead cross-functional teams to develop new strategies or tackle stubborn issues.

At level 5, IT capability is perceived as one of a select few strategic capabilities that are critical to the success of the company. IT capability is a differentiator for the company, a critical function that enables the company's core businesses, and a capability necessary for the company to remain competitive.

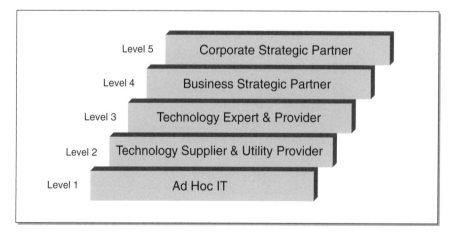

Figure 6.2 IT Capability CMF

The Need for a Theory of Business

Every firm or industry needs what Peter Drucker (1994) calls a *theory of business*—a fundamental model that describes how the firm adds value to the products or services that it offers to its customers. Drucker believes that a clear, consistent, and focused theory of business is extraordinarily powerful. Just as a conventional business uses its assets to create value for its customers, an IT business also has invested in assets that enable it to deliver value to members of the firm and, in many cases, to the firm's customers and trading partners. An IT organization with a clear, consistent, and focused theory of business will optimize this capability to create value.

Information technology by itself does not provide competitive advantage, nor does deploying IT systems guarantee a positive ROI. Instead, it is the *uses* of IT solutions that determine IT's value. What is needed is an IT capability that delivers the right stream of applications and solutions to sustain competitive advantage. As soon as competitors replicate the last IT innovation, the successful firm's IT organization should have the capability to deploy the next IT solution. Thus, the IT organization should aim to be one generation ahead in order to bring new solutions online in a timely manner.

The best way for an IT organization to determine how its capability is perceived is by asking its customers. In immature IT organizations, this conversation often takes place in unstructured meetings between business and IT managers. In more mature organizations, the assessment is made by using formal survey tools, recording key feedback and actions items, and maintaining survey histories over time to track progress.

IT Assets

Historically, IT assets have been somewhat difficult to describe and categorize. In 1997, Jeanne Ross and Cynthia Beath proposed that IT assets can be organized into three categories: *people*, *relationships*, and *technology*. To their model I have added an additional asset category: *intellectual capital*. I define IT assets as follows:

- IT *intellectual capital assets* consist of the business processes and know-how that are codified into enterprise solutions and applications, and the business data, information and knowledge that flow through the firm's solution and application portfolio.

- *Technical assets* are the sum of IT infrastructure including hardware, networks, storage, middleware, and databases.

- *Relationship assets* reflect the degree of trust and shared responsibility between the firm and the IT organization. In a conventional business, the relationship assets are called good will. Even though it is intangible, good will typically appears on a financial balance sheet to reflect the value of the organization over and above its tangible assets.

- *People assets* are the knowledge, skills and motivation of the IT work force that creates an ability to run world-class infrastructure and solutions and to turn IT and business know-how into winning solutions.

The IT Value Chain

IT assets lead to business value through their impact on an IT value chain, which consists of the sequence of processes that create value: dreaming up a solution, building that solution, and then delivering the solution as a service that meets the business need or capitalizes on the business opportunity.

The key inputs to the value chain are business opportunities and business needs that can be matched with potential IT solutions. The output of the value chain is a stream of solutions that solve business needs or capitalize on emerging opportunities. Another output of the value chain is future business opportunities that arise out of prior investments managed through the value chain.

In 1987, Cyrus Gibson, in his book, *The Information Imperative*, described the four basic value-chain activities of the IT organization as follows:

- Planning of applications and of technical infrastructure

- Development of applications

- Operations or use of developed applications

- Technical service and support of applications

Notice Gibson's focus on the technical aspects of the IT value chain and his focus on applications. A significant change in mindset has occurred over the past decade. The term *application* has been replaced by the term *solution*. This is a good development because delivering a solution emphasizes that a business problem is being solved rather than just that another application of information technology is being deployed.

At the same time, enterprises are increasingly coming to view their IT organizations as *service* organizations rather than *product* organizations.

An IT service provides a solution to a business need and typically has intangible benefits associated with it. In the old days, the IT organization would have delivered a server and a database as a product. Today, the IT organization delivers a customer care solution, an inventory management solution, and so on.

More recent research by Agarwal and Sambamurthy (2003) suggests that the IT value chain comprises both primary and secondary value-adding activities.

As shown in Figure 6.3, the primary value creating activities are *IT innovation*, *solutions delivery*, and *services provisioning*. IT innovation is the conceiving and prototyping of innovative new solutions that could provide competitive advantage; solutions development is the process of building and deploying solutions; and services provisioning refers to the flexible ongoing operation and support of these solutions.

Depending on the profile and maturity of the firm, the resource allocation profile across the steps in the primary value chain will differ. Many IT organizations place a significant majority of their resources on services provisioning. For these organizations, an objective for improvement may be to move resources back in the value chain by driving cost out of services provisioning and investing the savings in improved innovation and solutions development.

Resource allocation varies by global region as well. In November of 2003, I hosted a group of CIOs from Russia at Intel Ireland's IT Innovation Centre. In most western companies, the majority of IT resources are deployed in the services provisioning stage in the value chain. In contrast, in emerging markets there are fewer legacy systems to maintain. These IT organizations can afford to dedicate proportionally more

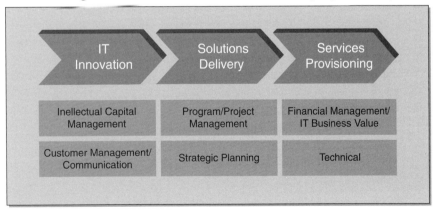

Source: Adapted from Sambamurthy and Agarwal

Figure 6.3 IT Value Chain

resources to IT innovation and solutions development. Also, since IT people resources in these countries are less expensive than resources in more developed economies, IT leaders have more people assets to put more *horsepower* behind IT innovation and solutions development.

Agarwal and Sambamurthy also describe secondary IT value chain activities that include processes such as strategic planning, financial management. These secondary activities provide a necessary foundation for the primary value chain. Quality leadership and management are other activities required in the IT organization.

Primary Activities in the IT Value Chain

I want to take a closer look at IT innovation, solution delivery, and services provisioning, which are the activities that define the primary stages in IT value chain.

IT Innovation. IT innovation is the process of creatively developing intelligent combinations of new and existing technology and knowledge to deliver new business solutions that can add new value or perform an existing function better, faster, or cheaper. While you might think that innovation is mostly about invention, the invention of entirely new technologies is generally only a small part of innovation. Innovation is all about knowing how to put technology to use to create or capitalize on new business opportunities, strengthen business competencies and customer relationships, and improve business processes. Along the way, IT innovators must ensure that innovation is in alignment with the strategic business thrusts of the firm.

Using a combination of satellite-based wireless WAN, peer-to-peer file transfer, and wireless LAN technologies to field eLearning at a remote site is an example of IT innovation. This combination of technologies can deliver near-broadband experience for learners while using narrow band connections. Once a single copy of an eLearning file is downloaded to the remote site, it can be replicated using peer-to-peer techniques. With a wireless LAN, learners are free to study lessons in their offices, in meeting rooms, or in the cafeteria.

While IT innovation in firms has generally taken place in *ad-hoc* fashion, firms are now trying to implement more systematic robust methods. Many firms cannot yet accurately identify the innovation activities underway in their firms. In the future, developing systems to support innovation and making the innovation visible will be increasingly important. At Intel IT, we are prototyping an IT innovation methodology aimed at capturing creative ideas, business problems, and enterprise needs. We expect this methodology to help systematically manage innovation.

Our methodology highlights the importance of rapid solutions prototyping. Moving quickly from thought leadership to working prototypes—analogous to the automotive industry's use of concept cars—allows us to run the pilot studies that evaluate the potential value and practicality of new ideas and innovations. If an idea or prototype demonstrates sufficient potential value, we can then shift to solutions delivery, which is the next stage in the IT value chain.

Solutions Delivery.   Based on the output from innovation, solutions delivery focuses on delivering the solutions either through internal development, external contracting, or through solutions integration using packaged software. The goal of the solution delivery stage is to ensure timely and cost-effective deployment of IT solutions to support business needs.

Depending on the profile of the company, IT organizations predominately either develop software solutions from scratch or integrate solutions purchased as building blocks. In the last decade, the pendulum has swung very much from *build* to *buy*. IT and business managers have come to believe that buying and integrating packaged software is more cost effective and carries less risk than developing custom software. However, I believe that we will see some rebounding in the years to come, with more organizations increasing their capability to develop custom solutions. Packaged software does not always fit an organization's need, integrating packaged solutions is increasingly complex, and more powerful development tools are available for custom solutions.

The Software Capability Maturity Model (S/W CMM) developed at Carnegie Mellon University's Software Engineering Institute (SEI) is the most widely recognized tool for improving competence in solution delivery.

The capability maturity frameworks (CMFs) that I put forward are based on the same principles that underpin the CMMs developed at Carnegie Mellon. For more information on CMM, look at the SEI Web site: *www.sei.cmu.edu.*

Services Provisioning.   Services provisioning is about delivering the primary services and products to support the firm. Activities include the allocation of IT services and resources, such as a share of the data center, the help desk, remote desktop management, and IT solutions. The primary objective of services provisioning is to deliver the services and solutions the firm needs in the most cost-effective manner. Rather than allocating fixed resources to users of IT within and outside the corporation, one objective of services provisioning is to be able to reallocate resources efficiently as workloads shift.

Service provisioning was once primarily an internal function and more recently has had an increasing external focus. The IT organization at Cisco Systems provides a case in point. While IT at Cisco supports 40,000 employees, it also provisions IT services to over a half million extranet users, the suppliers and customers of Cisco. It is a quantum shift for an IT organization to host more outsiders than insiders. Doing so puts new pressure on the services provisioning function and a stronger emphasis on security. The IT organization, once relegated to back-office activities, finds itself customer facing and supplier facing.

Many firms spend over 80 percent of their IT budget in the area of services provisioning. Surprisingly, there are few frameworks and approaches to support the formal development of services provisioning methods. Digging deeply into services provisioning is beyond the scope of this book, but I encourage readers to watch this area closely.

Here are activities that I feel are particularly important:

■ The IT Infrastructure Library (ITIL), formulated by the U.K government's Central Computing and Telecommunications Agency (CCTA), now overseen by its Office of Government Commerce (OGC) is a popular framework that specifies what tasks should be accomplished when building a foundation for provisioning. The ITIL defines a set of best practices in 24 IT disciplines.

■ The IT Service CMM is a practical framework for improving service provisioning competence. The IT Service CMM is being developed at the Software Engineering Research Centre (SERC), which is based in The Netherlands. For more information, check the SERC Web site://www.serc.nl.

Measuring and Improving IT Value Chain Performance

The performance of an IT value chain is ultimately measured by the business value it delivers. We have discussed many of these performance measures in Chapters 3 through 5. In terms of improving performance in a value chain, it is important to look at a number of different performance indicators:

■ Operational excellence—the measured ability to deliver and support solutions efficiently and reliably

- Creativity—the number of innovative solutions conceived, developed, and delivered

- Productivity—improvements in the amount of work output enabled by IT solutions

- Speed of delivery—the time elapsed between conceptualizing a solution and deploying a working solution that returns value to the customer

- Agility—the speed with which IT resources can be realigned with with changing business priorities

- Quality—the usability, accuracy, and reliability of new solutions aiming to address business needs

- Modularity—the degree to which an IT organization successfully minimizes the potentially complex relationships among solutions

Firms have high expectations for IT capability on each of these dimensions. Taken together, these performance indicators represent a broad-ranging agenda for the IT organization. Although delivering high quality, creative, productive, and efficient solutions with speed, and agility is a tall order, doing so means delivering business value and competitive advantage to the firm.

IT Program Governance. Managing the flow of products and services is often called IT program governance, which is a subset of portfolio management. IT staff responsible for program governance evaluate these services at checkpoints or stage-gates to re-assess expected future value based on risk, benefits, cost, and other factors. Managers responsible for program governance must decide whether to accelerate, stay the course, or halt IT initiatives depending on shifting business priorities or new estimates of contributions to business value. The ability of an IT organization to pick the right solutions and move them through the IT value chain quickly and in a cost-effective manner is a key determinant as to whether IT can provide sustainable competitive advantage to a firm. In some cases, the right decision may enable the firm to stay in business.

In my opinion, program governance is the single most important practice in the IT value chain because it provides oversight for all IT decisions in the IT value chain from initial concept to system testing, deployment to production, up to and including a solution's end-of-life. Program governance describes the key processes and tools used for developing and deploying new or incremental solutions in response to

Measuring Solutions Delivery Performance at ING

ING uses an integrated approach to measuring the performance of their value chain that reflects not only the solutions delivery process, but also the benefits that are delivered as the solutions and services are provisioned and operated. The integrated measure shown in Figure 6.4 reflects the real risks and trade-offs associated with solutions delivery and the IT value chain.

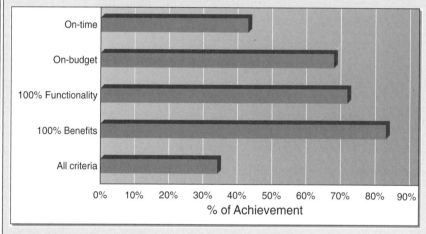

Source: ING

Figure 6.4 Risks and trade-offs for Solution Delivery

Business priorities and conditions determine which performance measures are most important. Time-to-market concerns may drive on-time delivery as the most important measure, with a willingness to exceed budget in order to drive on-time benefits delivery where these benefits are likely to be significant.

business problems or opportunities.   Program governance often maps directly onto the software development or solution development life cycle in a company. Typical stages in this life cycle include:

1. Conceiving the solution
2. Evaluating the investment's costs and benefits
3. Initiating the project
4. Analyzing the requirements
5. Designing, building, and testing

6. Piloting and validating

7. Implementing and deploying

8. Operating and supporting

9. Retiring the solution at the end of its life

As we have discussed earlier, ongoing measurement and accountability throughout the life cycle is crucial for benefit realization, keeping in mind that different phases in a program life cycle incur different costs. If a project is abandoned early in the life cycle, the sunken costs are generally small. However, abandoning a project just before deployment or, worse still, after deployment can be very costly. Efficient IT organizations should follow the example of product development in pharmaceutical companies by maintaining a pipeline of projects that have the potential to deliver future value.

Program Governance at Intel. Intel IT has adopted the program governance approach that our own product divisions use to develop Intel's microprocessors and communications products. Adopting a program governance methodology for IT solutions has been a major breakthrough for us. According to Keith Reese, VP of our supply network group, "First, program governance provides a framework that allows us to consistently manage a program from inception to completion using a system that has been proven by others. Second, program governance gives us a common language ... so that people can talk about where a program is and know what that means."

Intel's program governance revolves around a product development life cycle called Intel PLC. The three major components to the Intel PLC are phases, decisions, and program information. The phases for creating

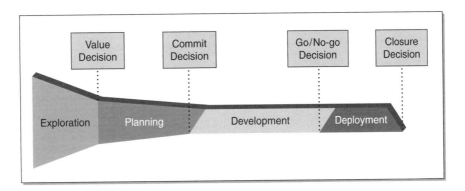

Figure 6.2 Intel's Product Life Cycle (PLC)

a product or service, shown in Figure 6.2, are exploration, planning, development, and deployment.

At Intel we use a stage-gate approach (described in Chapter 1 on page 19) that requires a decision at every transition between phases. The approach gives us the ability to accelerate, decelerate, or even halt programs depending upon their progress and depending upon their ongoing business alignment and importance. We believe in tracking benefits after IT solutions are deployed and we hold program managers accountable for post-deployment benefits. And, finally, we believe that program governance includes responsibility for retiring solutions from the firm's IT ecosystem at the right time.

An important component of program governance is developing standard templates and methods for each of the stage-gate review processes. Standard templates enable employees to focus on the content of their programs without having to worry about how to develop and present their evaluations. Similarly, standard templates simplify comparisons among IT programs and also help provide benchmark information at each stage gate.

IT Assets and the IT Value Chain: A Virtuous Relationship

IT assets and the IT value chain should be mutually reinforcing. As IT assets accrue, they need to be regularly reallocated to meet the changing needs of the business. At the same time, IT managers should strive to tighten the links in an IT value chain that delivers solutions more quickly and efficiently. In the process of delivering new business solutions, IT staff will gain new skills and the IT infrastructure will assimilate new hardware and software. The integration of the asset management and value chain optimization provides a useful conceptual model for the proactive management of IT.

I believe that the IT organization's theory of business should embrace the value chain and asset management. Here are six basic strategies that I recommend to systematically maximize business value delivered to the firm. I shall provide some examples of principles in action, and link this discussion on IT assets and IT value chain to topics covered elsewhere.

■ Develop and manage IT assets based on projected demand and growth.

Any business needs to scale its assets based on project demands and growth. For example, manufacturing firms build factories to a specific size based on projected growth. Similarly, the IT assets of a firm should be scaled to meet forecasts of future demand. For the

IT infrastructure, this means either having needed capacity in place or developing the ability to provision capacity in response to new demands.

At Intel we use a scale-up/scale-out approach when designing IT infrastructure. In response to increased demand, we can either scale up by adding more processors to make a single server more powerful or we can scale out by adding more servers.

In a similar manner, we manage our people asset as a flexible resource by using a mix of internal and external IT professionals to obtain the skill sets that we need. As skill sets at Intel change, we invest in developing new competencies for our people with vigorous training programs. In this way we upgrade the value of our IT people asset.

■ Focus on the highest leverage services and on strategic initiatives.

We make a point of identifying capabilities that are crucially important to Intel and improving the links in the IT value chain that delivers these capabilities. Input to the value chain is always a business opportunity or a business need. For some needs and opportunities, we need new and innovative approaches and for others, we need to tune the deployment and operation of the systems currently in place.

Investment governance, outlined in Chapter 4, is a key process area for ensuring that the IT value chain is focused on the right issues. The business capability roadmap (BCR) discussed in Chapter 4 is an example of locking of the IT value chain on a particular vector and sequencing a number of solutions along the vector based on priority and need for the business.

■ Improve speed and effectiveness of value chain transformation and execution.

The speed and effectiveness of the IT value chain needs to be continuously improved. I think the key issue is usually quality IT program governance. The value chain requires leadership and oversight. Governance assures that IT is focused on satisfying business needs and opportunities by efficiently and effectively delivering the right solutions in the time frame required by the enterprise. Methodologies such as *rapid application prototyping* or *Xtreme Programming* are examples of approaches that can be used to speed up the "beat rate" of the IT value chain, that is, how quickly the IT organization responds to new needs or opportunities.

Someone in the IT organization should be directly accountable for the IT value chain. That individual's challenge is to ensure that each stage in the value chain is performed effectively and that the links between stages are as tightly integrated as possible. I believe that the IT value chain itself is a candidate for a business process re-engineering exercise. Regular reviews to seek out improvements are often handsomely rewarded.

■ Improve conversion efficiency by raising asset utilization and improving alignment between IT and business objectives.

Redeployable IT assets, underpinned by open and scalable IT architectures, enable an efficient IT value chain. When the enterprise invests in new IT assets, the IT organization's goal is to create a virtuous circle where new assets are integrated with existing assets to provide useful new IT services at a small incremental cost. The goal is high utilization and I believe that infrastructure and people assets are often underutilized. Here are two examples:

- Highly skilled IT professionals are often bogged down in supporting IT customers in tasks such as resetting passwords. Such tasks as this are better performed by an automated system. The enterprise is incurring an opportunity cost because that same professional could be focused on delivering a higher-value IT solution to the firm.

- Many firms add computing assets, particularly servers and storage, on an application-by-application basis and lack an architecture that supports shared resources. As a result, server and storage assets are effectively stranded, and thus under-utilized. New technologies such as peer-to-peer computing and grid computing are aimed at enabling better IT asset utilization.

■ Sharpen customer focus by investing in improved customer account management.

The IT organization must understand the firm's information needs and opportunities in order to deploy IT capability accurately and effectively. Customer account management, discussed in Chapter 8, is a key part of running IT like a business. The ability to understand the needs of the firm and identify how information technology solutions can be used to meet or exceed business needs is essential in optimizing the use of the IT capability. Excellent customer account management will ensure strong business and IT alignment.

■ Migrate IT resources upstream in the IT value chain (*i.e.,* to the innovation and solution development states).

I believe that the IT organization should have a profile of budgeted expenses that is balanced across the IT value chain. Without aggressive management, resources tend to migrate downstream in the value chain. Over time, ongoing operations can consume nearly all resources. Lost is the opportunity to provide new and innovative IT solutions that might truly provide competitive advantage.

When resources can be directed upstream to IT innovation, there is a greater likelihood that more business value will be generated. I encourage IT managers to automate service provisioning as much as possible. Move the people asset freed by automation upstream in the value chain so that they can seek out better IT solutions.

I am not suggesting that services provisioning is not important. Keeping IT services running smoothly is a crucial first step in improving the IT capability. Only after successfully automating daily functions as much as possible will it be possible to shift resources to earlier stages in the IT value chain.

In the remainder of this chapter, I discuss strategies to develop and manage the IT assets. Other chapters cover the other strategies listed above in more detail.

Managing IT Assets For Value and Agility

IT assets are formalized in an architecture and that IT architecture includes both technology and people assets. As always, my objective is to manage all IT assets to gain business agility and to contribute to business value.

The Importance of IT Architecture

The IT architecture is one of the most important components that determine an IT organization's ability to develop and deliver IT capability. Prasad Rampalli, Intel's Chief IT Architect, defines the IT architecture as "the blueprint of stated intent for information technology." That is, the IT architecture is the document that identifies the component building blocks, shows how they fit together, and specifies the interfaces used to interconnect the components. Gene Meieran, who is an Intel senior technical fellow, likens IT architecture to the architecture of buildings, bridges, and towers.

I encourage readers who find themselves in the Silicon Valley to visit the Winchester Mystery House in San Jose, California. Its owner, Sarah Winchester, was the wealthy widow of the inventor of the Winchester repeating rifle. Armed with an unlimited budget and the belief that she would die if the house were ever finished, Sarah kept a corps of carpenters and craftsmen busy for 38 years. The result was a 160-room house that is a chaotic collection of rooms and doors added in an ad hoc manner, as well as several staircases leading nowhere.

The Winchester Mystery House is an extreme example of the consequences of constructing a building without an overall architecture. If the Winchester house were an IT architecture, I would describe it as ad hoc at best, with poor or missing interfaces, inefficient in its use of resources, and high maintenance.

In contrast, consider the Eiffel Tower in Paris, which was designed by Alexandre Gustav Eiffel. This structure clearly had an architecture and, as a consequence, the tower's design provided for additions, such as the shops and restaurants that have been added at different levels. After scaling up the tower, scaling out space for occupants was accomplished seamlessly. The overall impact of the Eiffel tower is high, and maintenance costs are relatively low.

The contrast between the Winchester House and the Eiffel tower is analogous to the decisions we make when building an IT infrastructure. Even with the best of intentions, I suspect that we all have a few staircases that lead to walls without doors.

Compared to architectural practices in the construction industry, IT architecture practices are relatively immature. Can you imagine a builder commencing construction of a building without an architecture? Yet we all know examples of IT solutions that start directly with programming before needs and requirements have even been defined. Defining a high-quality IT architecture is still perceived today as a black art with few tools, standards, and methods.

I believe that architecting IT assets for agility and value is the right imperative for IT planners. The configuration of the technical assets has significant impact on the ability of the firm to exhibit strategic agility and take advantage of new opportunities as well as react to emerging threats.

The basic four-tier enterprise model, shown in Figure 6.3, is a good starting framework. The bottom tier is a technical architecture, which comprises the processing, storage, and networking infrastructure. The technical tier supports a data and information architecture where enterprise information is well defined and available. Tier three is firm's application architecture and it consists of the software that provides IT services and solutions. Lastly, the technical, data, and application tiers support the business architecture, which comprises the functions that enable the enterprise to provide products and services to its customers, integrate with its supply chain, and provide the internal IT systems necessary to manage the enterprise.

I believe that IT architectures need to be defined and built for optimum flexibility to allow organizations to sense and respond to new environment changes or business opportunities and threats. Gone are the days when IT was primarily used to automate and support a few functions, such as general ledger or inventory management. Today IT is such an integral part of most firms that it is hard to separate IT and applications from the work of the firm itself.

It is beyond the scope of this chapter and this book to provide a systematic review of IT architectural choices. I freely admit that I have provided criteria for evaluating the important qualities of an IT architecture without providing the necessary engineering specifications or design heuristics for building one. From my point of view, it is the principles—such as adaptability and alignment with business value—that will prevail. Over the months and years to come, many technology solutions will emerge that address these operating principles.

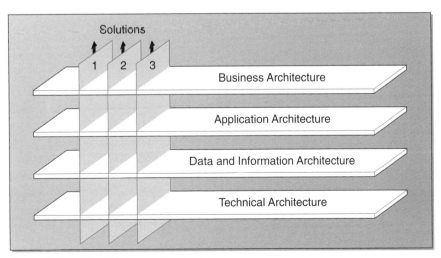

Figure 6.3 The IT Enterprise Architecture

IT Architecture Maturity

Jeanne Ross (2002), in her paper entitled "Creating a Strategic IT Architecture Competency: Learning in Stages," identifies four stages of maturity for an enterprise IT architecture:

1. *An application or solution silo architecture.* The architecture consists of several architectures for individual applications or solutions rather than an architecture for the entire enterprise.

2. *A standardized technology architecture.* The architecture is standardized throughout the enterprise with a limited number of hardware, network, and database components used to develop and deliver solutions.

3. *A standardized and clean-data architecture.* The architecture is standardized and, in addition, includes standards for structuring data and information.

4. *A modular architecture.* The architecture accommodates enterprise-wide global standards with loosely-coupled applications, data and technology components. The modular approach leverages enterprise standards while enabling some flexibility through loose coupling.

Moving up this architecture maturity curve structurally increases IT and business alignment to a significant degree. Having a modular architecture allows optimal flexibility and enables organizations to sense and respond to new environment changes or business opportunities/threats.

One example of a recent breakthrough for IT architecture is the concept of Web services—business or consumer service applications delivered over an intranet or the Internet, that users can select and combine for various activities. By using a set of shared protocols and standards, disparate systems can share data and services.

The concept of a service is all about creating a wrapper that hides internal complexity around an application or software module, exposing only a well-defined interface. Other software modules can call for services through this interface, easing the task of integration. The flexibility and reduction of complexity that the Web services architecture promises should deliver a significant improvement in speed of delivery, quality, and functionality for software.

The Web services model promises to improve agility and, I believe, the architecture is fundamentally changing the way that IT systems are built and integrated. The IT industry is on the cusp of building "plug-compatible" software components that allow easier integration, lower total cost of ownership, faster time to market and better integrated functionality. While similar breakthroughs have been claimed in the past, I believe that this time IT professionals will not be disappointed.

Developing IT People Assets

An IT staff that consistently solves business problems and addresses business opportunities through IT is a valuable IT people asset. In the past, IT professionals and particularly software developers were lampooned as wearing anoraks or pocket protectors and having little personality. Today, IT professionals in leading IT organizations are emerging as consummate IT and business professionals. Today's IT professional needs a solid foundation in technical skills from both the engineering and informatics cultures. IT professionals must be able to work cohesively in teams with increasing understanding of economics, market and business issues. In addition, IT professionals need to have good interpersonal skills, including problem solving abilities, awareness of the need for life-long learning, readiness to understand fully the needs of the customer and their project colleagues, and awareness of cultural differences when acting in a global environment.

Peter Drucker says that knowledge is the most important resource in today's economy—it is no longer labor, capital, or land. I agree and note that the knowledge resource is largely the people asset. Valuing people for both their intrinsic and instrumental worth is important. Maximizing the value of the IT people asset means cultivating an organization with IT professionals who have the right knowledge, skills, and motivation to do the right things right.

At Intel we looked for a framework for systematically developing our people asset and we chose the People Capability Maturity Model (P-CMM) developed at the Software Engineering Institute at Carnegie Mellon University (2002). We find the P-CMM to be a useful tool to guide continuous improvements in the management and development of the people assets of IT.

P-CMM is comprised of four strategies:

1. Characterize (measure) the maturity of IT workforce practices

2. Adopt a program of continuous workforce development

3. Set priorities for immediate action

4. Establish a culture of IT excellence

Table 6.1 shows the version of the P-CMM as we adapted it for our use. Intel IT integrated a category for safety because we wanted to align our safety practices (*e.g.*, data center safety, ergonomics) with our people initiatives.

Table 6.1 People-Capability Maturity Model

Maturity Levels	Process Categories				
	Developing Capabilities	Building Teams and Cultures	Motivating and Managing Performance	Shaping the Workforce	Safety
5. Optimizing	Coaching personal development	-------- Continuous workforce innovation -------			Injury free
4. Managed	Mentoring	Team building	Team-based practice, organizational performance alignment	Organizational competency management	Commitment to safety
3. Defined	Competency development, knowledge and skills analysis	Participatory culture	Career development, competency-based practices	Workforce planning	Compliant with safety
2. Repeatable	Training communica-tion	Communication	Meritocracy, performance management, work environment	Staffing	Reactive
1. Initial	--- Beginning ---				

Note: Adapted by Intel IT from SEI (2002)

Typically, P-CMM assessments are costly and require a lot of effort. At Intel IT, we implemented SAM-lite, a light-weight version of P-CMM that gives us results that are directionally correct (*i.e.*, approximate but sufficient) with significantly less effort and cost. SAM-lite is described in Chapter 7 and the details are in Appendix B. While a full explanation of P-CMM could fill a book in itself, I want to highlight the three key elements that I believe are pivotal to improving the IT people asset: career development, workforce development, and organizational competency management.

Career Development.   According to P-CMM, career development initiatives should provide a mechanism for employees to manage their own careers, identify and obtain the training and experience they need to progress through the IT organization, and add value in their work. At Intel IT, this goal translates into a process with five integrated components, as shown in Figure 6.4 and described as follows:

■ *Career paths*—illustrative paths for the most typical career trajectories paired with the skills required for new position.

■ *Job Descriptions*—standardized job descriptions with specifically defined competencies.

■ *Skills Builder*—a skills self-assessment tool with options to provide feedback to people on their readiness for a new position and to provide recommendations for a personal development plan.

■ *Development Plans*—a standardized template and development process for recording and tracking individual development plans.

■ *Training*—specific training resources organized by job type.

Workforce Development.   To implement workforce development, P-CMM requires a comprehensive documented process that provides IT managers with a framework for making the right staffing decisions and growing employee competencies. Workforce planning is concerned with putting the right number of people with the right knowledge skills, experiences, and competencies in the right jobs at the right time. Work-

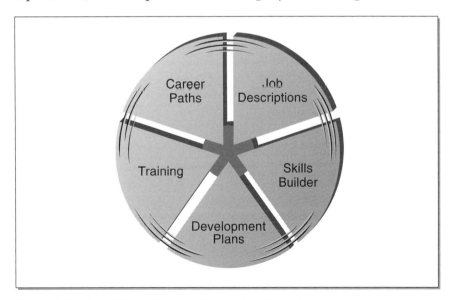

Figure 6.4 Closed Loop Process: Navigating Your Career

force planning and development occurs within the context of the firm's mission, strategic plan, and budgetary resources.

Competency Management. Competency management is concerned with defining, quantifying, and managing the current and future competencies required for the IT organization and for the enterprise as a whole. Organization-wide competency management is a process that is difficult to perform and can easily be overlooked because everybody assumes someone else is doing it. I encourage you to engage in competency management at the IT organization level to ensure that the competencies you begin developing now are the ones you need in two years time.

Motivation is important for IT employees. Even with the right knowledge and skills, if members of the IT staff are not motivated, they will not deliver the right solutions. Having a high level of intellectual capital means not only having the right knowledge and skills but also a high level of motivation. A critical task for CIOs and IT leaders is to create a compelling vision and emotional climate that leads to sustained energies and satisfaction for all IT employees.

The *soft* aspects of the people assets cannot be ignored—they are absolutely critical for long-term sustained success of the IT organization and, indeed, the firm. In his book *Beyond World Class*, Clive Morton (1998) quotes figures that provide a compelling case for the equal importance of soft people investments along with hard ones. Morton says "Good people management practices can give 20 percent productivity and profit improvement compared with 6 percent from a combination of research and development, innovation and quality."

Ireland's Intel IT organization takes a quarterly IT employee well-being survey to assess the emotional state of the organization and to gain feedback on potential current or future issues. In parallel, frequent informal *brown bag* lunches allow managers and employees discuss ongoing priorities and issues outside regular staff or operations meetings.

Developing the Relationship Asset

Relationships based on mutual trust are typically the foundation of all accomplishments. Trustworthy relationships generate possible solutions in risky situations, analysis of the possibilities leads to qualified opportunities and finally opportunities lead to results. I believe that trust between the IT and business organizations is essential to maximizing business value. IT and business managers should take shared responsibility for ensuring that benefits are delivered from IT projects. Often, quality technology amounts to only 20 percent of what is needed to make a project successful. Success depends in large measure on behavioral change and other relationship-based activities in the firm.

Developing an IT marketing organization is one good way to improve the relationship assets. The purpose of the marketing organization is to explain the solutions and capabilities of the IT organization to the firm as well as trying to understand the IT customers' needs. We at Intel IT have found that the creation of a professional IT marketing organization has been very useful in building credibility with our internal customers. The IT marketing organization has been successful in broadly marketing our successes, thus helping us build a track record of success. Marketing has also helped us recover from unexpected delays, project failures, and other unfortunate events such as virus attacks.

Encouraging Relationship Asset Maturity

I use a sales-based model for developing the maturity of the relationship asset. You might ask what has IT got to do with selling. In a less mature IT organization, trying to convince the firm of the value of your services and trying to obtain funding for new initiatives is all about selling. In an IT organization with a well developed relationship asset, selling is de-emphasized because the firm is well aware of the value that IT brings. Partnering is emphasized because the firm and the IT organization exists in an almost symbiotic relationship.

In his books on improving sales abilities, Holden (1990, 1999) develops a four-level selling model. The model describes an evolutionary path from low impact selling to strategic partnership between vendor and customer. I added Level 1 to Holden's model, which is shown in Table 6.2 on page 174, to recognize that in some firms, IT isn't considered a solution provider at all. The IT relationship asset may have no value or even negative value when, for example, major competitors of a firm are using an IT solution to perform a standard industry function and are deriving competitive advantage.

The relationship asset maturity model describes levels for each of four key dimensions involved in selling; relationship, firm intent, buying focus, and customer value. The goal is to move to higher levels on all of the dimensions. Notice that at level 2, IT is viewed as a *Band-Aid* or *quick buck* solution and at level 5, IT has emerged as partner and key contributor to the firm's new product lines or even to transforming the industry.

Table 6.2   Relationship Asset Maturity Model

Focus Area	Level 1	Level 2	Level 3	Level 4	Level 5
Relationship	Vendor not considered	Vendor on demand	Increasing trust and commitment	Strong mutual dependency	Symbiotic relationships— business partners and advisors to each other
Firm Intent	Use of IT not considered	Solve a problem	Acquire a solution	Capitalize on a business opportunity	Create new business opportunity
Buying Focus	None	Product or service features	Product or service benefits	Supplier expertise and resources	Supplier strategic ability and commitment
Customer Value	None or negative because IT not used when it should be	Low cost, quick fix	Ability to purchase reliable solutions	Ability to co-develop and create customer offerings to solve complex problems	Has constant insight to business issues/opportunities and applies ongoing creativity to solve/seize them

Source: Adapted from Holden (1999)

The buying focus dimension traces the evolution of IT decision making from a focus on features and benefits onward to realizing that IT is a strategic partner. Participating in firm strategy is the holy grail when selling IT to your business partners at your firm. To earn a role in the strategy, you must move through each level, sell IT successfully and then meet or exceed the value proposition that you made on a consistent predictable basis.

As the IT organization and its business partners take on harder problems and larger opportunities, it is important that risk and reward are shared between the parties. Scenarios of unbalance risk or reward may jeopardize deliverables. Both the IT organization and the relevant business partner need to be held accountable for delivering the benefits from a particular solution and should be recognized for success when it is achieved.

One last word on growing the relationship asset: don't expect to move from level 1 to level 5 in a quarter or two. Maturity requires patience and, above all, predictable. Say clearly what you intend to accomplish and then do what you said.

The IT Organization

I believe that how IT is organized has a profound effect on IT efficacy. I also believe that there is no single correct organization. It is better to view the IT organization (or, indeed, any organization) as a complex adaptive system that is continuously morphing and adapting to its changing environment. In the face of a rapidly changing business environment, increasing demand for IT services, and trends such as globalization, a restructuring of the IT organization should occur frequently to adapt to these challenges.

Increasingly, IT organizations are forced to become more outward facing. Rather than a back-office operation, IT is part of the supply chain communicating with the firm's training partners over business webs. The IT function must enable the firm to mobilize resources quickly, leverage expertise, and apply it to emerging business needs and opportunities. Unfortunately, few models are available to advise IT managers on how to organize for outward-directed services.

In the research literature, alternate IT organizational structures are typically measured along three axes to illustrate the competing forces of efficiency versus flexibility. The three axes are:

- *Centralization versus decentralization of the IT organization—* Centralization of IT means that primary authority for IT resides with a core group while decentralization means the primary authority and resources are distributed among business groups.

- *Centralization versus decentralization of the IT architecture—* The IT architecture of the company also affects the IT organization. For example, if a company depends mainly on centralized computing systems, there is a greater likelihood is that the organization will be centralized.

- *Global versus site-based IT coordination and control—*In global companies, IT organizations can be organized along a continuum which begins with site-based management, regional management, and fully global management with end-to-end responsibility residing with each global function.

In reality, each firm's IT organization will fall somewhere along each of these axes and their position will shift as the firm's business, industry, and markets change.

Table 6.3 shows some different organizing options for the IT function in enterprises. Each of these organizing models and variants thereof have advantages and disadvantages. Like the pendulum swinging between centralized and distributed computing architectures, there have been regular swings in organizational center of gravity over the past few decades. In the late 1990s, as firms struggled to manage total cost of ownership of distributed platforms, there was a significant shift towards centralized IT organizations to drive standardization and reduce costs.

In a centralized IT organization, a major advantage is greater economies of scale that reduce cost for IT resources and for products and services. In theory, a centralized IT organization should have reduced coordination overhead within IT. However, a fully centralized IT organization may have weaker customer relationships and limited business area knowledge. Lack of relationships and knowledge can limit IT's ability to customize solutions and develop IT in alignment with strategic business needs and opportunities.

Table 6.3   Organizing Options for the IT Function

Organizing Strategy	Description
Centralized	A single corporate IT organization is responsible for IT and solutions.
Decentralized	Divisional IT units or units aligned with firm divisions are responsible for IT and solutions.
Federated	Both the corporate IT and divisional IT units work together on solutions delivery.
Outsourced	An external outsourcing organization is primarily responsible for IT and solutions. Typically a small core management team managers the outsource.
Independent IT Subsidiary	An independent IT subsidiary firm is responsible for IT and solutions.
Fusion	The IT organization and the operations organization become one.

Source: Adapted from V Sambamurthy

Some organizations have built a hybrid model in which the centralized organization has dedicated account managers with deep IT and business expertise. It is the job of these IT evangelists to match business opportunities and needs with IT solutions and help the IT organization build and field the right solutions. This organization structure is likely to improve customer relationships and consequently better solutions being delivered to meet business needs.

Outsourcing has had a significant impact on the IT organization. Essentially, outsourcing works when the outsource provider can gain some form of an economy of scale and that the ensuing cost reduction is passed on to the client. IT managers have come to realize that, in certain situations, a third-party provider may be better positioned than the internal IT organization. Over the years, the drive to outsource all of IT has lessened as firms have come to grips with the associated risks and costs. Outsourced IT still requires in-house expertise to manage the outsource contractor, for example. Customers will attribute an IT outage at the outsource provider of a customer care system to the firm, and not the contractor.

Finally, a new kind of IT organization is emerging, one that CSC Research Services call *fusion*, in which the line organization and the IT organization become one. This is happening where the operation of the business and the IT processes that underpin it are becoming indistinguishable. Microsoft is the prime example of this; their CIO runs business operations as well as IT. Intel also has a business operations group, which is a complement to the IT group. Sandra Morris, Intel's other CIO, leads Intel's eBusiness operations.

At Intel we emphasize the importance of a centralized IT organization with global responsibility. We have made the transition from a mainly site-based IT structure, onward to a region-based structure, and finally to a global organization. Figure 6.5 on page 178 shows how we were organized in 2003. Our global functions were broadly clustered in three groups, business process, products and services, and infrastructure. Steering committees monitor and manage each of these groups. Note that the Intel IT organization has morphed approximately every eighteen months, either in reaction to business changes or to prepare us to become more proactive.

For our IT organization, the three steering committees (SCs) were formed to allow IT decisions to be made by appropriate stakeholders rather than involve all of the CIO's staff in every decision. This has improved and streamlined the decision-making process. The infrastructure SC is responsible for making strategic infrastructure decisions, the product and services SC for managing the product and service offering and delivering business value. The business process SC is responsible for the business processes that IT uses to run itself.

A key innovation in Intel IT's organizational design aimed at improving agility is the IT Flex service organization. The IT Flex service organization actually runs as an IT business within a business. Flex services at IT is an internal consulting service that is able to respond quickly to new requests and emerging needs in the company. The group uses a flexible resource model with a mixture of Intel permanent and contract employees. The

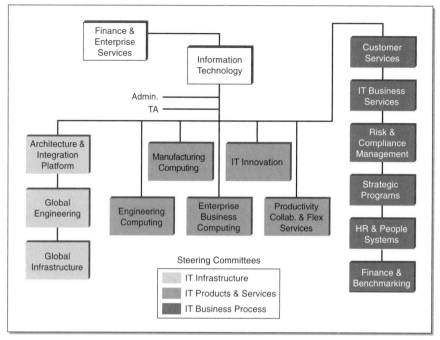

Figure 6.5 Intel IT Organization in 2003

number of contractors can be adjusted to match fluctuations in demand. The use of a flexible staffing function like IT Flex Services coupled with the stability of the other functions, provides a stable IT organization that can respond in an agile fashion to new requests.

Summary

In this chapter I have introduced a maturity framework for IT capability. I introduced the framework to help understand and systematically improve the IT capability with the end of goal of optimizing IT business value and agility. I have also introduced capability maturity frameworks for the IT people and relationship asset and for the IT architecture. I have discussed how IT assets and the IT value chain are related and offered strategies to improve both. Finally, I enumerated several ways that IT staff can be organized to improve contributions to both business value and agility.

Chapter 7

Measuring the IT Capability

If you can't measure IT, you can't manage IT.
—modified from Andy Grove, Intel Corporation

Managing the IT capability for business value calls for two separate but complementary approaches. The first approach, proactive management of key IT assets and the core IT value chain, was discussed in Chapter 6. In parallel with this approach I recommend an integrated organizational assessment process that identifies areas to focus on and measures improvement on an ongoing basis. Such an integrated assessment of the IT organization is the focus of this chapter.

Why is measuring and improving the IT capability important? Many enterprises spend similar amounts of money and have similar numbers of IT employees. However, enterprises do not derive the same business value and competitive advantage from their IT investment. Gains in business value vary significantly, and I believe that IT capability is the key to understanding why. Successful management requires that an IT organization realize systematic capability improvements that improve the organization's overall performance.

Whether your organization is large or small, some form of ongoing capability assessment is important. You will need to determine the appropriate level of ongoing assessment for the size of your organization.

Taking an integrated, 360-degree view of the IT organization capability allows you to avoid any blinds spots. In assessing the maturity and capability of an IT organization, the best perspectives come from the customers and the users, as they are ultimately the people who can determine the value from IT products and services. IT employee opinions are important because they can give the inside view and provide information about what is really going on in the organization.

Figure 7.1 suggests a holistic approach that considers customers, users, and IT employees.

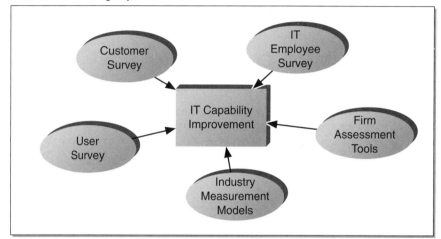

Figure 7.1 Integrated View of IT Capabilities

Figure 7.1 distinguishes between customers and users. Customers are those people who pay for services, such as general managers of a product division. Users are the actual users of the IT organization's systems. Clearly, feedback from both of these groups is useful. Feedback from customers, however, should probably be more heavily weighted in driving improvement plans, as customers are the constituency funding the services.

Tools for Assessing IT Capability

Having some internal assessment models and quality awards can be excellent tools to help an IT organization improve and achieve recognition throughout the company for its progress. Intel has established an award called the Intel Quality Award that is the most prestigious award that an internal organization can receive. Intel IT uses this award as its key yardstick for measuring progress; winning the award in 2001 was a signal to us of a high level of excellence and would communicate this excellence to our customers and employees. In addition, industry assessment models are very useful as they contain IT-specific improvement and reflect many man-years of effort in their creation.

Intel IT Vendor of Choice Program

IT organizations can often adopt business practices used by their parent organization to good effect. A good example of this is the Vendor of Choice (VOC) program that Intel uses to measure and improve relationships with customers such as Dell and IBM. Driven by Louis Burns, then CIO, Intel IT has adopted the same approach used by Intel with its external customers to help determine priorities and manage the relationship with internal customers. Before this approach was established, the IT organization had a poor reputation with its internal customers, and the level of respect for the IT organization was relatively low. The consistent and repeated use of the VOC process has led to sustained ongoing improvement, and Intel IT is now rated as one of the best organizations inside Intel. With the help of the VOC program and other tools, Intel IT has moved from being perceived merely as a supplier to being viewed as a strategic business partner.

The IT VOC program strives to assess the perceived value of Intel's IT services as measured by senior IT managers and end users. By surveying IT customers, we are able to identify areas of strength and areas for improvement on an ongoing basis. When we started the program in 1997, we initially surveyed only a few senior managers. Each year, as we learned more about the information-gathering process, we included more IT consumers, we improved survey questions, and—most importantly—we set higher goals. Today, we request IT VOC input from both senior managers and IT service end users, as each provides a unique perspective that, when combined, assesses the value that each of our IT services provides.

As the IT VOC process evolved, we honed in on the answers to two key questions posed to our IT customers:

- What is your overall satisfaction level with Intel IT?
- How did Intel IT perform this year as compared to last year?

At each VOC cycle, we cross-tabulate responses to these two questions and apply scoring rules. As shown in Table 7.1, we set a target for the percentage of responses to land in four numbered cells, the cells for excellent or good overall satisfaction and for equal or better year-over-year service.

Table 7.1 IT VOC Matrix: User Responses to Two Key Questions

| | What is your overall satisfaction level with Intel IT? | | | |
	Excellent	Good	Fair	Poor
How did Intel IT perform this year as compared to last year? Better	1	2		
Equal	3	4		
Worse				

Scoring:
0.5   if > 80% of responses in cells 1–4
1.0   if > 85% of responses in cells 1–4
1.25 if > 85% of responses in cells 1–4 and
        > 55% of responses in cells 1–3

Scores of 0.5 or 1 are achieved if the total number of responses in the four cells exceeds 80 or 85 percent, respectively. As a "stretch" goal, we also looked to cells 1–3. Ideally, we would like our customers to say that either we are excellent and getting better (cell 1), good and getting better (cell 2), or excellent and holding steady (cell 3).

Figure 7.2. illustrates how our half-yearly IT VOC scores have increased over time, as Intel IT has applied a closed-loop approach to assessing user satisfaction and developing improvement plans based on the issues identified. Since IT VOC was introduced in 1999, managers' scores have jumped from an average of 60 percent to close to 90 percent. End user

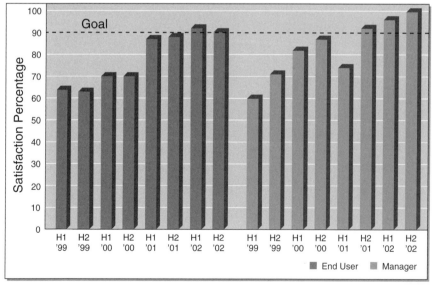

Figure 7.2 Increase in IT VOC Scores

satisfaction, which we began measuring through an online survey in 1999, increased from 64 to 88 percent. The user survey is open to anyone at Intel, and user response rates are surprisingly high. Interested and satisfied customers are a great indicator of improving capability.

To ensure motivation from each IT employee, we link these IT VOC scores to each employee's annual bonus. Each year, Intel IT identifies its key goals through an employee bonus (EB) program and attaches bonus payments to whether or not these goals are achieved. It is important to note that the EB goals include a mixture of top-level company goals and Intel IT goals. The goals are multi-dimensional, and they are agreed upon and scored with the CEO of Intel at the beginning and end of each year. This process works well in achieving alignment between Intel's IT and business organizations and ensures that efforts are focused on the initiatives that will have the most impact in producing value for the company. Tracking performance against these EB goals (of which IT VOC is an important component) on an annual basis gives a good idea of how an organization is performing. Figure 7.3 shows our success in improving EB scores, of which IT VOC is an important component. The increased success in achieving VOC goals correlates directly with an improving IT capability.

In parallel with conducting surveys on an annual or semi-annual basis, it is important to conduct real-time surveys with the IT organization's end users. This practice can take the form of an e-card presented to a user when a particular service request has been handled (*e.g.,* a help desk

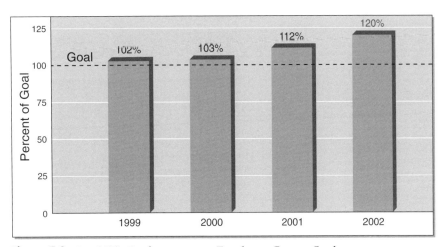

Figure 7.3 Intel IT's Performance to Employee Bonus Goals

call), asking whether the problem was fixed quickly and whether the customer was satisfied with the call.

Integrated Organizational Capability Assessment

If your firm already has an organizational performance tool in place, you should consider seriously using this tool to drive performance improvement for the IT organization. If you do not have a tool in place, I'd strongly recommend the tool that we use at Intel IT. This tool is substantially based on criteria for the Malcolm Baldrige National Quality Award in the United States, shown in Table 7.2.

Table 7.2   Malcolm Baldrige Award Criteria

Criterion	Definition
Leadership	Examines the behavior of senior leaders who set performance expectations, create and sustain organizational values, and set strategic direction.
Strategic Planning	Evaluates a company's strategic directions, and how key action plans are determined. The plans are also examined to see how they are translated into the management system.
Customer and Market Focus	Assesses the degree of customer focus along with the market focus. A key feature of this criterion is measures of customer satisfaction.
Information and Analysis	Examines the effective management and use of data and information to support key company processes including the company's performance management system.
Human Resource Development and Management	Assesses how the firm's work force has developed and is utilized to its full potential while implementing the company's objectives.
Process Management	Evaluates the organization's management of key processes. Common processes are customer-focused design, delivery methods for products and services, partnering activities with suppliers and other organizations in the enterprise.
Business Results	Evaluates business values, including customer satisfaction, financial performance, supply chain performance, and operational efficiency.

Source: National Institute of Science and Technology (NIST)

The seven criteria address key components or pillars common to most organizations that underpin an organization's performance. For example, organizations exist to produce business results measured by financial performance. Successful organizations emphasize quality system alignment and foster ongoing learning. The criteria also encourage breakthrough thinking, leveraging benchmarking, and provide a metric that challenges an organization to be the best. The criteria outlined in Table 7.2 represent a model of organizational behavior that is illustrated in Figure 7.4.

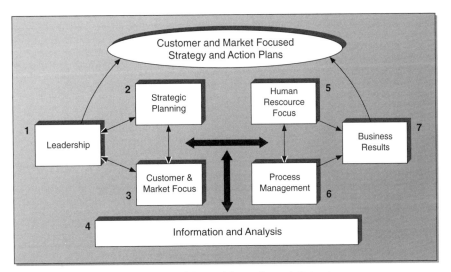

Figure 7.4 Organization Model for Baldrige Award Criteria

SAM-lite

A large distributed organization such as Intel IT—with over 4,000 employees located at 50 different sites in nearly every time zone—requires a structured and repeatable approach to organizational capability improvement. To achieve this, in 1990 Intel created a streamlined self-assessment method, called SAM-lite, based on The Baldrige Award's tried and trusted organizational performance model and associated assessment criteria.

Intel's self-assessment process is called *lite* because it focuses on a few key items that Intel believes will identify the largest portion of improvement for an organization. While used across all of Intel, SAM-lite has emerged as our IT organization's primary tool for assessing the maturity of its IT capability.

SAM-lite is based on the premise that processes (*i.e.*, what you do) produce outcomes and that identifying and improving systematic processes will produce and sustain incremental improvement. The assessment criteria are intentionally non-prescriptive and are generally based on core organizational values and concepts. SAM-lite takes a holistic view of the full organization and provides managers with rich data to fuel focused improvement. As a side effect, SAM-lite also helps build organizational morale. Furthermore, because the method typically employs cross-organizational teams to perform the assessment, the SAM-lite process brings people together who might otherwise not have a reason or opportunity to interact.

The SAM-lite Assessment Process

As shown in Figure 7.5, the SAM-lite process is cyclic, with seven recurring steps. The organization periodically assesses its performance, analyzes the results, identifies major opportunities, and develops action plans to seize opportunities and improve performance.

Repeating the SAM-lite process on a regular basis allows us to track trends in performance improvement. Figure 7.6 shows Intel IT's SAM-lite scores from 1997 through the end of 2002. As this figure illustrates, the organization has matured from being mediocre (*i.e.*, scores of 400) to an organization with a world-class score (*i.e.*, a score in excess of 700),

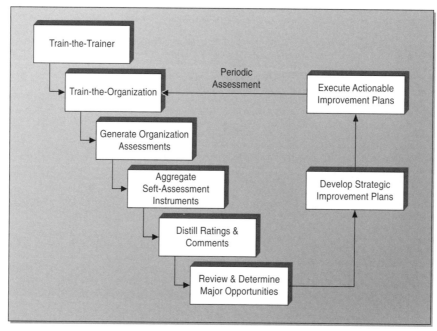

Figure 7.5 SAM-lite Cyclic Process

showing that Intel IT's performance and capability has effectively been doubled over a five-year period. Profiling scores over time also helps identify exceptions, such as the drop in our score for the second quarter of 2000. This dip was associated with a change in the leadership of the process team that resulted in a change in scoring methodology. In addition, the evaluation was done during a period of high organizational stress associated with a major reorganization.

At each cycle, Intel IT identifies a small number of key issues and develops improvement plans and actions aimed directly at these key issues. Then, in the following scoring cycle, we pay particular attention to the area that scored lowest in the previous cycle. Thus, over time, SAM-lite serves as both a roadmap and a progress report on our organization's performance. It also functions as an effective tool for communicating to senior business management the ongoing improvement of the IT organization.

A data collection sheet for each category calls for both qualitative and quantitative data. Typically, a cross-IT assessment team is formed, and some continuity is maintained across assessment cycles. Assessors provide a quantitative score—a number that represents the maturity of the area being measured—and also collect qualitative evidence that is used to identify specific improvement actions or to underscore high-performance processes and activities that ought to be encouraged in the

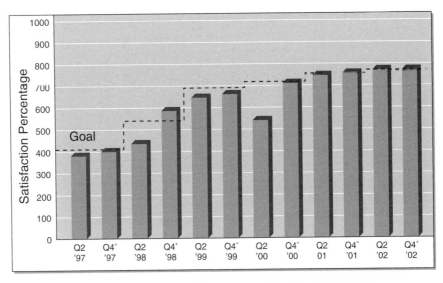

Figure 7.6 Intel IT's SAM-lite Self-Assessment Results: 1997–2002

organization. Qualitative annotations on the assessment sheet are crucial to understanding the score, the organizational behavior upon which it is based, and the activities and actions that should be put into strategies and plans for the future.

We find it particularly useful to have two teams performing the assessment in parallel, one comprising CIO staff and the other composed of a cross-section of IT employees across many grade levels. Thereafter, the scores from each group are compared, providing excellent data on the difference in perceptions between senior management and general IT employees.

A particularly good way of viewing SAM-lite findings over cycles is to use a spider diagram (*i.e.*, a polar graph) such as the one shown in Figure 7.7. In this graph, we use the consensus score for each category of assessment. It is important to note that the spider diagram does not indicate any priority of one category over another, but rather highlights differences.

Year-over-year plots provide a view of how an organization's performance is or is not improving. Our objective at Intel IT has been to achieve a balanced organizational score at around the 75th percentile. A quick look at Figure 7.7 reveals exactly where we met or missed this target. The graph also shows where we are improving, where performance is slipping, and where performance remains steady. For example, when the

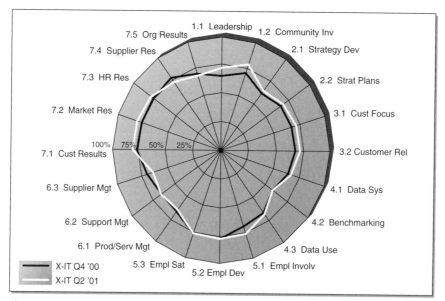

Figure 7.7 SAM-lite Cross-IT Q2 2001 to Q4 2000 Comparison

graph showed performance for item 4.2—benchmarking— to be low and not increasing, we identified benchmarking as an area to target for improvement.

For readers interested in including SAM-lite in their IT assessment processes, I have provided questions and scoring criteria for each of the seven core categories in Appendix B.

IT Employee Assessment

Often the harshest critics of an organization's performance are the individuals who make up the organization. I recommend surveying your IT organization on a regular basis, either annually or biannually to see how your IT employees perceive organization's IT capability. While the SAM-lite approach provides excellent feedback, it is impractical to use it to solicit feedback from an entire organization.

At Intel IT, we developed the IT Organizational Assessment (ITOA), and we use web technology to poll every IT employee once or twice a year. Our response rates are typically over 75 percent and provide us with statistically valid information that can help improve the IT organization. Table 7.3 shows a portion of a report generated from the Intel IT ITOA survey of the fourth quarter of 2002.

Table 7.3   IT Organizational Assessment: Partial Results

Items 1–5 of 15 items	Average response	Standard deviation	Total responses	5 - Strongly agree	4 - Agree	3 - Neutral	2 - Disagree	1 - Strongly disagree
1. IT partners with its customers to understand their needs and mutually identify solutions.	3.98	0.74	3518	752	2114	510	126	16
2. IT has a good reputation with its customers.	3.80	0.82	3534	579	1948	738	243	26
3. Customers find it easy to do business with IT.	3.59	0.86	3492	397	1690	1022	343	40
4. IT provides support to help customers resolve their problems in a timely and efficient manner.	3.98	0.76	3543	786	2060	551	125	21
5. IT's services meet customer expectations for stability and performance.	3.94	0.75	3531	699	2082	592	142	16

All inputs are gathered and reported anonymously, but IT managers can see aggregate scores for their organizations. IT staff are given the ability to enter both quantitative and qualitative feedback. We obtain quantitative feedback by having employees score tailored questions on a scale of 1 to 5, and we obtain qualitative feedback by allowing the IT employee to enter comments or suggestions for improvement.

The output of the ITOA is reviewed by both the CIO and by individual managers to determine what actions need to be taken for improvement. Year-on-year comparisons of the aggregate survey results identify trends in organizational performance and provides valuable information from an insider's perspective.

Intel's IT Organizational Assessment is provided in its entirety in Appendix B.

Industry Assessment Methods

The best known methods by far for improving capability performance in IT are the Capability Maturity Models (CMMs) developed at the Software Engineering Institute at Carnegie Mellon. Software CMM, and now CMM-I, are used extensively by software product development organizations. These two CMMs are useful for IT organizations, but I believe that two other CMM models can be even more useful for IT organizations: P-CMM and IT Service CMM. P-CMM, introduced in Chapter 6, is a particularly good tool for assessing the organization's workforce and people practices.

P-CMM-lite Assessment

If you have not participated in a CMM assessment process, be aware that the process is expensive and time-consuming. Generally, the effort and cost is paid back handsomely through improved capability and ultimately improved products and services. For those looking for more information on the CMM models, I suggest visiting the SEI web site: *www.sei.cmu.edu/cmmi*.

At Intel we introduced a "lite" version of P-CMM that allowed us to obtain actionable results that were directionally correct for much lower cost and less effort than a formal assessment would have taken. We adopted a new scoring mechanism and drafted a core team of assessors who had the best visibility to our workforce and people practices. The assessment process is an adaptation of the SAM-Lite process and is shown in Figure 7.8.

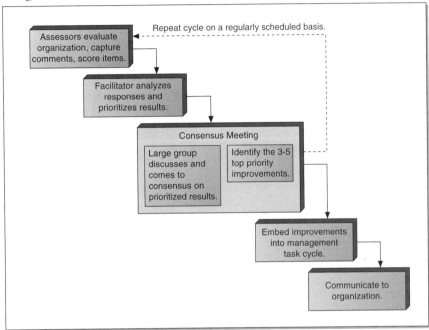

Figure 7.8 P-CMM Assessment Process

Table B.2 on page 274 of Appendix B shows the assessment criteria we use to evaluate each key process area.

Each assessor completes the assessment independently. A facilitator then aggregates and analyzes the results, and we look at the aggregated results in a consensus meeting. After discussion, we identify and agree upon key areas for improvement. Solutions are embedded then into our management roles. Figure 7.9 shows the result from one of the first P-CMM assessments performed at Intel IT using this streamlined assessment method.

Analyzing the results showed us that we had most level-2 key process areas under control, but we had not made as much progress as we would have liked on the level-3 key process area. Based on these results we prioritized training and communication on level 2 and most of the level 3 key process areas for investment and improvement in the following assessment period. Performing this kind of assessment is very useful in that it uses a recognized standard industry improvement model and uses it in a very efficient way. Presenting data like this can help some technical

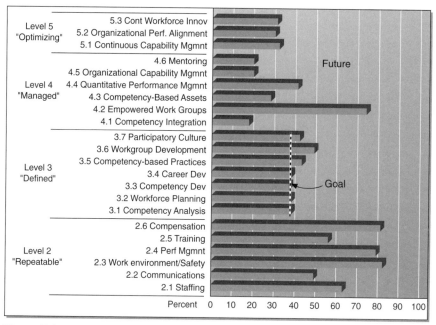

Figure 7.9 P-CMM Assessment Results

managers who have not yet got the message that people practices are as important as all other IT technical practices.

An emerging industry assessment model that will likely prove useful is the IT Service CMM. At the time of writing this book, the IT Service CMM is not yet complete. I encourage you to check progress at *www.serc.nl.*

IT Benchmarking

Benchmarking is an important business practice being used by IT organizations to see how they compare to other similar organizations, to provide the information required to reduce cost systematically, and to demonstrate value to sometimes skeptical business customers. Benchmarking is ordinarily facilitated by a third party organization. Competing firms offer cost and quality data to the third party and receive in exchange a statistical summary of the results. Confidentiality is maintained while each participating firm can then compare its operating parameters with global industry-wide averages, regional averages, or averages for firms categorized by size or type.

In the past, some firms have simply benchmarked against cost. While this information is somewhat useful, it often requires a good deal of subjective judgment, as it is difficult to achieve an apples-to-apples comparison.

A better way to benchmark is to measure performance related to cost and quality, because one firm may provide a very high quality email service at a high cost, and another may provide a low cost service with poor quality. It is important to be able to differentiate between these. Taking quality as well as cost into account provides for a more complete benchmarking result, and it becomes obvious that the lowest cost IT solution is not always the most competitive.

Benchmarking can be a labor-intensive activity for a few resources, but it can produce results beyond the committed resource because of what is learned and what actions are taken. The results can be compared and analyzed. When your organization is not identified as best in class, various questions can be posed: Are there further cost savings to be sought? Are other companies using IT differently, and what competitive advantage does this bring them?

Annual benchmarking provides longitudinal data to enable progress monitoring over an extended period of time. And, not only can members of the IT organization track its own costs and quality, they can also gain perspective on trends across the industry. An increase in average IT spend by the company's competitors may signal the launch of an IT system aimed at raising the bar for customer care, for example.

An increasingly important additional value of benchmarking is the provision of data and information that can build credibility with customers and enable business–IT relationships to develop beyond cost debates to business partnership and value discussions. Without benchmarking, customers can claim that IT is too expensive and without benchmarking, IT has no data to refute this claim.

Figure 7.10 on page 194 shows the results of Intel's 2002 benchmarking activity for our top 12 products and services. Through an aggressive improvement process, we were able to move all of our top IT products into the right hand quadrant, with leading cost and quality performance. This performance was achieved through quick learning from prior benchmarking and aggressively implementing action plans to capitalize on what we had learned to resolve issues.

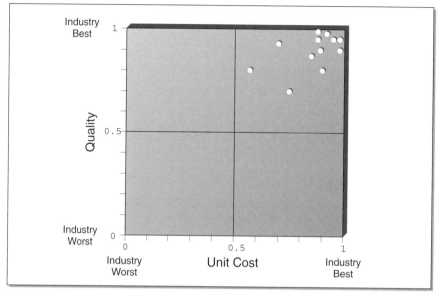

Figure 7.10 Intel IT Top Twelve Product and Service Benchmarks

Getting into an Assessment Rhythm

It is a valuable exercise to create an integrated annual calendar of assessment events, such as that shown in Table 7.4. This calendar identifies which assessments will be done when. It also institutionalizes a culture of using assessments for performance improvement. While some initial effort is required in defining and implementing the first assessment, subsequent assessments generally require less effort and proceed more smoothly.

Using an annual assessment calendar allows the assessments to be spread out evenly over the year, avoiding a "death by survey" syndrome. Spacing of different assessments allows the IT capability to be assessed from different angles throughout the year avoiding any blind spots. Regular execution of the annual assessment cycle will drive systematic improvement as IT employees and customers become accustomed to providing feedback at regular intervals. From a customer standpoint, this regular disciplined assessment is also a indicator that an IT organization has its act together.

Table 7.4   Annual Calendar for IT Assessments

Q_1	Q_2	Q_3	Q_4
• Develop Organizational Improvement plan • Launch IT VOC program • Submit benchmarking data to industry organization	• SAM-lite checkpoint to verify schedule • CIO to review SAM-lite revisions, if any • Benchmarking data back from industry organization, reported to CIO	• Submit applications for Intel Quality Award • Complete IT VOC program • Conduct P-CMM assessment benchmarking	• Perform IT Organizational Assessment survey • Perform safety self-assessment • SAM-lite surveys in and analyzed • Submit draft Organizational Improvement plan to CIO

Summary

In this chapter, I have discussed a number of different organizational and capability improvement techniques that, when integrated together, give a panoramic view of the organizational performance. By tracking these various assessments over time you can detect trends in the improvement or decline of the IT capability. You might argue that you don't have the time to perform these kinds of assessments. My response would be that you cannot afford not to be doing at least some of these assessments. Failing to do these is to fail to "sharpen the saw" and is likely to guarantee continued mediocrity. I would encourage you to choose the assessment methodologies that best meet your needs and put them to use.

Chapter 8

Running IT
Like a Business

Whenever you see a successful business,
someone once made a courageous decision.
—Peter Drucker

The phrase "…running IT as a business…" is increasingly seen in the trade press and heard at IT conferences. However, I prefer to use the phrase "…running IT *like* a business." To me, running IT like a business implies adopting business practices to run the IT operation with the goal of maximizing the overall business value that IT contributes to the firm. On the other hand, when the IT operation is run as a business—that is, with the primary goal of maximizing profit (however that is measured) for the IT organization—the IT operation is not likely to be properly aligned with the firm's business objectives.

I have observed a number of efforts where IT organizations were set up as separate entities, and I have seen varying results. Delta Technology, which develops and provides IT services to Delta Air Lines, is operating very well. In contrast, some years ago the IT organization at a large oil company put into place a business operating model that ultimately failed and had to be reversed.

Peter Drucker, in his 1963 Harvard Business Review article entitled "Managing for Business Effectiveness," states that the first duty of a business manager is to strive for the best possible economic results from the resources currently employed or available. In the context of IT, I would refine this statement to say that the first duty and continuing responsibility for IT managers is to strive to deliver the best possible IT business value from the resources currently employed or available, with IT business value defined as the contribution that IT makes to the firm's ability to achieve its objectives.

In a 2003 *Computerworld* article entitled "Survey Shows Common IT Woes Persist," Julia King cites research from the Hackett group reporting that the biggest factors separating world-class IT departments from the "also-rans" were their respective levels of business alignment and the sophistication of their internal IT processes. My notion of running IT like a business conveys two similar ideas. First, it is businesslike to align IT operations with the firm's overall business value strategy. Second, it is equally businesslike to operate IT with sophisticated processes and governance.

This chapter primarily focuses on the internal business processes used to run an IT organization. It introduces a maturity framework for running IT like a business and outlines a key process for enabling this approach.

Maturity Framework

I see five levels of maturity with respect to an IT organization's business processes. These five levels have not been empirically derived, but are based on my observation. The five levels are illustrated in Figure 8.1.

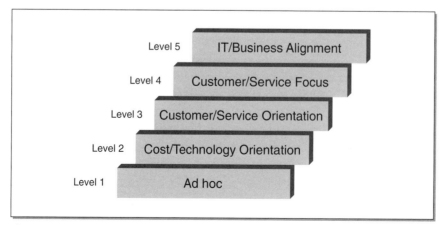

Figure 8.1 Running IT Like a Business CMF

At level 1, the IT organization is completely focused on technology and has few or no asset or cost-management systems in place. Systems are provisioned on an ad hoc basis, or perhaps even at high velocity, but no asset management, cost control, or tracking exists.

In evolving to level 2, the IT organization adopts basic IT asset management and cost management practices. However, at level 2 the IT organization is still very much focused on the technology itself.

As the IT organization matures to level 3, it begins to become customer oriented. In other words, the organization is thinking less about what information technology can be implemented and more about providing what the customer actually needs. It is also starting to adopt an orientation toward service, recognizing that IT is primarily providing services, not just products. At this stage, the organization is beginning to implement service-delivery and management processes, surveying customers to obtain feedback on performance and value proposition, and querying for current and future needs of the business.

As an organization makes the transition to level 4, concepts of IT chargeback and flexible funding mechanisms begin to take root. This means that the business has more control over the IT budget, and that the budget is being driven more by business strategy than by external benchmarks or targets defined arbitrarily by the CIO.

Level 4 IT organizations have a measurable customer and service focus. They have implemented proactive customer relationship management systems, possibly including customer segmentation. At this level, the IT organization also has key service support and delivery processes in place.

At level 5 the IT organization has a strong business orientation, and there is a high level of business–IT alignment. At level 5 the IT organization complements its comprehensive service- and customer-focused practices with key business practices, such as using tools like the balanced scorecard and publishing an annual IT performance report similar to the annual report a firm publishes for its shareholders. Also, at level 5 continuous innovation of IT business processes is the norm.

In some level 5 organizations, business operations and IT organizations fuse so that there is complete alignment. However, a word of caution: Professor Paul Tallon has identified an alignment paradox where if the business and IT are too closely aligned then business value and flexibility can degrade.

IT Asset Management

In a level 1 IT organization chaos is typical, with users often provisioning their own IT, unpacking boxes, and loading their own software. There is no strategic focus; IT is used in an opportunistic and uncoordinated fashion throughout a firm. At level 1 there are no business processes in place, and every IT product or service that is provisioned is done in an a ad hoc fashion. Typical issues include nobody really knowing where IT assets are nor the status of software licences and maintenance contracts. Disaster recovery plans are unheard of. Staying at level 1 is not an option for any self-respecting firm who uses IT.

Progress to level 2 of the maturity framework requires putting in place a number of fundamental business processes or practices. A cornerstone practice is IT asset management, that is, knowing what IT assets the organization has and where they are. IT asset management involves managing and tracking IT assets through their full lifecycle of usage from receipt through disposal, and viewing IT assets from an acquisition, financial, contractual, and inventory perspective. Having IT asset management in place enables a second key practice: product and service costing—a practice that is, of course, fundamental to the success of any business.

In level 2 firms, an IT organization exists and IT asset management and product costing have been put into place, however, there is little strategic focus or business alignment for IT. IT is used as a tool, and the emphasis is still on the delivery of the technology.

While IT organizations can develop their own IT asset management systems, it is often more efficient to procure a system from an external vendor. External vendors experienced in implementing management systems can quickly bring IT organizations up to speed and can give advice on how to connect these systems to a firm's finance and ERP systems. Another option is to use asset management systems that are already in place to manage a firm's physical assets for IT asset management. However, the different characteristics that hardware and software assets have compared to physical assets (*i.e.,* rate of refresh, complexity, information intensity) can make this an awkward solution.

Product and Service Costing

When an organization has an asset management system in place there are a number of ways of performing IT product/service costing. The simplest method is calculating the cumulative cost of providing IT services and dividing that figure by the number of employees or number of customers. More complex models include allocating all IT organization costs against a portfolio of IT products and services. Still more sophisticated is the automated metering and measurement of consumption of IT products and services.

The best way for an IT organization to compute its product and service costing is to use the firm's financial systems of record as the basis for costing. In most firms, the system of record is the General Ledger, which contains the operating budgets for IT. Given that these data are readily available, department costs can be allocated to products and services in a way that is "directionally correct," that is, accurate enough that IT and IT's customers agree with the methodology.

Before proceeding, I want to briefly distinguish between IT products and services. At a basic level, a product is something that is tangible and can be touched or seen, such as a PC or a server. An IT service is essentially a set of intangible activities or benefits provided by one party to another, for example, email or data warehousing services.

To measure the total cost of products or services accurately, an IT organization must understand factors such as how assets are used, what degree of outsourcing is employed, and how IT employees spend their time. I recommend running an IT organization like a professional services firm where IT employees keep track of their time and allocate it against different activities or projects. Since IT employees' salaries are often among the largest line items in IT budget, it is important to understand how their time is being spent.

Not collecting and analyzing this kind of data can lead to a scenario where an expensive resource is being managed without important data. Simple automated solutions exist that IT employees can quickly use to enter their weekly or monthly time spend. These time-tracking systems provide management and aggregate reporting. Seeing where employees time is being spent can drive important resource reallocation decisions.

Total cost per user can be derived by allocating used portions of products and services to the customer. This can be accomplished either by observing how the product is used by the customer, which is sometimes difficult to measure, or by directly metering its use. Tying costs to customer behavior by measuring or estimating what each customer group is using is called "measuring demand."

Overhead costs must also be monitored to ensure that activities such as research and development and strategic planning are funded to keep IT competitive in the future and to ensure that these costs are in line with what the business can afford.

When costing products or services, it is important to consider the degree of accuracy required. While greater accuracy improves costing and billing systems and output, it can also increase the cost and resource time of compiling the data. The optimal level of accuracy depends upon the business strategy. At Intel, our goal is to be accurate enough to ensure that directionally correct decisions are made—in other words, to ensure that the cost associated with the product or service is reasonable.

Intel IT's Cost Model

Intel IT's cost model started with the definition of the product and service (P/S) list offered to customers. All IT departments distribute 100 percent of their spending among three categories: *products and services*, *infrastructure*, and *overhead*.

- Due to the large number of IT products and services that Intel IT offers, the spreadsheet workbook that held this information came to be called the MOAT (*i.e.,* the Mother Of All Templates). The MOAT is the basis for Intel's product and service cost analysis.

- Infrastructure product spending is split into two categories: computing platform spending (*i.e.,* spending attributed to a P/S based on the number of servers in support of that P/S) and network spending (*i.e.,* spending attributed to number of kilobytes transferred in support of that service).

- Overhead remains a category for costs that cannot be otherwise assigned. Our goal, however, is to assign costs to products, services, or infrastructure whenever possible.

As we refined the costing methods, we realized that our asset management systems were not as accurate as they should be. In talking to other IT managers, I have learned IT asset management is a common problem in large companies. Many IT organizations find that their asset costs are a significant part of their budget, and if IT asset management is not in place, it is very difficult to manage these costs successfully.

Tracking the individual unit costs for key products and services enables focused cost reduction and improves the ability to track results. To calculate the unit cost, divide the sum of all spending for a particular P/S by the number of units consumed (*e.g.,* Sum of LAN costs / Number of LAN users). For example, at Intel we were able to observe and drive a 60 percent cost reduction in WAN unit costs and 19 percent reduction in LAN cost from 2002 to 2003 based on a number of different cost initiatives.

Fixed Versus Variable Costs

A key measure for an IT organization is understanding the flexibility in their budgets vis-à-vis fixed and variable costing. Examples of fixed costs might be a three-year equipment maintenance contract or physical IT assets that are depreciated, typically over four years.

Variable costs include services such as teleconferencing, video conferencing, and consultant costs. Different types of variable costs are associated with different levels of control. For example, when firm budgets are constrained, the use of external consultants may be minimized, reducing costs in that area. However, under those same conditions, teleconferencing and video conferencing costs may spiral upwards with limited control. At Intel, when travel budgets are restricted, the demand for these virtual conferencing services usually escalates.

As many us have witnessed in the last couple of years, budget agility—the ability to modulate the budget up or down, depending on business conditions and cycle—is important. An interesting trade-off is that the lowest cost for purchased services or for a maintenance contract is usually tied to longer commitments that result in a lessening of budget agility and flexibility. Generally, IT shops need to look for the "sweet spot" that maximizes flexibility and minimizes cost. For example, some firms are looking at leasing PCs as an effective way of managing their PC refresh programs.

Closed Loop Management

As an IT organization matures to level 3, its focus shifts from technology and cost to customers and services. A key component of this transition is increasingly mature internal business processes. At level 3, technology and cost are delivered to meet an agreed-upon set of objectives. IT organizations at level 3 have established a mission statement and strategic objectives and have installed a closed-loop management system.

In a closed-loop management system, as shown in Figure 8.2, a number of activities take place at different times in the annual calendar. Firm-wide strategic planning provides input to the IT department's mission and vision statements, which are reviewed and revised on an annual basis. The mission statement focuses on the core objective for the IT organization while the vision statement paints a picture of what IT will look and act like in the future. The vision statement is a compelling motivator for the IT organization employees.

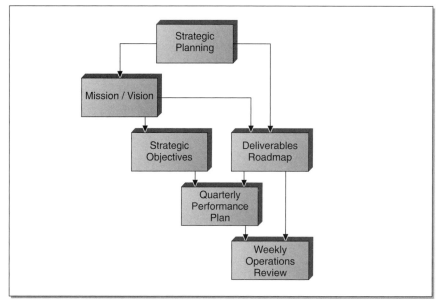

Figure 8.2 Closed Loop Management

A key outcome of the strategic planning process is a set of strategic objectives and an annual calendar of key deliverables. On a quarterly basis, priorities are determined and a quarterly performance plan is established for the IT organization as a whole and each key organization within it. The quarterly performance plan states the goals and measures of their success.

In a closed-loop system, IT managers are held accountable for their quarterly performance plans. Often a weekly operations meeting is held to track progress and identify issues or areas where help is needed to achieve the quarterly performance plan. Incidentally, this closed-loop approach is useful for both project and service deliverables. Frequent operational reviews will flag any potential issues early. The closed loop management system described is, of course, not unique to IT organizations. In fact, such internal business processes are fundamental to any business operation. Having a closed-loop management system ensures that the IT organization has strategic objectives in place and that the actions of IT employees are marshaled to achieve these objectives.

Ensuring Business and IT Alignment

Once an IT organization has implemented a closed-loop management system and can proactively deliver against stated objectives, it is ready to look at close alignment between business objectives and IT objectives. It is crucial to align the IT planning cycle with the business planning cycle. At Intel, we use a four-stage process for business planning that begins with a strategic long range plan (SLRP), which describes Intel's business direction for two to five years into the future. The corporate SLRP (pronounced *slurp*) identifies the "vital few" corporate objectives and supporting goals that must be met for Intel to be successful. Based on the corporate SLRP and IT's assessment of large environmental changes happening in the IT industry, Intel IT prepares its SLRP, which is aligned directly with and supports the corporate SLRP, as shown in Figure 8.3. The IT SLRP is presented annually to senior business executives in the firm to ensure alignment.

In Intel's planning process, the next step is a corporate product line business plan (PLBP) that defines the roadmap of products, how they will be delivered, and how resources will be allocated. A PLBP typically has an 18 to 24 month time frame. Just as we prepared an IT SLRP, our IT organization follows the same procedure to complete an IT PLBP in support of corporate needs.

On a yearly basis, every organization at Intel, including Intel IT, completes a yearly plan (PLAN) that is updated on quarterly basis. The updated a quarterly plan is called the plan of record (POR). Corporate PLANs and PORs call for IT PLANs and PORs, and the planning system shown in Figure 8.3 is complete. The quarterly POR process implements regular checkpoints for projects and to re-examine IT's alignment with corporate business objectives. Tight alignment between the business and IT planning process with a focus on different time durations can ensure alignment both at the strategic level and at the execution level as well.

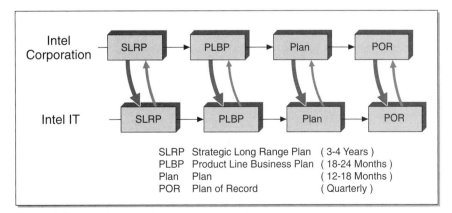

Figure 8.3 Synchronized Planning at Intel

IT Chargeback

Love it or hate it, IT chargeback has been a reality for many firms and IT organizations over the past twenty years. IT chargeback methodologies address how best to allocate the costs of providing IT products and services to internal customers within a firm to achieve cost recovery. In addition, IT chargeback systems typically have a demand management function, as without some sort of accounting methodology, users might assume that IT services are free and can consume these resources without constraint.

Chargeback systems can provide management information that is useful for improving IT products and services. Reviewing the management information or reports provided from an IT chargeback system offers a high-level perspective on cost and consumption. For example, the IT chargeback system at Intel showed us that nearly 70 percent of our IT spending was for workstation office products used to provide email and collaboration tools to Intel's distributed employees. This spending was not visible because the organization that supplies the office tools was one of the smaller functional organizations within our IT organization. In reality, this group and the products and services they delivered were consuming vast resources. This discovery was very helpful in restructuring our spending to achieve a better return on the overall IT investment.

IT costs can generally be charged back either on a proportional distribution basis or on a usage basis. In my experience, few IT organizations have good usage tracking systems in place. Typically, their focus in the hectic nineties was more on provisioning systems to meet rapidly growing user needs than on tracking usage. With the intense cost focus of the first few years of the current decade, more and more firms are moving to tracking consumption and usage. Traditionally, many IT organizations spread their total IT costs like peanut butter across the number of employees in the firm and allocated costs on this basis to each internal organization based on the number of employees in each organization. While this approach achieves cost recovery, it does not function as a demand management tool. Demand management is desirable because it enables better allocation of scarce resources, influences user behavior, promotes good corporate citizenship, and motivates cost savings through consolidation and optimization.

Managing Supply and Demand

One of the toughest challenges for an IT organization is managing the balance between supply and demand for IT products and services in a way that maximizes value for the company. Firms can use IT to extend the reach of the company, to improve productivity, to shorten design lead times, to improve factory yields, and more. The promise of benefits leads to a great thirst to deploy more IT solutions.

At the same time, firms need to manage their IT spending. Like the cost any other service, IT expenses impact the company's bottom line. Increasing spending typically carries two punches: reduced ability to compete and reduced profit margin. Putting the right mechanisms in place to balance these spending decisions should be a key focus in IT business planning efforts.

IT spending adjustments made in the best interests of a firm will be based on ROI. ROI, as discussed in Chapter 3, is the ratio of the benefit a firm receives a from a product or service divided by its cost. An aggregate ROI summarizes the contribution of IT products or services even when they are consumed in small increments. Every decision—from provisioning a desktop application, to providing shared file storage, to supporting a data warehouse—should depend on ROI. In every case, the question is "Do the benefits exceed the costs?"

Putting both the decision to spend and the budget impact in the hands of the IT consumer is a good way to manage the incremental cost and consumption of IT services. Pooling the cost of IT products and services and spreading costs over the firm's employee population can easily produce two negative effects: First, customers are often dissatisfied because they feel they are paying too much; more importantly, customers have no incentive to limit their use of IT products and services.

Empowering the Customer

Based on our experiences at Intel IT, I recommend shifting more decision-making authority to IT's customers. We all pay more attention to cost of products and services that impact our budgets directly, and different business units will require different levels and types of IT investment. Wireless mobility, for example, will be less important for desk-centric workers but absolutely crucial for the firm's road warriors. IT customers should elect to consume more IT services when doing so leads to an attractive ROI. Informed by analyses prepared by the IT organization, customers will likely shift spending among IT products or services to achieve greater business value.

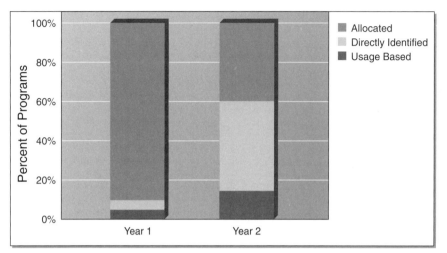

Figure 8.4 Expected Trends in Billing over a Two Year Period

To empower customer decision making, IT organizations will need accurate and fine-grained estimates of cost and benefit. The need for a reliable chargeback system may demand restructuring the way the IT organization accounts for its products and services and their costs. Moving to customer empowerment is a critical step in running IT like a business and enabling market dynamics to work in favor of the IT organization.

Upgrading Chargeback at Intel IT

In the late 1990s, Intel IT made the decision to change its chargeback systems. Traditionally, we pooled nearly all costs into one bucket and allocated the aggregate costs to organizations and departments in proportion to head count. We decided to reduce the general allocation significantly and, instead, to tie expenditures directly to individual organizations or businesses.

Identifying and tying expenses directly to IT customers allowed us to share more control of IT expenditures with business managers. Especially in conjunction with our developing portfolio of product and service offerings, we were able to support business managers making their own calls on how to spend their marginal dollars. We were able to help business managers decide which IT investments provided the greatest return, both among IT choices and with respect to investing dollars in non-IT resources or assets. Figure 8.4 shows the degree of change in allocations and directly billed expenses we would expect to achieve over a two-year period at Intel.

Armed with this information, IT customer account managers can work with individual business units with comprehensive information, detailing which products and services they are consuming and how much each costs. Business units make the right trade-offs, and the IT organization adjusts investments in the IT portfolio. In addition, the IT organization has a better understanding of which IT products and services are most important to the firm. High-priority solutions should be the focus for gains in efficiency. When running IT like a business, offerings are tailored to customer needs.

Service Orientation

IT organizations that want to run like a business need to adopt a service—rather than a product—mindset and introduce end-to-end accountability for service delivery. This will likely mean a reorientation from an internal technical IT perspective to a customer-driven perspective. Until this mindset change occurs, there is typically no single owner for issues resolution. Instead, the many different owners of individual components of a product or service will say that the problem is not theirs and no one will be held accountable for an actual integrated problem resolution.

Service orientation is a key principle when running IT like a business. The business of IT is predominately service, and a service organization should not be using business processes designed for delivering products. The product model is appropriate when the value added by an organization is derived mainly from the quality and quantity of standardized products. Focusing on efficient, reliable, and repeatable processes, and on continuous improvement is very important, but it is not sufficient.

When the value added by an organization depends mainly on customer relationships, the organization's focus should also be on responsiveness and flexibility. The main variables are the rapidly changing needs of your customers. In fact, an IT organization needs a bit of both the product and service approaches, but with an increasingly strong bias towards service.

For those of you who are wondering what it might take to start putting in service-oriented processes, help is at hand. Thanks to the UK Government and its Office of Government Commerce (OGC), a standard methodology exists for implementing service support and delivery mechanisms. This is called the IT Infrastructure Library (ITIL).

IT Infrastructure Library

Although it is relatively new, ITIL is fast becoming a popular approach for both implementing and validating service management in IT. ITIL provides comprehensive guidelines that support best practices for aligning IT services with business needs. ITIL supports increased process maturity by improving management control and increasing the organization's ability to respond to customer needs. It also increases cost effectiveness by improving the quality of services provided and by reducing the cost of those services.

If you are ready to adopt a service-oriented approach, I would recommend that you invest in the series of ITIL reference books. The foundation of ITIL is its service management functions (SMFs), which primarily describe service support and service delivery. Service support identifies the primary disciplines that enable IT services and service management about the delivery of the services themselves.

Service Support

The service support SMFs focus on day-to-day operations and support of IT services, and affect the day-to-day user of the service. Service support includes the following:

■ Configuration management is the implementation of a system that contains details of the elements in an organization that are used in the provisioning and management of its IT services. This system tracks assets, records how assets are configured, and looks at critical dependencies among assets.

■ Problem management is a process that addresses the resolution and prevention of incidents that affect the running of an organization's IT services. This process involves tracking issues, assigning ownership for resolution, and assuring that resolution occurs. Many organizations have daily operations meetings to manage open problems. An IT organization needs to become a learning organization so it does not repeat the same mistakes over and over. Ideally, this can lead to a *double-loop* learning situation where problem management trends are analyzed, systemic problems are identified, and root-cause solutions are installed to address the problems. The implementation of double-loop procedures can substantially reduce help desk calls.

■ Change management is the practice of ensuring all changes to configuration items are carried out in a planned, tested, and authorized manner. This is one of the most fundamental business processes an IT service organization needs to have in place. As complexity of IT solutions continues to increase, change management becomes crucial. It is impossible for an IT organization to develop mature business processes without having a comprehensive change management system.

In the early 90s, Intel's IT and factory automation organizations struggled with change management because changes were having unpredictable impacts on systems and sometimes resulted in downtime. Our solution was to adopt the change control process that Intel's manufacturing organization used. This solution consisted of setting up a change control board with a formal process for submitting white papers on changes to a panel of experts prior to implementing any change.

■ Help desk is the first point of contact when users of IT services encounter a problem. While many companies are adopting internal web-based self-help systems and are moving toward using web-based systems for initial problem reporting, these systems are almost always backed up by a help-desk staff. Although the help desk is often considered to be at the bottom end of the IT food chain, getting company employees back online and productive when they have an IT problem is critical to ongoing company performance. Companies such as Dell have been very successful at creating help-desk positions with a viable IT career path.

■ Software control and distribution are the systems that manage software development, procurement, installation, and support. Program governance, discussed in Chapter 6, is a key part of software control and distribution. Increasingly, automated software distribution systems are used to deliver new applications, upgrades and patches to firm employees.

Service Delivery

Service delivery is the management of the IT services themselves. The five recognized disciplines described by ITIL are as follows:

■ Service level management is the discipline of formalizing an agreement between IT and its customers to ensure that services are delivered when and where they are needed. Fundamental to service level management is the concept of service level agreements (SLA), discussed in Chapter 2.

■ Capacity management is the discipline that ensures that IT infrastructure is available, cost-effective, and efficiently managed. Predicting demand with reasonable accuracy and maintaining a scalable, flexible, and modular IT architecture underpin the IT organization's ability to provide high-quality capacity management.

■ Contingency planning is the process by which plans are put in place to ensure that IT Services can recover and continue should a serious incident occur. Contingency plans typically address business continuity, disaster recovery, and the ability to back up and restore data.

■ Availability management is the practice of identifying and negotiating levels of IT service reliability for discussion and agreement with customers. Availability should be measured end to end and should accurately reflect customer experiences. It is not acceptable to report high availability for components and subsystems while users experience system-wide outages.

■ Cost management is the discipline of ensuring that IT services are obtained at the most cost-effective price. Cost management involves calculating and communicating the total direct and indirect cost of providing IT services so that IT customers can understand the cost structure that underlies IT services.

Resource Management

To ensure continuous alignment of IT with the business objectives, IT organizations need a mechanism to flexibly realign resources as business priorities shift. While many of the services provisioning and operations roles are often unaffected in the short term by changes in business priorities, a change in strategic direction requires a shift in development resources to fulfill the new requirements. It is important to create a flexible IT workforce with the right skills to deliver solutions that meet new requirements. Resources may need to be redeployed on short notice to address new strategic initiatives.

Redeployed resources are typically a mix of program managers and technicians who work together to deliver solutions that meet the new requirements. At Intel IT, this role is played by an organization called IT Flex Services, which comprises a mix of Intel IT employees and external contractors. Including external contractors in this resource mix is important because it enables us to scale this resource up or down, depending on the overall demand for new IT services. The decision to reallocate resources is typically made within the framework of IT program governance, discussed in Chapter 6.

Both ends of the IT value chain need to be managed. In the next sections I first discuss customer account management, which focuses on the ultimate value delivered to the customer from the IT value chain. I will briefly discuss IT strategic procurement as an approach to managing the supplier input to the IT value chain.

Customer Account Management

Account management is a standard function used in many businesses today and it is typically carried out by customer account managers (CAMs). The same function and role is equally valuable in IT organizations. CAMs understand the needs of the firm, the portfolio of available solutions and the potential IT solutions that could be developed. CAMs recommend solutions to IT's customers, negotiate service agreements, and ensure that appropriate solutions are delivered.

Demand from customers comes in two categories: tactical and strategic. The request to provision a PC is a tactical or operational demand. As a firm's IT processes mature, tactical requests can be satisfied automatically with online systems to receive and approve the request and send it onward to a supply chain for fulfillment. A call for IT's help in improving inventory management, however, is an example of a strategic demand. It is the CAM's responsibility to understand the nature of the business problem and match it to IT solutions. Highly competent CAMs with specialized knowledge of IT and the firm's business can anticipate strategic opportunities and offer solutions to business managers proactively. These opportunities or even problems may not be visible to the business managers, who are, of course, primarily focused on the business.

CAMs can develop business capability roadmaps (BCRs) within the firm or in a division. BCRs define the capabilities needed in the future to improve the efficiency and effectiveness of the organization. These roadmaps specify when the investment will occur, when the solution will be deployed, and when the new capability will return value. Managing

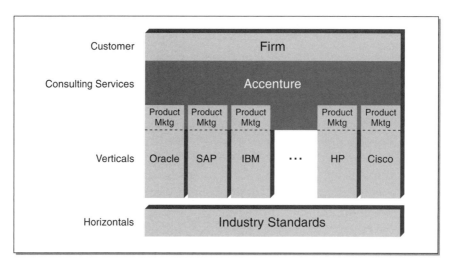

Figure 8.5 Solution Integrator Business Model

demand and opportunities using a BCR methodology can help to optimize business value.

CAMs must fully comprehend the IT service offerings as well as the business opportunity and needs. Account managers are responsible for adding value to the business, managing the customer relationship, and maintaining and communicating account profiles and strategies. Account management also provides input and feedback to the IT organization regarding the appropriateness of their proposed solution offerings. They may oversee the administration of the design and execution of account-specific beta or pilot programs, as well as new service or product deployments.

An IT customer account manager may need to operate like a consultant from a company like Accenture, as depicted in Figure 8.5. Companies such as Accenture pair industry experts with technology experts when recommending solutions to clients. The team evaluates the needs of the client, surveys available solutions in the marketplace, recommends solutions that most closely meet the customers' present and future needs, and, in some cases, manages the vendor selection and implementation processes.

CAMs, like consultants, should add value with their knowledge of available technology, knowledge of business needs, and their ability to orchestrate tailored solutions based upon standardized IT building blocks available from a range of suppliers. Finally, like consultants, CAMs work with the IT customer to define and negotiate implementation milestones and success metrics.

IT Strategic Procurement

An increasingly important business process is that of using an IT strategic procurement function to manage suppliers and understand their future roadmaps. This function comprises three primary activities:

1. Building strategic relationships with key suppliers
2. Aggregating purchasing requests for products or services across the entire firm and all IT organizations
3. Negotiating the most advantageous purchases for the firm

Strategic procurement can deliver important cost savings even before solutions are deployed at a company. Procurement staff should actively manage suppliers through the post-contract period to ensure that quality products and services are delivered within the terms of the contract.

Customer Segmentation

In the late 90s, as many organizations wrestled with the concept of TCO, many IT organizations took a "one size fits all" approach to delivering IT services, deciding to offer only a single product or service—such as a single configuration for all PCs—to drive down costs through consolidation and standardization. Upon realizing that a single offering may not satisfy the needs of some users, organizations began to segment users into different groups with shared needs and preferences with the goal of providing better service to each segment and achieving greater business value. Today, segmentation of IT customers is a standard business practice.

It is important to distinguish between customer management and user segmentation. Both concepts are equally important. The customer that the IT organization is managing is the business unit manager who has the authority to approve spending for IT services or products. IT organizations need to partner closely with this customer to ensure current and future needs are met. In contrast, users are the consumers of IT services—the employees of the companies and people outside of the firm who use the company's extranet or eBusiness systems.

The segmentation approach typically leads to business value benefits because it puts the IT organization in touch with actual business processes and with the behavior and attitudes of users. Understanding how users actually work today and how their work might evolve in the future enables IT organizations to anticipate and prepare for future solutions. Segmentation can also identify specific business process re-engineering opportunities.

IT Marketing

In any reasonably sized organization, I strongly recommend creating a small, focused IT marketing team whose role is to manage the IT organization's image and communications. Communication takes two forms: first, the IT organization needs to communicate and market its services to customers and users; second, it needs to communicate with its own IT personnel. Unless marketed properly to a broad base of customers, a successful IT organization may go unrecognized and undersupported. Thus, IT marketing can be an important tool in enhancing the customers' and users' perception of the IT function. Finally, having an IT marketing and communication capability in place is essential for public relations when responding to service interruptions or incidents such as virus attacks.

Adopting New Solutions

As new solutions are introduced, IT organizations would do well to understand key principles of high technology adoption and how those principles apply to the firm. Depending on strategy and industry, companies have different approaches to technology adoption. While some companies may make a strategic decision to be early adopters of IT for competitive advantage, others, in slower moving industries, may choose to be late adopters or even laggards with respect to new IT solutions adoption. A company's appetite for adopting technology will also be influenced by the adoption behavior of competing companies.

The IT organization's track record in delivering next-generation IT solutions that deliver competitive advantage at reasonable cost also matters. Another important factor in adopting new IT solutions is how IT markets the proposed solution. If the fundamental business value of a proposed investment can be emphasized, marketing gets easier. The innovators in the IT organization are wise to identify which business managers have an affinity for early adoption and work with them to become sponsors for new innovations.

IT organizations looking at innovation would do well to read one of Geoffrey Moore's books on high technology adoption. I particularly

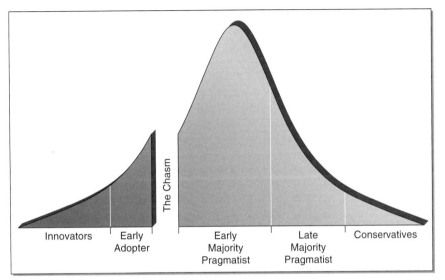

Source: Intel, modified from Moore (1991)

Figure 8.6 Geoffrey Moore's Adoption Curve with Chasm

recommend *Crossing the Chasm* (1991), which provides a framework for understanding how new IT solutions can be introduced and diffused into an organization. Moore's framework, shown in Figure 8.6, shows the predictable path of marketplace adoption when a new high technology product is introduced.

■ Initially, only innovators buy or build the product. Innovators are looking for products with high strategic value. They are willing to live with solutions that are not quite polished. They like new ideas and are always on the outlook for breakthrough technologies.

■ Innovators are soon followed by early adopters—those who are willing to take on high-risk products in return for expected high rewards. Note that innovators and early adopters are leaders that make up only a small portion of the total available market for a successful new technology.

■ The next step for new technology is to cross what Moore calls *the chasm*. Technology suppliers must understand that the vast majority of the market are not visionaries and early adopters. They must cross the chasm in order to survive, and the majority of the market often has different requirements for products.

■ Moore identifies an early majority and a late majority made up of pragmatists. Pragmatists are only comfortable buying products that require significant change if they know that other pragmatists are already using them. Pragmatists are cautious, and only want to use products that are well-established and well-supported.

■ Finally, Moore acknowledges conservatives on the far right of his market adoption curve. Conservatives comprise the small group of troglodytes who are guaranteed to be the last to accept and assimilate a new technology.

I have observed Moore's adoption path at work when organizations adopt new IT solutions. Generally, a only small number of business visionaries can see the potential of a compelling new IT solution, and they are the ones who are willing to sponsor pilot studies and prototype development. Pilot studies generally attract the attention of early adopters who want to determine whether the technology shows promise.

Moore recommends that new technology be targeted to a niche market in which people are able to communicate more easily, so that the existence and benefit of a new solution can be diffused quickly among members of the community. This approach translates to deploying a new solution into an individual business or product group. Another key lesson from *Crossing the Chasm* is that for a new IT solution to achieve mainstream adoption, a complete solution must be provided, including supporting services. In other words, even inside the firm, there is a chasm to cross.

One last word on the migration path illustrated in Figure 8.6. When Geoffrey Moore originally segmented the market, he divided the early and late majority exactly at the highest point of the bell curve. At Intel IT, we shifted the distribution of the early majority to the right to indicate that we want to stay ahead of the curve. That is, we want the average IT user to have access to more advanced IT platforms and solutions than most users in other businesses. And, according to Compass Benchmark results, we have achieved exactly that.

Governance

Most firms need governance structures not only to operate successfully but also to have as formal legal entities. Increasingly, IT organizations are adopting a governance approach to both help maximize the return from IT and to meet legal obligations from new legislation, such as the Sarbanes-Oxley Act of 2002 in the United States, which tightened restrictions related to corporate governance, financial disclosure, and the public accounting practices.

There are a number of different definitions of governance. One defines governance as an overarching approach to running an organization that is based on high-quality, well-defined and repeatable processes. At a more detailed level, governance outlines policies, highlights procedures, requires meticulous documentation, and establishes a plan for constant improvement. Currently, several comprehensive IT governance models are gaining popularity, the most popular of which is Control Objectives for Information and Related Technology (COBIT). COBIT was created to align IT resources and processes with business objectives, quality standards, monetary controls, and security needs. Other definitions are much looser; for example, one defines IT governance as a methodology for keeping IT operations such as spending and labor under control.

Opinions about the value of IT governance are as numerous as its definitions. At a recent debate on IT governance held at a Cutter conference (April 2003), panel members strongly disagreed on whether IT governance best practices could be transferred successfully from one company to another. Harvard professor Rob Austin was quoted as saying "You'll be fixated by best practices that work at very different types of organizations and trying to transplant those directly to your company." This quote is somewhat reflective of my view, and I recommend that first you decide what you need to govern before deciding how you want to do it. Once you have decided what needs to be governed, you can then put the processes that make the most sense for your company in place.

Governing IT for Business Value

With respect to IT governance and maximizing business value, I particularly like the definition and approach proposed by Peter Weill, director of the Centre for Research in Information Technology (CISR) at MIT. He defines IT governance as specifying the decision rights and accountability framework to encourage desirable behavior in the use of IT. Effective IT governance requires defining which critical decisions need to be made, defining who makes them, and stating how they are communicated and implemented. MIT CISR recommends that governance cover at least the following five critical domains of IT:

- ▪ Principles
- ▪ Infrastructure
- ▪ Architecture

- Applications
- Investment and prioritization

In developing a governance framework, Weill and fellow researcher Richard Woodham from CISR hypothesized that firms achieving above industry-average returns from IT investments must be making consistently better IT-related decisions and consequently embarked on a comprehensive research program to investigate this. Their findings were significant. They found that an effective IT governance structure is the single most important predictor of achieving value from IT and that a key measure of an effective governance structure is the ability of IT and business managers to consistently describe their governance structure. This is a test you should try in your own company.

Another major finding was that top-performing firms governed IT differently, with governance structures linked to the performance measure in which they excelled (*e.g.*, growth, return on assets, margin, market capitalization, productivity, and so on). Thus, depending on your company's strategy and primary goals, you should consider potentially different mechanisms for governance.

The Key IT Decision Domains

Building on Weill's research, effective IT governance for business value can be enacted through deciding who will make what decisions and how these decisions are communicated and implemented. Let's discuss each one briefly.

IT Principles

IT principles are overarching statements about how IT is used or should be used in the firm. These principles are often related to a firm's strategy intent or cover general principles of IT use. A good example of an IT principle related to a significant business future direction is Intel's eBusiness transformation. In 1999, Intel set a three-year goal of becoming a 100 percent eBusiness with an associated IT principle statement that IT would be used to restructure and automate Intel business processes. This statement and its associated goals drove an IT-enabled transformation of Intel business systems. Today, all Intel revenue is booked online, all employee transactions with the company are electronic, and, finally, over 95 percent of suppliers are connected electronically.

If you do not have IT principle statements, think about what they might be for your company. For example, do you have an IT principle about providing the same level of IT service to your employees, irrespective of their location?

IT Infrastructure

IT infrastructure strategies describe the approach to building the IT foundation for the firm. IT infrastructure is made up of the shared and standard IT services that are centrally coordinated including PCs, networks, storage area networks, middleware, and databases. In many companies, the IT infrastructure is akin to a digital nervous system that senses and enables relatively seamless transfer of information through the company. The flexibility and scalability of the IT Infrastructure is a crucial factor in enabling new business solutions to be implemented quickly.

IT Architecture

IT architecture, as discussed in Chapter 6, is defined as a blueprint for strategic intent for IT, oriented around providing for future business value. It generally consists of elements such as modules, components, and interfaces. Typically, architecture includes the standards and guidelines for technology usage, use of data and information, and design guidelines. Essentially, an architecture provides an integrated set of technical choices to guide the organization as it will endeavour to fulfil future business needs.

IT Applications

IT applications and business solutions are described by the business capability roadmaps that identify what solutions need to be delivered and when. The architecture of an individual solution is the representation of the most important decisions about the design, construction, operation, and termination of that solution, enabling a common understanding among the stakeholders.

IT Investment and Prioritization

I discussed IT investment and prioritization extensively in Chapters 3 through 5. This function includes the complete decision-making process for IT investment. Investment and prioritization activities include developing business cases, managing solution portfolios, creating investment review boards, and so on.

Designing IT Governance: Summary

Designing an effective IT governance structure is important so that an integrated approach can be taken and than decisions can be effectively made, communicated and implemented. Key questions that need to be addressed include the following:

- Who has decision rights and input to the key IT decisions?
- Does the CEO or the CIO make the key IT decisions or are they jointly made?
- What mechanisms are used to decide, communicate, and implement decisions?

I recommend using the IT governance framework developed from the MIT CISR research. Further details on how this approach are available in the book by Weill and Ross entitled *Don't Just Lead, Govern!* A variety of mechanisms (*e.g.,* a senior management steering committee) are needed to manage the different areas that need to be governed. As you approach IT governance design for your firm, you should recognize that it takes time to design and particularly to implement and get the various mechanisms operating properly.

Performance Management and Alignment

In managing the performance of an IT organization, I recommend that the IT organization adopt the standard business planning processes used in the firm and then be held accountable for these. These processes will likely include strategic planning, development of service or product line annual plans and quarterly or monthly performance plans in which the key goals are set out. Regular review of the strategic plan and any performance plans with business executives are likely to lead to both improved alignment and performance.

Business Value Program Office

Based on our experience at Intel IT, I recommend setting up a formal IT business value program office (BVPO). The BVPO comprises a set of resources focused on managing a formal business value program. Initially, creating a formal BVPO communicates to the IT organization and beyond, the increasing importance of seeking to create and measure value from IT investments.

The BVPO should manage any templates and tools associated with IT business value and be the developer and steward of the process for measuring and creating business value. A key role of the BVPO should be to educate and drive a culture change so that IT professionals are thinking about business value first, rather than as a postscript. As the maturity of the IT organization develops with respect to business value, it should ultimately be possible to disband the BVPO as the business value processes, tools, and mindset become inculcated and embedded across the organization. In this stage of maturity, the organization is autonomically focused on maximizing business value.

CIO Dashboard

We at Intel have found two tools particularly helpful in monitoring both performance and alignment: the CIO Dashboard and the Balanced Scorecard.

The CIO Dashboard is an important innovation for measuring and improving the capability of IT organizations. The dashboard is an easy-to-read, one-page, high-level summary of IT operations that also provides IT managers with the ability to drill down to details of the key performance variables in an IT organization. For us, the dashboard approach has had significant impact on improving organization performance. Many of today's dashboards are based on the Balanced Scorecard approach developed by Kaplan and Norton (1996).

The Balanced Scorecard

The balanced scorecard was developed in the early nineties by Robert Kaplan (Harvard Business School) and David Norton (Balanced Scorecard Collaborative). To bolster known weaknesses and vagueness in previous management approaches, the balanced scorecard approach provided a more prescriptive approach as to exactly what companies should measure in order to produce a balanced financial perspective. The balanced scorecard assesses an organization from four perspectives: learning and growth, business process, customer, and financial.

The balanced scorecard is not just a measurement system; it is a management system that can enable organizations to clarify their vision and strategy and translate that analysis into action. It provides feedback about both the internal business processes and external outcomes in order to improve strategic performance and results continuously. When fully implemented, a balanced scorecard methodology transforms strategic planning from being a useful but abstract exercise into a concrete management system that drives the organization on an ongoing basis.

The essence of the Kaplan and Norton message is that information age companies need to be measuring performance through more than just financial metrics. Kaplan and Norton use the analogy that you can't fly a modern airplane on just air speed; you need many more indicators, for example, altitude, fuel tank readings, and so on.

Intel IT uses a variant of the balanced scorecard approach. On an ongoing basis we track performance across five categories: *financial, customer, operations, people and environment,* and *key programs.* Our dashboard, shown in Figure 8.7, uses a traffic light color-coding scheme and directional arrows to immediately identify areas with problems or trends that are heading in the wrong direction. Online links allow both IT managers and business managers to hone in to find out more specific information.

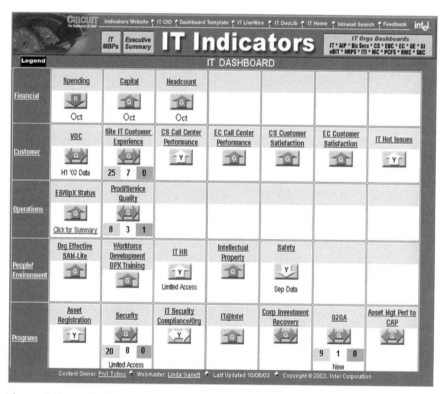

Figure 8.7 Intel IT's Dashboard of IT Indicators

Figure 8.8 shows a typical graph from the Intel IT CIO Dashboard. It is a business value chart showing how actual business value delivered compares with the business value estimate in our plan for the year 2002. Many other snapshots can be created to zoom in on metrics such as customer satisfaction or operating parameters such as availability.

Prior to implementing Intel's online dashboard, CIO Doug Busch implemented a walk-the-wall process. Each month, directors of each IT organization were required to post their key indicators boldly and explicitly onto an entire wall of the meeting room where the CIO staff met. Following a review of the key indicators, the CIO's team was encouraged to ask hard questions both about the validity of the indicators and particularly about the status or trends of the indicators. After a period of time, it became clear which indicators were the most important, and these were the ones that were codified into the online CIO dashboard. The CIO staff continues to allocate important CIO staff meeting time on a monthly basis to allow IT directors and review indicators and then ask the hard questions raised by the values and trends of the indicators.

IT Annual Reports

Finally, leading-edge, business-oriented IT organizations have adopted regular business practices such as publishing an IT annual report that details achievements in the prior year and outlines challenges, outlook, and opportunities for the year ahead. Intel IT has published an IT annual report for the past two years, and has found it to be not only an impor-

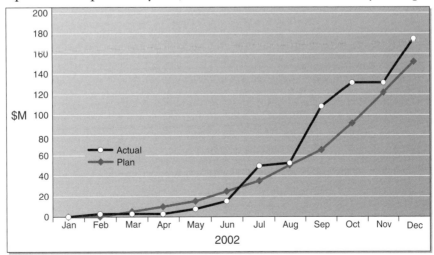

Figure 8.8 Q4 2002 Indicators: Actual and Planned Business Value

tant tool for building credibility with customers but also a motivational tool for IT employees, who can reflect on the track record of accomplishments in the last year as they look forward to some exciting challenges and opportunities in the year ahead.

Summary

I believe that IT organizations ought to be run like a business. Gartner analysts call this the ISCo, where the IT organizations are challenged to compete with external providers. Adopting a business mindset can be a real breakthrough for an IT organization. Businesslike thinking can drive the implementation of new business processes focused on delivering high-quality services and optimizing IT business value. However, as business and IT complexity increases and the demands on an IT organization increase, adopting a business mindset is not just a good idea, it is becoming a necessity.

A growing need is emerging for an integrated enterprise application to help run and manage IT like a business. This enterprise application would be comparable to an ERP system like SAP or a CRM system like Siebel. These enterprise applications have added significant value in their respective functional areas. In my opinion, too much time and energy is consumed actually running and managing IT systems. Of course, this is a reflection on the relative immaturity of the technologies and applications.

The emergence of autonomic computing and integrated IT management enterprise application software over the next few years should help IT organizations quickly make the transition to running IT like a business. It should also ensure that the majority of the IT organization's effort is focused on figuring out how IT can add more competitive advantage rather than just trying to keep systems running while driving costs down. Finally, as the IT organization matures, it ultimately will move from being perceived solely as a cost center to being perceived as a value center.

Chapter **9**

Putting It All Together

Overnight successes take about two years to accomplish, on average.
—Kerry Horan, Partner, PricewaterhouseCoopers

Information technology is an unconventional resource. Those of us who have used IT over the past decade or two have learned this through osmosis. But because we are dealing with this change on an ongoing basis, we sometimes forget its dramatic nature. To help illustrate the degree of change, consider a thought experiment: What if Moore's Law described improvements in aircraft technology over the past 25 years?

In 1978 a commercial jet aircraft took approximately 8 hours to fly from New York to Paris and a seat on that aircraft cost approximately €900. In 2004, aircraft still takes approximately the same flight time and the cost is about the same as well. If Moore's Law had applied to aircraft technology, the trip from New York to Paris would be completed in 1 second and would cost half a cent.

I wonder if the management structures and techniques would have remained the same in the air travel industry with this level of change. IT management practices have not changed all that much in the last twenty years. With the last 25 years having been marked by orders of magnitude improvements in information technology, a complementary question emerges: What magnitude of information technology change lies ahead?

John Gantz, IDC's Chief Research Officer, recently addressed this question. Gantz (2003) pointed out that today's Internet connects three quarters of a billion devices and that these devices include not only traditional computers, but also handheld devices, e-mail terminals, cell phones, automobiles, and cameras. In 10 years time, Gantz forecasts an increase of greater than three orders-of-magnitude—over a trillion networked devices. Of that trillion, a billion will be what we think of as computers today. The vast majority of devices will be active sensors and tags that communicate over wireless networks.

I believe it is safe to conclude that the need for strategists to re-examine the practicality of IT solutions due to technology change will continue into the next decade. Looking back and looking ahead, I see IT as an unconventional resource that will continue to provide dramatic new business solutions.

In this chapter, we discuss some approaches to managing IT as an unconventional resource to maximize business value delivered.

Managing an Unconventional Resource

How IT is organized and managed will lead to vastly different results. At Intel we have over 4000 IT employees and spend over a billion dollars on IT each year. An IT operation of the same scale in another enterprise may delivery significantly different value. There are two extremes in the continuum of IT's contribution to business value: on one extreme you have high value and managed costs and on the other extreme low value and high costs.

I think it is difficult to deliver high IT value on low costs. Most organizations recognize that IT is a competitive necessity and that the most realistic approach is to manage, not minimize costs. In industries that might be described as having lower clock speeds (*e.g.,* longer product lifetimes, slower introduction of new products, lower level of IT turnover), perhaps aiming for the lowest possible IT costs might be plausible.

In managing IT, I believe a firm's executives and its IT organization must come to an agreement about the current value proposition for IT and what a future value proposition ought to be. Conversation between the business and IT should reveal any dissonance in opinions.

As shown in Figure 9.1, the optimal situation is to be in the top left-hand quadrant, achieving both high value and low costs. However, I think the most realistic trade-off is to aim for high value and *managed* costs.

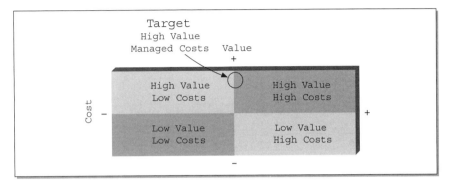

Figure 9.1 Business Value versus IT Cost

Business managers understand that IT does not come for free and that efforts to cut corners may save money in the short term but often have poor consequences longer term. Business managers also realize that they have no other option than continuous investment in IT; affording IT resources is as essential as affording human resources to run a business.

I suggest that you use a chart like this to quickly plot where business and IT leaders locate the firm's solutions and its portfolios of solutions. Pitting business value against IT cost can help stimulate productive discussions as firms attempt to transform how they deal with business value.

IT Management and Methodologies Matter

Research from Tallon, Kraemer, and Gurbaxani (2000) at CRITO shows that different levels of IT business value can be achieved with similar levels of IT spend. The researchers studied survey results from over 230 respondents in firms with revenues ranging from $300 million to $3 billion.

In one analysis, Tallon et al. classified the companies in a 2×2 table with low and high IT flexibility on one axis and low and high degrees of strategic alignment between business and IT on the other axis. The investigators collected ratings of average IT payoff and strategic flexibility, each measured on a seven-point scale. They also asked respondents to report IT investment as a percentage of overall revenue.

The results from the study are shown in Figure 9.2. Notice that firms in both the best and worst performing quadrants spent about the same amount of money on IT. In other words, firms in the top quadrant (*i.e.,* those that exhibited high IT flexibility and high business-to-IT strategic

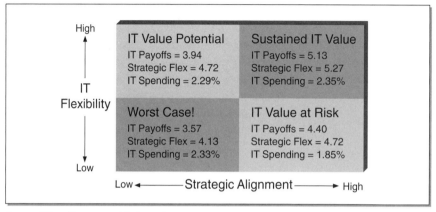

Source: Tallon, Kraemer, and Gurbaxani 2000

Figure 9.2 IT Flexibility versus Strategic Alignment

alignment) had a mean IT payoff of 5.13 on the seven-point scale, with average spending on IT of 2.35 percent of revenue. Firms in the worst performing quadrant (*i.e.*, those with below average scores on IT flexibility and low strategic alignment) had an IT payoff of 3.57 with average IT spending of 2.33 percent of revenue.

These findings tell me that two factors—the degree to which IT is aligned with strategy and the level of IT flexibility—have an impact on the business value delivered from IT. The lesson for IT managers is that alignment and flexibility can and should be management objectives, and achieving those objectives can have a significant impact on the IT business value delivered to your firm and consequently on firm results.

- Tallon et al. describe companies with high strategic alignment between IT and the Business and high IT flexibility as having *sustained IT value*. This assessment is commensurate with a strong IT capability.

- When high IT flexibility is accompanied by low business-IT alignment, companies are said to have *IT value potential* if the alignment issue can be addressed.

- *IT value at risk* identifies the problem for firms with high business-IT alignment but low flexibility. Strategic alignment is necessary but not sufficient.

- *Worst case* describes companies with inflexible systems and a lack of alignment. And again, it is ironic that *worst case* spend and *sustained IT value* spend are virtually identical.

Identifying where your particular firm is on this chart will help identify appropriate management objectives to improve IT business value.

Defining the IT Posture of the Firm

A well-known maxim says, "Attitude and aptitude give you altitude." I think this statement appropriately describes the use of IT in a firm. The maxim is in sharp contrast to analyses aimed at improving the yield on information technology. The yield approach implies that IT is an expense to be managed, and it also conveys to me that incremental improvement is the expectation. I have a different expectation: I view IT as a transformational resource enabling breakthrough business innovations.

Ireland's RyanAir is an excellent example of a company that has used IT as a transformational tool to achieve competitive advantage. Today, RyanAir is one of the largest carriers in Europe, and it competes on a low cost, no frills basis. The introduction of an Internet reservation system (for very low cost) broadened the audience for its products to include all of Europe and enabled a dramatic shift of bookings from travel agents and call centers to RyanAir's online automated Web site.

Today RyanAir uses its Internet reservation system as part of a proactive yield management system. When seats are available, RyanAir advertises special discounts to fill planes. When planes approach full capacity, the yield management system increases prices in real time. RyanAir's success with commonsense solutions is surprising because in its early years, RyanAir was a laggard in the adoption of IT. However, RyanAir's CEO, Michael O'Leary, spotted a strategic opportunity and almost overnight RyanAir was transformed.

The RyanAir Web site helped to create a virtuous circle as the reservations Web site underpinned aggressive expansion to new destinations. In turn, the company's aggressive route expansion drove more people to the Web site to make bookings. It is also significant that the reservation Web site was implemented with a small capital investment. Automated online transactions improved IT efficiency and enabled RyanAir to reduce the percentage of call center staff.

Interestingly, RyanAir continues to use an antiquated check-in system for seat assignment at the airports. For this function, RyanAir chooses to minimize cost and not invest in new IT solutions because it sees no strategic advantage from them. Operating as a point-to-point airline requires no inter-lining, that is, no coordination with other airlines for passengers flying multiple segments on different carriers.

Thus, I argue, the business value delivered to a firm from IT is heavily influenced by the firm's posture or attitude towards IT. Aptitude is equally important; insofar as the IT organization is able to develop new solutions quickly and base them on an open, scalable infrastructure, then the possibilities and opportunities for using IT strategically expand appreciably.

However, current success does not guarantee future success. The IT organization needs to be routinely identifying its future core competencies and investing in developing those competencies on an ongoing basis. Maintaining an anticipatory posture ensures that the IT organization is competent and prepared to help the business seize new opportunities.

People in the company can have short memories at times. When the Intel finance organization gets a little too picky on ROI analyses, Intel's CIO, Doug Busch, offers them the option of closing Intel's books without PCs and spreadsheets, using calculators or pen and paper. This example, although jovial, illustrates how critical IT is to businesses and how it has become embedded in nearly all day-to-day business processes.

Impact of IT Posture

Be prepared to define and defend the IT posture of your company. You may be postured as an IT leader, an early adopter, a fast follower, a mainstream adopter or even a late-majority laggard. Any of these positions can be valid in your industry. Don't assume, however, that firms in slow-moving industries should necessarily be laggards with adoption of IT. In some cases, business innovation through the use of IT can provide significant advantage in such an industry. What's important is to understand your strategy and communicate it clearly within the company as a whole.

An excellent example of defining and defending IT posture can be seen in the case of Laing O'Rourke, the fastest growing construction company in the UK. The strategic use of IT at Laing O'Rourke has been a key enabler to driving the firm's growth at a time when the revenues of other construction companies are declining. An innovative use of mobile and wireless technologies is providing Laing O'Rourke with a cost and performance advantage in new construction, as the company's engineers are using wireless laptops on the building site to view construction drawings. They have also developed radio frequency identification (RFID) and enterprise resource planning (ERP) systems to support just-in-time delivery of construction materials to their constructions sites.

Moreover, Laing O'Rourke is adding value to their product by leaving the wireless LANs they use for construction in place after they complete their work, as part of the building infrastructure.

Govern for IT Business Value

According to research from Weill and colleagues, good IT governance apparently pays off. Firms with better than average IT governance have at least 30 percent higher return on assets than other firms with the same strategic objectives. Weill and colleagues also found that top-performing firms govern IT differently from the typical firm and from each other depending on the performance metric they lead on. Clear accountability and clear decisions are critically important to structurally positioning IT for optimized business value. Chapter 8 reported the work of Weill and Woodham, who identified the areas noted in Table 9.1 as crucial for IT governance and, ultimately, for delivering business value.

Table 9.1   Five Key IT Governance Decisions

Business Decisions	
1. IT Principles	Overarching statements defining how IT should be used in the firm
2. Business Solution Needs	Roadmaps specifying the business need satisfied or the business opportunity created through a new IT solution
3. IT Investment and Prioritization	Decisions about where and how much to invest in IT
IT Decisions	
4. IT Infrastructure and Capability Strategies	Strategies for the foundation of infrastructure (PC's network etc.) and IT personnel based on a planned budget
5. IT architecture	An integrated set of technical choices to guide the enterprise in satisfying business needs

Adapted from Weill and Foglia, MIT CISR (2003)

In follow-up research, Weill and Foglia (2003) looked at who should make these IT and business decisions for best firm performance. In their sample of over 250 enterprises, they found that in top performing enterprises, business managers and IT professionals make the business-oriented IT decisions jointly.

Interestingly, Weill and Foglia also found that top-performing companies favored no best method for arriving at IT-specific decisions. It is difficult for me to imagine that business managers could make better decisions than IT managers on these IT-specific issues.

With respect to these key decisions that structurally impact IT contribution to business value and consequently the firm's performance and agility, I recommend that you ask two key questions:

1. Who is accountable for the five key IT governance decisions?

2. Are these decisions clearly communicated and reviewed at an appropriate frequency?

If the answers to these questions are unknown or unclear, you have a great place to start when improving the business value contribution IT can make in your firm.

In determining your governance approach, I would recommend you leverage the research and recommendations from Peter Weill and associates at MIT CISR. The optimum governance approach should align with your firm's central strategic objective.

- If your firm is focused on maximizing return on assets then a dual-governance approach may be most appropriate with IT and the business collaborating nearly equally on IT decision making and keeping a clear focus on IT principles of asset reuse and utilization. The horizontal view of a firm that IT uniquely has is important as it can identify good opportunities for reuse and overlap areas that can be eliminated.

- If your firm's focus is leading on profit, then decisions should be made by business leaders who also possess substantial IT acumen. According to Weill, leaders in profit made effective use of senior business management committees to achieve cost control and standardization. There is also a clear sense that the business architecture is driving the IT architecture.

- Finally, if your firm's focus is growth, you should implement governance structures that help to balance individual business units' entrepreneurial spirit with the firm-wide need for efficiency. In such cases, business units should be empowered to drive IT investment decisions that enable innovation and market responsiveness.

In his research, Weill identified a governance archetype called "business monarchies" with IT principles that focus on growth and not necessarily on standardization and cost management. This governance approach is likely to be beneficial for firms focused on growth.

Seven Action Statements for IT Business Value

In the remainder of this chapter, I provide some guidelines and recommendations for maximizing the business value of IT in your firm. These recommendations take the form of action statements accompanied by explanations and justifications.

Over-invest in IT

IT is an unconventional resource because its capability has improved so rapidly. IT is the only business resource that delivers twice the capability every eighteen months at less or equal cost. Moore's Law does not apply to other business assets, such as staff and manufacturing equipment. People become more capable, I suppose, by Darwinian evolution, which is a slow process at best. However, when people are empowered by increasingly powerful PCs, their capability is enormously enhanced. Compared to IT, other capital assets become more expensive year over year. For these reasons, I suggest that organizations should over-invest in IT vis-à-vis other business assets and that this investment should be on a regular schedule to ride the improving performance wave.

IT over-investment does not mean that organizations indiscriminately invest in IT as they often did in the irrational exuberance of the late 1990s. However, over-investment does mean avoiding the extreme conservatism that came about as a backlash to the late 90s IT splurge. I am suggesting that companies will deliver business value by maintaining aggressive IT investments based on solid business cases and strong program governance. In addition, Eric Brynjolfsson's research, cited in Chapter 1, showed that while IT investments returned about the same other types of investments viewed on a one year horizon, they significantly outperformed other investment types over a 5 to 7 year period.

I introduced an IT Business Value CMF in Chapter 2 as a means to improve the relative immaturity of management and financial controls and competencies for the corporate IT function. Without an improvement in maturity, organizational politics will generally overrule economics.

Invest in IT on a Cyclical Schedule

As IT is changing so rapidly, I believe that firms and IT organizations need to make an explicit decision to invest in IT on a regular schedule. They should be planning investments and upgrades and sticking as much as possible to the plan unless something fundamentally changes. Important lessons can be learned from the Delta case study shown in Appendix A, and none is more important than trying to avoid the dreaded bow wave of investment requirement created when IT investment is deferred from one year to the next. Apart from the bow wave, two other significant impacts result when an IT investment is deferred: a cost impact and a performance and value impact.

Many companies realize that three years is the optimal refresh rate for their corporate PCs, although not all companies can afford to purchase PCs this often. In early 2003, I spoke with Vladimir Tikhonov, CIO of AutoVAZ, a Russian car manufacturer, who confirmed this rule of thumb. when his data showed that the optimal refresh rate was 3 years, but his CEO found this refresh rate unaffordable, AutoVAZ opted for a four-year cycle.

In late 2003, I met with Vladimir again, and AutoVAZ had found an innovative solution to maximizing business value and minimizing TCO with respect to their PC refresh. Vladimir had a negotiated a leasing agreement that refreshed PCs every two years at the same annual cost AutoVAZ was paying for a four-year refresh through purchasing the assets. This solution delivered greater business value, as AutoVAZ employees have higher performing PCs in their hands earlier, and they also experience fewer PC problems because the PCs are still relatively new when they are refreshed. AutoVAZ's leasing solution is likely to be replicated as a mechanism for investing in IT on a regular schedule.

Cost is important, but I would be more concerned about the impact of performance by not upgrading on a short enough cycle. While several years ago the difference in speed between new and older PCs was a few hundred megahertz, today that gap can be several gigahertz. I would be interested to see the results of pilot studies contrasting the performance of an organization equipped with older PCs and an organization running on PCs with more capable processors. These results are likely to be significant productivity improvement benefits that become magnified across an organization of hundreds or even thousands of employees.

The question then becomes:

> "Can your organization afford not to invest in IT on a cyclical basis?"

Find the Sweet Spot: IT Business Value and IT Efficiency

In the late 1990s, when the Internet fever was raging, few IT or business people were concerned about business value, and fewer still were concerned about IT efficiency. Now both topics are salient in most IT planners' minds. I strongly recommend using the Intel IT Business Value Matrix and Business Value Index as tools to better understand the trade-off inherent in IT investment prioritization decisions. This approach allows decision makers to evaluate proposed investments based on their business value, IT efficiency, and financial attractiveness. You should be targeting your investments to land in the win-win space shown in Figure 9.3, to both add IT business value and improve IT efficiency.

When such an outcome is not possible, you should aim to make IT investments that improve either business value or IT efficiency but do not have a negative impact on the other, as Figure 9.3 also shows.

Intel achieved a win-win IT investment by developing a distributed solution called the Intel® Distributed Computing Platform. The solution provides Intel design engineers access to available CPU cycles on other engineering workstations. Intel Distributed Computing Platform is fault-tolerant, distributed peer-to-peer middleware capable of balancing workloads across heterogeneous compute platforms. The software enables compute workloads (*i.e.,* jobs) to be migrated transparently to other systems within the engineering environment connected by a LAN or to systems at remote sites connected by the Intel WAN.

Access to remote sites in other time zones enabled engineers in California, for example, to run compute jobs on idle workstations in Europe, and vice versa. Not only did compute-intensive design solutions run faster, moreover the utilization of workstations was improved. With

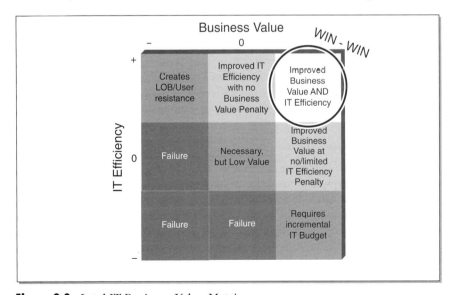

Figure 9.3 Intel IT Business Value Matrix

the Intel Distributed Computing Platform, the average utilization of workstations was increased from 35 percent to a sustained 70 percent.

From a business value perspective, time to market for Intel processors was routinely shortened, realizing tens of millions of incremental dollars by bringing new Intel products in the market earlier than the competition. From an IT efficiency perspective, tens of millions of dollars of capital expense avoidance was achieved by spreading workload across idle machines. We were able to reduce our purchases of workstations while meeting escalating demand. In engineering computing at Intel, computing demand has grown on an average at 88 percent annually. With the use of the Intel Distributed Computing Platform and the introduction of Linux on workstations using Intel processors (*cf.* Linux on IA for Engineering Workloads in Appendix A), the annual capital run rate for engineering computing has been kept flat.

Sequence IT Investments

Sequencing IT investments correctly has a significant impact on the value delivered and the cost to deliver a new solution. Imagine trying to deliver an executive information system without having the fundamental infrastructure and automated transaction systems in place to provide the needed information. A robust infrastructure makes it possible to deliver new solutions that make smart use of the data and information flowing through the firm and makes deploying any solutions more cost effective.

It often makes sense to split the delivery of new solutions into phases, as shown in Figure 9.4. For example, when introducing a new eLearning solution for Intel, we decided to focus the first phase on IT efficiency. We replaced a mainframe database solution with a SQL database running on a server. Despite the neutral business value of this solution, this project allowed us to quickly reduce the total cost of ownership of the existing solution from an IT standpoint. Phase 2 of the investment will be focused on transforming learning at Intel and leveraged the new more flexible IT infrastructure installed in phase 1.

Compound IT Investments

If you can sequence your IT investments correctly, you can achieve the compounding of fielding new investments that build on prior investments and deliver even higher returns at lower costs. For example, a yield analysis system built atop a core process-control system (*i.e.*, a system that collects process and product data) leverages the existing

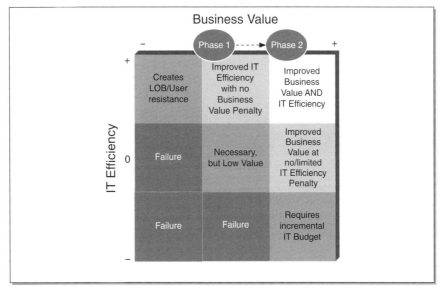

Figure 9.4 Sequencing IT Investments

investment and delivers incremental value that could probably not be delivered if the process control system were not already in place.

Also, enterprises are finding compounded value from their investments in wireless-enabled laptops, such as those based on the Intel Centrino™ platform. While many firms have justified the move to mobile and wireless based on internal efficiencies, they are finding that the build up of external hot spots allows them to extract even more than the original value. Employees in the field are able to connect quickly and economically from remote locations, send mail, and use other corporate applications.

Invest in IT Flexibility

IT flexibility can be enhanced by using open and scalable platforms and adopting standards and methods that allow increasingly seamless connectivity (*e.g.,* IP networking, XML, and enterprise application integration products). At Intel IT we use a scale-up, scale-out architectural approach for IT flexibility. "Scale out" means that we can add new servers quickly to increase capacity. In contrast, "scale up" means that we add more processors to a server or workstation to build a more powerful computer. We believe that using both scale-up and scale-out techniques provides us with a balanced approach to provisioning computing capacity wherever it is needed quickly and efficiently.

We deploy *rich clients* (*i.e.,* high performance PCs) to our knowledge workers to ensure that they have the computing power to perform their tasks quickly and efficiently and to provide headroom for new applications. I explained earlier that at Intel we had to write off 20,000 PCs at a cost of $40 million because the value PCs could not support an operating system upgrade and new solutions. Using rich clients puts the best tools available in the hands of firms most expensive resource—people—and provides for headroom and flexibility for new solutions deployment.

For example, at Intel we were able to deploy a high value multi-task solution for eLearning, executive video communications, and knowledge management across our distributed PC platform at a very low incremental cost and with a robust ROI. This solution was enabled by peer-to-peer computing middleware that takes advantage of the power of PCs on people's desktops. Implementing a similar solution on value PCs would not have been possible.

In other cases, we find it cheaper to scale out by provisioning a new server. Adding a server often costs less and takes less time than it would take for an IT professional to engineer two or more applications to coexist on a single server. With the introduction of server blade technology (*i.e.,* servers that provide a backplane for a multitude of blades, which are independent SMP computers), I expect to scale out by adding a new blade.

At Intel IT we are increasingly adopting what we call an "occasionally connected computing" (OCC) approach. We design solutions that work irrespective of whether an application or a solution is running on a device connected to the network. As we move to support an increasingly mobile workforce, we are discovering that our employees find themselves alternately to have high bandwidth connections, to have a low bandwidth connection, or to have no connection whatsoever. Improving our OCC architecture contributes to higher IT flexibility. You can find more information about designing mobilized software applications at *www.mobilizedsoftware.com*.

Invest in IT Innovation

IT is an important tool for business innovation. IT innovation is about putting together intelligent combinations of new, emerging, and existing technology and knowledge to deliver superior business solutions. One could argue that the greatest future value to a company from IT is the conceptualization of future business solutions. I encourage IT leaders to explore implementing solutions that help make innovations systematic by studying needs, opportunities, solutions, and knowledge across the company.

At Intel, we have developed an IT innovation engine that effectively acts as two solutions: a customer relationship management system for IT's customers and a solution for identifying the best innovations and accelerating them into production. I expect that software to support systematic innovation will start to appear in the marketplace over the next few years.

Making Something Happen

In conclusion, I want to discuss action plans that integrate the four complementary strategies discussed throughout the book. To recap:

- ■ I have reviewed a strategy around "Managing for IT Business Value," that is, how to maximize benefits from existing investments, how to choose the right IT investments for the future, and how to use portfolio management techniques to optimize the overall business value to the firm.

- ■ In "Managing the IT Budget" I discussed the importance of performance against budget to build credibility with the firm, techniques to systematically reduce costs to improve IT efficiency and to enable shifting of funds into innovation and new areas. This discussion, of course, takes place in the context of a growing demand for IT services irrespective of business cycle and firm revenue trends.

- ■ In "Managing the IT Capability" I discussed how to systematically develop and assess the IT capability to enable the delivery of sustainable competitive advantage.

- ■ And, finally, in "Managing IT like a Business" I reviewed how the adoption of IT business practices can improve the efficiency and effectiveness of an IT organization, ultimately helping information technology transform into a strategic capability for the business.

The current maturity of your IT organization determines where you will need to begin, if you are to improve or transform your organization. The capability maturity framework has been designed to allow you to choose areas to focus upon. Unlike traditional CMM models that on focus on descriptions of what should be done, I have tried to integrate a mix of what should be done and how it should be done.

When beginning the transformation process, it is important to understand the baseline state of your firm and IT organization today. From the baseline you can look ahead to develop a vision of where your firm's use of IT and the IT organization needs to go. The roadmap you develop from the baseline into the future then becomes the basic tool for your journey.

Mindset, Motivation, Methodologies, and Tools

Depending upon where you are on the maturity framework for delivering IT business value, different steps and initiatives must be taken. However, regardless of the maturity level, the common threads are mindset, motivation, methodologies, and tools.

First, an IT business value mindset needs to be in place. IT employees need to consider IT business value as a "first things first" priority when evaluating new opportunities. Similarly, business executives and managers need to recognize IT as not merely a cost item in their P&L statement, but as a function that has the potential to transform their business. Achieving this business value mindset can usually be accomplished only through an education process and a demonstrated track record of success.

Recognition and reward are two of the first tools that organizations use to motivate mindset changes. Employees who take an IT business value perspective should be recognized as role models and rewarded. If the firm is serious about leveraging IT for business value, it may choose to tie IT employee bonuses to achievement of business value goals. Through frequent communication and clear rewards and recognition, the company can motivate IT personnel to be oriented towards achieving business value.

In parallel with mindset and motivation, new methodologies for managing and measuring IT business value need to be introduced. For maximum effectiveness, these methodologies should be supported with automated or semi-automated tools that help focus the energy on IT business value.

To determine the IT organization's level of maturity I use the IT Business Value Maturity test. Sample items are shown in Table 9.2, and the entire survey is included in Appendix B. The goal of this assessment is to identify quickly your firm's level of relative maturity and then to help prioritize where new processes or resources need to be added.

Based on this quick assessment, you will have a result that is directionally correct. Your scores in each section will reveal your weakest maturity thread and where you should likely focus your efforts.

Table 9.2 IT Business Value Maturity Test: Selected Items

1.0 Managing for IT Business Value	5 Strongly Agree	4 Agree	3 Neutral	2 Disagree	1 Strongly Disagree
1.1. A standard business case template for reviewing proposed investments is in place (including lifetime costs of supporting the solution).					
1.2. A formal set of proposal valuation criteria that maps to key business variables is deployed.					
2.0 Managing the IT Budget					
2.1. A structured IT cost reduction program is in place.					
2.2. Financial performance with respect to budgets is predictable and within the variance range.					
3.0 Managing the IT Capability					
3.1 Integrated IT organizational capability assessment methodologies are in place (e.g. organizational quality, CMM, etc.).					
3.2 Formal customer survey processes are in placed and are acted upon.					
4.0 Running IT as a Business					
4.1. A high level of Business and IT alignment exists.					
4.2 IT Governance structure exists and is clearly known across business and IT.					

Figure 9.5 shows the output from a hypothetical assessment. In this example, the managing for IT Business Value strategy is the least mature and clearly the area where effort should be focused first.

Depending on the maturity of your organization, you may need just incremental improvement or you may require radical transformation. If you have identified that you need radical transformation, I would recommend creating a business plan for the IT organization, with accountability assigned to a key member of the CIO staff. Developing a business plan for the IT function or organization can be a very effective way of driving a transformation. In building a transformation plan, it is very important to have both employee and leadership involvement.

I suggest that you perform the IT Business Value Maturity assessment on an ongoing basis to check your progress. Meanwhile, we at Intel are busy conducting further research with industry partners to build out the

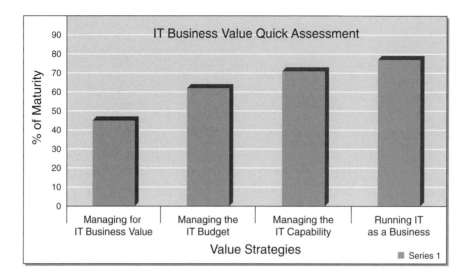

Figure 9.5 Value Strategies

IT Business Value Maturity Framework into an IT Business Value Capability Maturity Model.

The BV-Maturity Framework is still evolving. Typically CMM models are very comprehensive, and we will add detail as our research progresses. The intent is that the framework's well-defined strategies and approaches will help you identify key processes or structural changes to help your firm achieve more business value from your IT investments.

You Get What You Measure!

If you read this book and do only one thing, I would recommend that you start to measure and track the benefits from existing IT projects and programs. This is money and resources that you have already committed! I have noticed that as soon as I start to measure something, it improves. Introducing a standard business case and and ROI template that is reviewed regularly is a good second step toward ensuring accountability for delivering business value with IT.

As I continue to collect new ideas, examples, and case studies, I shall be publishing them on the *Managing IT for Business Value* Web page, which you can visit at *www.intel.com/intelpress/sum_bv.htm*.

Good luck on your journey!

Appendix **A**

Case Studies

Well done is better than well said.
—Benjamin Franklin

It is common to cite examples of the outcomes of IT projects and investments and less common to study the key decisions that led those projects and investments. And yet it is the struggle to formulate the problem, weigh the risks inherent in taking a different course of action, and making hard decisions that is most interesting. In the tradition established by schools of business, I include two case studies that focus on the process as well as the outcome of managing IT for business value.

The first case study, The Delta Technology Operating Tail, was developed with IT leaders at Delta Technology and explores the IT organization's attempts to communicate the issues of IT in terms and analogies familiar to the parent company, Delta Air Lines.

The second case study, Linux on IA for Engineering Workloads, was drawn from Intel IT and looks at the tough decision leading to a migration of our firm's engineering hardware and software platform from a UNIX operating system and RISC processors to the Linux operating system and IA-32 processors.

The Delta Technology Operating Tail

By developing a common language for success, Delta and Delta Technology have partnered to create new technological innovations, changing the face of the airline business and lifting Delta above our competitors.
—Michele Burns, EVP and CFO, Delta Air Lines, and Chair of the Board, Delta Technology

"Let's try to speak to Delta in air carrier terms, not IT terms," counseled Curtis Robb, CEO of Delta Technology, a wholly-owned subsidiary of Delta Air Lines, to his direct reports. "We need our customers to understand the challenges of IT, many of which are related to the cost of ongoing operations after a capital investment has been made."

Robb, who joined Delta Technology as CTO in 2000, was rallying his troops as they prepared for the annual presentation of Delta Technology's budget, operations, and multiyear plan. The air travel industry was booming and Delta was a leader in deploying IT to streamline its operations and improve its competitiveness.

Information Technology at Delta Air Lines

Delta wasn't always a technology leader in the airline industry. In fact, some might say that Delta has undergone a technology transformation to move from a technology laggard to a technology leader.

The Delta Air Lines board of directors made a conscious decision in 1997 to invest heavily in technology. Over the next five years, Delta spent more than $1.5 billion on information technology. This investment addressed the challenges of Y2K, completely overhauled Delta's IT infrastructure and helped transform Delta's airports. As a result, customers now enjoy web-based ticketing, kiosks and virtual check-in. Employees are using state-of-the-art workstations to board passengers, and Gate Information Display Screens answer customers' top 20 questions, enabling employees to assist passengers with more complex transactions.

Also included in that $1.5 billion investment were the critical, but less visible infrastructure investments, such as moving from ad hoc integration techniques to the consistent use of middleware products. Delta and Delta Technology were quick to face up to the limitations of data and operational "silos" that have plagued many companies over the past decade. The dynamic digital network called the Delta Nervous System (DNS) was developed by Delta Technology to receive, store, organize, filter, and distribute essential data in real time. By making this bold investment, Delta has been able to accelerate its focus on customer self-service, while keeping its technology operating costs flat.

Explaining the Logic of the IT Budget

IT managers have long known that the cost of development and initial deployment of IT systems is quickly equaled by the cost of maintaining those systems. For Curtis Robb and his management team, explaining the logic of the IT budget was particularly crucial. While there was a period of high investment and demonstrated success, Robb's challenge was to continue innovative programs while affording the ongoing costs of maintaining existing systems.

Still, in 2000, Delta Technology needed a way to communicate to its parent company that a budget was needed just to keep things running, that the budget would be significant in magnitude, and that the budget would grow over time as IT systems aged.

The Delta Operating Tail

In 2000, Curtis Robb, Brian Leinbach, Delta Technology Senior Vice President of Operations, and their colleagues developed the Delta Operating Tail. The Delta Operating Tail is a graphical way to display the accumulating cost of building and operating IT systems. The resulting graphic looks like the vertical stabilizer, which is a part of the tail of an airplane.

In its basic form, data are presented as a stacked bar graph with cost on the Y axis, as shown in Figure A.1. The first bar on the left is the initial

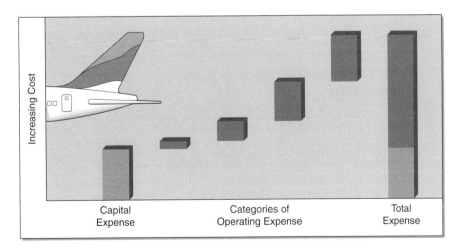

Source: Delta Technology

Figure A.1 The Delta Technology Operating Tail

development expense (*i.e.,* a capital expenditure) and the last bar on the right is the cumulative total cost. Categories of operating expense are displayed along the X axis.

"Our operating tail is a picture of what IT managers call the total cost of ownership," Robb explained. "However, this graphic organizes the information into a visual representation that is memorable. And, the operating tail is a comfortable fit with the terminology used by air carrier personnel."

Fleet Mix

"Another analogy we find helpful when briefing our parent company is fleet mix," added Brian Leinbach. "We could say to Delta executives that we have an increasingly homogeneous IT infrastructure, and they might not understand what we mean by that."

"Did you know that Delta Air Lines flies an all-Boeing fleet of aircraft?" Leinbach queried. "That's the air carrier's version of homogeneity—and the benefits are much the same. Fewer skill sets are needed for a standardized fleet mix.

"Further, like the aircraft fleet mix, our IT fleet mix should contain the right ratio of newer and older equipment and a plan to retire older systems. So, when we talk about our investments in servers and storage systems, we call it our fleet mix."

Managing Growth at Delta Technology

"I believe that we've been successful in reining in costs and focusing IT investment on projects that make a difference for Delta," Curtis Robb reflected in mid-2001. We've developed a rapport with our customers by establishing regular reporting techniques, such as the Delta Operating Tail. This helps Delta understand what we are doing and why."

The Delta Technology board of directors was scheduled to meet in Fall 2001 to define the next major technology initiatives. However, following the events of September 11, 2001, things changed. As a result, Curtis Robb and his colleagues began an unexpected new chapter in IT management. Would the techniques and metrics that Delta Technology used to manage growth remain useful?

Managing the Downturn

September 11, 2001 marked a turning point for the entire air carrier industry. In its March 2002 annual report for the fiscal year ending on

December 31, 2001, Delta Air Lines CEO Leo Mullin described the magnitude of the downturn as follows:

> With depressed revenues, fewer customers, high costs, and increasing expenses for security and insurance, the situation for the airline industry remained grim throughout 2001 and into 2002.

Not surprisingly, cost cutting was a major objective across all of Delta's operations, including Delta Technology. Curtis Robb and his colleagues studied their cost structures and revisited their assumptions about fixed and variable costs.

"We were particularly frustrated with fixed versus variable costs," Brian Leinbach explained. "We came to realize that our cost of maintenance was related to the number of applications that we support, and none of those applications were optional to the everyday activities of Delta. Ongoing operating expense could not be reduced in proportion to fewer flights and fewer customers."

"The Delta Operating Tail remained a useful communication tool for us," said Curtis Robb. "Our working assumption for most IT systems was that they would serve us for three to five years before being replaced. To reduce spending, we cut our capital expenditures for renewals sharply. The Operating Tail showed that not all of those savings could be realized."

The Delta Operating Tail shown in Figure A.2 illustrates the problem. In 1999, Delta Technology rolled out extensive systems to improve customer service at the airport. Budgets were in place for an Operating Tail spanning three years time, and that time was up.

As Figure A.2 shows, not replacing these systems meant encountering two more years of operating expense not budgeted for. Moreover, the cost of maintaining equipment increases as the "fleet" ages—maintenance for the airport customer care systems was forecast to be larger in year 4 and 5.

Thus, Delta Technology found that the Operating Tail was equally good at communicating budget issues during times of growth and times of downturn. Curtis Robb and his colleagues could show their customers that rising operating expenses would erode savings in capital expenditures and the problem would grow quickly over the coming years.

The Bow Wave of Accumulated Cost

"To highlight the accumulated costs, we created a variant of the Operating Tail we call the Bow Wave." Robb explained. "The Bow Wave illustrates graphically that failing to invest in new systems incrementally over

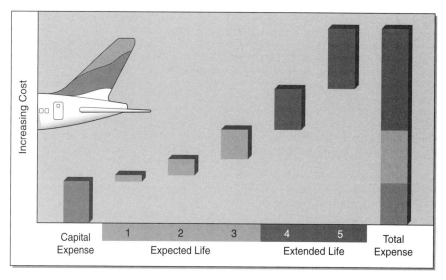

Source: Delta Technology

Figure A.2 Delta's Operating Tail and Delayed System Retirement

the years causes a buildup of expense. The Bow Wave is critical to thinking through strategic plans for different periods of downturn. Weathering a two-year downturn is dramatically different than weathering a four-year downturn, as the Bow Wave indicates."

The Bow Wave shown in Figure A.3 is typical of situations such as PC replacement programs. IT sets a schedule to replace machines when they are five years old. If the schedule slips, then the cost of catching up grows with each passing year. By combining the Operating Tail in Figure A.2 and the Bow Wave in Figure A.3, the full nature of the cost-cutting dilemma is crystal clear. A restriction on spending leads to retaining PCs, thus incurring increased maintenance costs. That same restriction triggers an accumulation of costs necessary to get back on track.

"These are not pretty pictures," Brian Leinbach hastened to add. "But, we believe that they communicate the nature of our operations during 2002, so that we can think through different scenarios and build contingency plans as necessary.

Given the economic climate, Delta Technology quickly realized that the Bow Wave was larger than Delta could afford to solve in one year's time. To communicate this, Delta Technology developed a Business Risk Analysis tool that defined the various methods to resolve the Bow Wave over a multiyear time frame. This tool is used to measure the risk of Delta's aging technology assets by reviewing the following character-

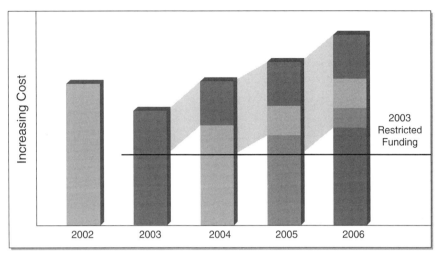

Source: Delta Technology

Figure A.3 Delta's Bow Wave for Deferred Investment

istics: technology age, business value at risk, platform supportability, platform complexity and risk of failure.

For each IT asset, risk is categorized as unacceptable, affordable, and unaffordable. After reviewing and ranking the five characteristics, the scores are combined to identify a compiled rating.

In Figure A.4, the unacceptable region of the graph represents an asset that must be self-supported by Delta Technology, and has security risks that could have an enterprise-wide impact. The area between

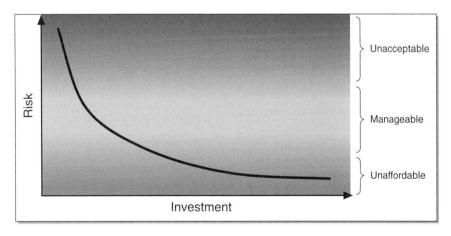

Source: Delta Technology

Figure A.4 Risk versus Investment at Delta Technology

unacceptable and manageable represents assets that would require support at a premium price through the vendor and security risks that are manageable. The manageable area represents those assets that are supported by the vendor at no cost and that have no easily exploitable security risk in the environment. By using this tool and graphic, Delta Technology was able to explain to Delta the context of risk at various spend levels.

Lessons Learned

A major thesis of this book is that IT ought to speak the language of business value. The leaders of Delta Technology have taken this thesis a step farther by saying, "Speak the language of the enterprise to be better understood." By casting IT in air carrier terms, Curtis Robb and his colleagues are anchoring the concept that they intend to be part of the fundamental business of Delta Air Lines. By establishing clever and insightful graphical views of the IT budget, Robb and his staff are increasing the understanding that they need when talking about new opportunities or tough challenges with their customers.

Linux on IA for Engineering Workloads

Designing Intel processors with Intel processors is the right thing to do,
and Linux makes that possible.
—Doug Busch, CIO, Intel Corporation

"So that's what they have in mind..." thought Elwood Coslett as he reviewed an e-mail message in late 1997 that suggested what his next assignment ought to be. Coslett, a ten-year veteran at Intel, had just finished a proof-of-concept project to explore the possibility of a wide-scale migration to servers with Intel processors as the primary platform for engineering computing at Intel.

"Well, if it's visibility that enhances a career, then this is the project for me," Coslett mused. Intel was asking him to turn that proof-of-concept demonstration into a new engineering platform and roll it out in time to support the development of the Pentium® 4 processor, code-named Willamette, which was slated for design and validation in late 1998.

Engineering Computing at Intel

The engineering computing (EC) organization at Intel Corporation manages the computing resources used by engineers to design and test the company's products. Electronic design automation (EDA) software from both internal and external suppliers assists semiconductor device designers in building and validating new products. Intel products, particularly their line of microprocessors, are developed and released to original equipment manufacturers (OEMs) on aggressive schedules in a highly competitive marketplace. EC resources are critical to delivering quality products on time.

Prior to 1996, the EC environment at Intel was primarily servers using RISC processors running UNIX. Thousands of servers were employed by hundreds of engineers to run a multitude of packaged EDA and custom Intel design and testing applications. At the end of each product design cycle, EC managers examined the resources consumed and estimated the investment needed in providing sufficient resources for the next product generation.

What Migration to the Intel Architecture Entails

"Let's pencil it out," Mark Aitken said to himself as he began to formalize the problem. "Porting our register transfer language (RTL) will be a major activity. And, we'll need to establish a stable, trustworthy hardware and operating environment consisting of at least 1,000 servers. We'll need to train hundreds of engineers to use the new system."

RTL comprises a few hundred computer programs laced together with 750,000 lines of UNIX scripts. RTL is used to validate the microprocessor's logic design, which is the most compute-intensive activity in the design lifecycle (*cf.* Validating a Processor Design). Up to 50,000 RTL jobs are submitted per week and jobs vary in CPU usage from minutes to days.

With such intense computational demands, EC hardware and operating environments must remain available. Problems such as system crashes or freezes can quickly erode progress and threaten the time box assigned for processor validation.

Coslett was interested in using Linux, a relatively new Open Source operating system similar to UNIX. Would Linux be up to the task? And, how would Intel support Open Source software? Previously, Intel looked to the provider of its RISC-based servers for system maintenance. Was the move to Linux and Open Source on Intel architecture processors timely or too aggressive?

Formulating the Decision

In their briefing to management, Elwood Coslett and Mike Janes framed the decision by identifying three major risks associated with a migration to servers using Intel processors and the Linux operating environment. They also forecast the financial savings that could be expected if the migration were successful.

Beginning with the benefits, Coslett and Janes told their managers to expect about $100 million in savings by 2000 due to the lower cost of servers based on the Intel architecture processors. To achieve equivalent computing capability, RISC-based servers cost roughly five times as much as servers based on Intel processors. The risks were stated as questions and Coslett's replies explained how the risks should be weighed or mitigated.

■ Can we implement mission-critical production systems on an Open Source operating system, namely, Linux?

"At this time, most Linux installations are not running critical applications." Coslett explained. "However, the operating system is solid and has proven to be resilient in other uses."

■ Will support issues threaten Intel's tight production schedules?

"Linux is a lot like UNIX, and so retooling our EC staff to support this new platform will demand far less effort than a shift to an

Validating a Processor Design

Validating the design of a complex semiconductor device such as an Intel microprocessor is a five-stage process. Initially, engineers design and validate the overall architecture, as shown in Figure A.5.

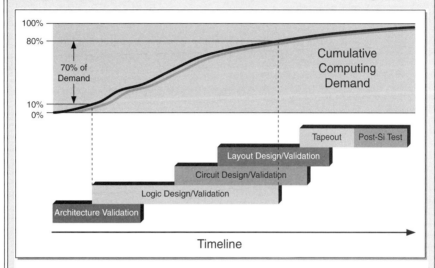

Figure A.5 Compute Demand over the Design Time Line

At the second stage, engineers design and validate the chip's logic. This stage consumes 70 percent of the total computing resource for a engineering project. Thousands of computers run millions of simulations as engineers exercise the processor's functionality.

Circuit design and layout follow logic validation. The final steps in the process are tapeout, which is the process of writing the processor's description to magnetic tape, and post-silicon testing of the actual processor.

entirely different operating environment." Janes argued. "And, we can contract with our server providers for additional help in this area."

■ Can we ramp up quickly enough to deploy the thousands of servers with Linux and all the necessary tools our engineers need without hitting an unexpected limitation?

"With an aggressive schedule we can deploy 1,200 servers. We have some experience to build on," Coslett reminded his managers. "Results of our proof-of-concept testing were very good."

Linux and Open Source

In 1991, Linus Torvalds implemented a version of UNIX that ran on a personal computer with an Intel processor. Linus and UNIX melded to Linux and, influenced by Richard Stallman's Free Software Manifesto, Torvalds released his source code and licensed the software using Stallman's General Public License.

By 1998, Linux was a well-recognized operating environment in academic and engineering communities. Under the auspices of the Open Source Initiative, computer programs were certified to work with Linux. Scripting languages and other utilities were in place and companies had formed to provide support for Linux for those customers who planned to put systems into production environments.

On Thursday, December 10, 1998, after a final presentation of testing results, a review of the stability numbers, and discussion on understanding and managing the risks, Elwood Coslett and his managers came to a decision.

Deploying Linux on IA

"Ninety days should do it," Elwood Coslett estimated. "In the first 30 days, we'll aim to bring up a farm of 300 servers equipped with all necessary applications and scripts. In the next 30 days, we'll double the size of the farm. In the final 30 days, we'll double again to a final total of 1,200 servers."

In typical Intel fashion, small teams were assembled to address the specific challenges. A team of platform builders began by downloading Linux and assembling UNIX tools drawn from GNU, the venerable Open Source supplier. GNU tools had the added benefit of being familiar to Intel IT, since they had been used for years in traditional UNIX environments. A second team of six people ported nearly 750,000 lines of code to bring the RTL test environment to life.

System stability testing began in earnest. Table A.1 shows the results for failures and frozen jobs for three parts of the RTL application suite. These error rates were within acceptable bounds and, in fact, the new Linux-on-IA platform was more stable than other platforms running other versions of UNIX.

Table A.1 Stability of RTL Applications Running on Linux and IA Processors

Criteria	RTL on Linux		
	AV	DV	MPV
False Failures	0.2%	0.2%	0.0%
Frozen Jobs		0.12%	

Support and training were obtained by contracting with a global IT systems and service provider. Doing so allowed Intel IT staff to focus entirely on rolling out the new platform, migrating the software, and testing the systems.

Ninety days after deciding to migrate the engineering design to a new computing platform, Intel engineers began validating the Pentium 4 chip on schedule and in late 1998, also on schedule, the processor code-named Willamette successfully taped out.

Intel Achievement Award

There are ten names on the Intel Achievement Award given in 2002 "for driving the migration of Intel's design environment from RISC to IA." Elwood Coslett, Mark Aitken, Mike Janes, Inderjit Puri, Kevin Wheeler, Randy Steck, Guru Bhatia, Igal Iancu, Kurtis Dayley, and Greg Spirakis were the major contributors to a project that Intel described as follows:

Researched and delivered an IA/Linux computing environment with improved reliability (99.9 percent success rates). Also drove substantially lower computing costs ($100 million savings) for our design engineering customers without compromising performance. Overcame open source software stability concerns by implementing rigorous change control processes resulting in the use of IA/Linux as a mission critical production capability for all processor/chipset design teams across Intel.

Four Years Later

In November of 2002, Elwood Coslett reflected on the decision to port EC to Linux and the Intel Architecture processors in a presentation to Intel Capital. The estimated savings for the first two years ending in 2000 was $99 million. Cumulative savings through 2002 was an astonishing $452 million! Computing demand grew by 86 percent a year in 2000 through 2002 elevating projected spending on equivalent RISC capacity.

At the same time, improvements in price/performance for servers with Intel inside continued.

Lessons Learned

In his book *The Innovator's Dilemma*, Clayton Christensen described the effects that disruptive technologies have in a marketplace. Competitors are able to enter markets with relatively less sophisticated products using new technology, grow the sophistication of those products, and topple market leaders. Christensen's observations are valuable to strategic planners defending market share.

For managers of IT, however, the message is different. With great regularity, IT suppliers have offered up what first appears to be an inferior offering that grows in its capability. Linux is a good example. Who would expect that a reliable operating system would be developed in an attic in Finland? Further, when in the life of the Open Source movement was it first apparent that Linux and its companion tools would achieve high quality?

Elwood Coslett and his team recognized Linux and Open Source as disruptive technologies that were ready to be exploited. It is interesting to note, as well, that Linus Torvalds wrote his operating system for the Intel Architecture, which is itself a disruptive technology.

Appendix B

Assessment Tools

We are what we repeatedly do.
Excellence, then is not an act, but a habit.
—Aristotle

This appendix contains four assessment tools used by Intel IT for systematically surveying our operations.

■ SAM-lite was created in 1990 at Intel as a streamlined self-assessment tool based on the evaluation criteria for the Malcolm Baldrige National Quality Award. The tool is called *lite* because it focuses on a few key items that will identify the largest portion of improvement for an organization. Use of SAM-lite is discussed in Chapter 7.

■ The IT Organizational Assessment (ITOA) is a 46-item questionnaire designed for internal assessment of the IT organization by its own staff. The instrument was developed by Intel IT and is used on a regular basis. Use of the ITOA is discussed in Chapter 7.

■ P-CMM-lite is the simplified People Capability Maturity Model assessment criteria that we use at Intel IT. This assessment classifies an organization on one of the five CMM levels. Use of the P-CMM-lite is discussed in Chapter 7.

■ The IT Business Value Maturity test is a tool that Malvina Nisman and I are developing for use at Intel. This assessment is new and has not yet been formally validated.   The IT Business Value Maturity Assessment is discussed in Chapter 9.

New assessment tools and updates to the assessment tools in this appendix can be found at the *Managing IT for Business Value* Web page, which you can visit at *www.intel.com/intelpress/sum_bv.htm*.

SAM-lite

SAM-lite Scoring Criteria: Approach and Deployment

Score	Factors to Consider
0%	• No systematic approach evident; anecdotal information
10% to 30%	• Beginning of a systematic approach to the primary purposes of the item • Early stages of a transition from reacting to problems to a general improvement orientation • Major gaps exist in deployment that would inhibit progress in achieving the primary purposes of the item
40% to 60%	• A sound, systematic approach, responsive to the primary purposes of the item • A fact-based improvement process in place in key areas; more emphasis is placed on improvement than on reaction to problems • No major gaps in deployment, though some areas or work units may be in very early stages of deployment
70% to 90%	• A sound, systematic approach, responsive to the primary purposes of the item • A fact-based improvement process is a key management tool; clear evidence of refinement and improved integration as a result of improvement cycles and analysis • Approach is well-deployed, with no major gaps; deployment may vary in some areas or work units
100%	• A sound, systematic approach, fully responsive to all the requirements of the item • A very strong, fact-based improvement process is a key management tool; strong refinement and integration - backed by excellent analysis • Approach is fully deployed without any significant weaknesses or gaps

SAM-lite Assessment

1.1 LEADERSHIP SYSTEM

How does our organization's IT leadership system work? Do our senior managers provide effective leadership throughout the entire organization while taking into account the needs and expectations of all key stake holders?   Score: ___ %

Clarifying questions:
1. How does our leadership system address performance expectations, focus on customers and other key stakeholders, learning and innovation?
2. How do our senior managers set and communicate organizational direction? How do they seek future opportunities for the organizations, taking into account all key stakeholders?
3. To what extent and level do our senior managers participate in and use the results of organizational performance reviews?
4. How do we evaluate and improve our leadership system? How are the organization's performance and employee feedback used in the evaluation?

1.2 ORGANIZATIONAL RESPONSIBILITY AND CITIZENSHIP

How, and to what extent, do we include our responsibilities and impacts to the public or other Intel organizations in our policies, improvement practices, and plans? To what extent are we a leader in this area?   Score: ___ %

Clarifying questions:
1. How do we contribute to our community and business environments?
2. Compared to organizations of like size, do we contribute accordingly?
3. How do we manage our responsibility to our customers and communities?

2.1 STRATEGY DEVELOPMENT PROCESS

How effective is the process by which we set the organization's direction to strengthen our performance and competitive position?   Score: ___ %

Clarifying questions:
1. Is the process used systematic? Are there cycles of evaluation and improvement of the process?
2. How do we take the following factors into account: customers/clients, market requirements (including price/cost), customer/market expectations, new opportunities, and our competitive environment?
3. How do we include financial, societal, and organizational risks?
4. How do we include our human resource needs and capabilities: systems, processes, and people?
5. How do we include organization capabilities such as technology, R&D, innovation, business/work processes, and supplier/business partner capabilities as we look for new opportunities?

2.2 ORGANIZATION STRATEGY

How well are our short- and long-term strategies and plan known, clearly understood, and used? How do we measure performance of these plans?

Score: ___ %

Clarifying questions:

1. To what extent do our plans adequately cover all major areas of: our current business, our future business, our human resources, quality, product/service development, customers, suppliers.
2. Do we have both short- and long-term plans articulated? Are they tied together and linked?
3. How do we communicate our plans throughout our organization?

3.1 CUSTOMER AND MARKET FOCUS

How well do we determine near- and long-term requirements, expectations and preferences for our customers, markets and potential customers/markets?

Score: ___ %

Clarifying questions:

1. How frequently does our senior management engage with the customer base? How is this information fed into our planning?
2. Do we group like customers or segment our markets? How well do we do this and use the information? Are different methods necessary for each group or segment?
3. How do we use information regarding our customers and markets to determine or project products, service, potential customer value, and new opportunities?

3.2 CUSTOMER SATISFACTION AND RELATIONSHIP ENHANCEMENT

How well does our organization determine and improve the satisfaction levels of our customers/clients?

Score: ___ %

Clarifying questions:

1. How effective is our customer complaint management process at resolving complaints quickly? How do we assure that all complaints received by our organization are aggregated and analyzed for improvement?
2. How well do our measurements of satisfaction and dissatisfaction capture actionable information that reflects the likeliness of future business and or positive referral?
3. How effective and proactive are our follow up processes regarding products, services and recent transactions so we receive prompt actionable feedback?
4. How effective are we at providing our customers access to us, determining their satisfaction, and building relationships with customers? How well do we evaluate and improve these on an ongoing basis?

4.1 SELECTION AND USE OF INFORMATION AND DATA

How effectively do we select, manage, and use information and data that we need to support key organization processes, action plans and improve our performance?　　　Score: ___ %

Clarifying questions:

1. How do we determine the appropriate information and data that we need to run our key processes and help drive our action plans?
2. How do we manage the issues of data availability where/when needed, speed of access, and timeliness of data/information and data reliability?
3. How well do we evaluate and improve the data and/or information that we use to keep pace with our changing business (or process) needs and strategies?

4.2. SELECTION AND USE OF COMPARATIVE INFORMATION AND DATA

How effectively do we select, manage and use comparative information and data to improve our organization's performance and competitive position?　　　Score: ___ %

Clarifying questions:

1. How well do we establish needs for comparative information/data? How do we do this, taking into account things such as our processes, action plans and improvement opportunities?
2. What types of criteria and methods do we use in the selection of appropriate sources for comparative information and data?
3. How effectively do we use comparative information obtained to set goals and/or stimulate innovation and creative thinking throughout the organization? How well have comparative data and information been used to improve our performance in achieving business results?
4. How well do we evaluate and improve our processes and methods relating to the organization's use of comparative data and information to keep up with our changing business needs and strategies?

4.3 ANALYSIS AND REVIEW OF ORGANIZATION PERFORMANCE

How effective are we at using data related to our overall performance, quality, customers, and financial results to manage and improve?　　　Score: ___ %

Clarifying questions:

1. What types of data are used? Are they adequate for our performance tracking and improvement needs? How they are systematically collected and analyzed?
2. How does the information obtained feed into our planning processes?
3. How are the data integrated and analyzed to assess our performance and improve our products/services?
4. How are the data used to improve business results?

4.4 Organization Culture

How well does our organization's culture foster knowledge sharing and knowledge leverage? To what extent do our senior managers encourage and model knowledge sharing and knowledge leverage practices and behaviors?

Score: ___ %

Clarifying questions:

1. To what extent do the leaders of the organization foster innovation, open dialogue, learning and knowledge sharing through the questions they ask, the direction they provide, and the actions they take?

2. How well do our compensation, and reward and recognition practices support and encourage knowledge sharing, knowledge reuse, and individual and joint learning?

3. To what extent do our senior managers establish and communicate behavioral expectations for knowledge sharing and knowledge reuse? To what extent do employees in the unit practice these behaviors?

4. To what extent is it "natural" for employees to share their knowledge and expertise, helping each other solve problems, make decisions, and take action?

4.5 INTERNAL KNOWLEDGE ACCESSIBILITY AND APPLICATION

How well do we learn from our work experiences and from each other? How well do we apply what have learned and what we already know inside the Sort VF, and from the rest of Intel?

Score: ___ %

Clarifying questions:

1. To what extent do we take the time to learn from past projects, decisions, or actions before we begin a new project or major task, take action or make decisions? To what extent do we learn from others across Intel who have faced similar issues? To what extent do we learn from experience and expertise outside of Intel? ("Learn Before")

2. How effective are we at understanding what we have already learned as we progress through an activity or project, and modifying our subsequent activities and work processes based on those learnings ("Learn During")?

3. How effective are we at taking the time after an action or project is completed to conduct a post mortem, and then making use of the learnings the next time we go through a similar activity or project ("Learn After")?

4. How well do we utilize dialogue and open debate to surface varied perspectives and expertise on issues and/or to stimulate innovation and creative thinking and problem solving?

5. How well do we share our knowledge with our customers and our suppliers to enhance our mutual productivity, performance and success?

6. To what extent do we have ready access to our own knowledge assets?

4.6 EXTERNAL KNOWLEDGE ACCESSIBILITY AND APPLICATION

How well do we make use of knowledge and expertise that is available outside   Score: ___ %
of Intel or about the external environment?

Clarifying questions:

1. How effectively do we disseminate customer and market knowledge to inform decisions and actions across the business unit?

2. How well do we learn from complaints? How effectively do we incorporate these learnings into what we do? How well do we share these learnings with others across Intel? Do we know who else could benefit from these learnings?

3. How effective and proactive are our follow up processes regarding products, services and recent transactions so we receive prompt, actionable feedback? What do we do with the feedback?

4. How well do we incorporate the use of knowledge and expertise from outside of Intel into our plans and decision making? Do we know what external knowledge sources could add value to what we do?

5. To what extent are suppliers and supplier knowledge included in new development, improvement activities, problem solving, and decision making?

4.7 KNOWLEDGE ACQUISITION AND PRESERVATION   Score: ___ %

How effectively do we understand and plan for our knowledge needs, acquire
that knowledge, and then preserve critical knowledge?

Clarifying questions:

1. To what extent do we understand and plan for the risk of loss of critical knowledge?

2. To what extent do we take staff profiles, potential retirements of key people, and our talent pool (backfilling and mentoring) into consideration during our business planning?

3. How well do we understand and plan for the knowledge and expertise needed to achieve strategic objectives?

4. To what extent do our plans adequately cover our knowledge needs and knowledge gaps?

5. How well do we understand what knowledge, skills, and competencies are necessary for effective performance?

5.1 WORK SYSTEMS

How effective is this organization at involving all employees in achieving our stated plans and goals via work design, recognition, and reward?   Score: ___ %

Clarifying questions:

1. How do we encourage employees to contribute? How do we design and manage our work processes consistent with our business and human resource plans, to encourage individual initiative, accountability, and responsibility?
2. How do we design and manage our work processes to encourage communication, cooperation, knowledge and skill sharing within the organization?
3. How well do we address the issues of flexibility, repaid response and learning relative to our customer, operational, and business requirements?
4. How effectively do our compensation, reward and recognition practices reinforce our values, objectives, performance improvements, and learning?

5.2 EMPLOYEE EDUCATION, TRAINING AND DEVELOPMENT

How effective is our organization at identifying the needs for delivering, reinforcing tracking and improving training and development opportunities in support of our plans and employees growth?   Score: ___ %

Clarifying questions:

1. What types of education, training and development opportunities are provided? How do we know that they are required for success of the business? The employee(s)?
2. How effectively do we address the needs of all levels of employees, including managers and supervisors?
3. How effective is the instructional design approaches that we use in transferring the knowledge or skills necessary? How well do we utilize employee and organizational feedback to improve our offerings and/or our designs?

5.3 EMPLOYEE WELL-BEING AND SATISFACTION

To what extent does our organization maintain a work environment and work climate that supports employee well-being, satisfaction and motivation?   Score: ___ %

Clarifying questions:

1. What are the specific ways in which safety, health and ergonomics are assured? Are there specific approaches to improve them? How are the results monitored?
2. How effectively are employees involved in the approaches? Are there feedback mechanisms?
3. What do we do that enhances our work climate for the well-being, satisfaction and motivation of all employees?
4. How effective are we at assessing and relating employee well-being, satisfaction and motivation results to business results?

6.1 MANAGEMENT OF PRODUCT AND SERVICE PROCESSES

How effectively do we design, implement, improve, manage, and deliver our products and services?　　　　　　　Score: ___ %

Clarifying questions:

1. How well do we incorporate changing customer and market requirements into our products and services. Changing technology?
2. How well are our product and service delivery processes designed to meet customer, quality, and operational performance requirements?
3. How do we evaluate and improve our product and service design and delivery processes?
4. How effectively do we manage our delivery processes to meet both customer and operation performance requirements?

6.2 MANAGEMENT OF SUPPORT PROCESSES

How effectively do we design, implement, manage, and improve our key support processes which enable the delivery of our main products and services?　　　　　　　Score: ___ %

Clarifying questions:

1. What processes are used to support the rest of the organization? Are there indicators and goals for these?
2. How are control mechanisms established for support processes and/or organizations? How are they improved? How do we know?

6.3 MANAGEMENT OF SUPPLIER PROCESSES

How effective are our supplier processes and relationships? How is performance measured, managed and improved?　　　　　　　Score: ___ %

Clarifying questions:

1. Is there a certification or qualification process? How is it designed, implemented, managed, and improved to meet performance requirements?
2. How are suppliers included in new development and appropriate improvement activities?
3. How are supplier performance and capabilities included in the organization planning activities?
4. How well do we manage the supplier relationship to enhance our mutual productivity, performance, and success?

7.1 CUSTOMER SATISFACTION RESULTS

What are the key customer satisfaction and dissatisfaction results and trends and how do these compare with other organizations and competitors?   Score: ___ %

Clarifying questions:

1. What measures are used to determine satisfaction? Dissatisfaction? What are the levels and trends?
2. Are the measurement timely, accurate and comprehensive to meet the needs of the business? How do we know?
3. How well do our results and performance compare with competitors or other appropriate comparisons?
4. Do we measure often enough to have leading indicators that will cause behavior changes in our organization?

7.2 ORGANIZATION FINANCIAL AND MARKET RESULTS

How well do our key performance measures meet short- and long-term plans and objectives?   Score: ___ %

How well do they compare with other appropriate organizations?

Clarifying questions:

1. What are the key measures of success?
2. Do they include both financial and market performance?
3. What are the levels and trends of these measures?
4. How well do these compare with competitor or other appropriate comparisons?

7.3 HUMAN RESOURCE RESULTS

What are the key human resource indicators, measurements and trends for this organization? How do they address employee well being, satisfaction, development, and work system performance?   Score: ___ %

Clarifying questions:

1. What are the critical measures that we use to determine the health of our people systems? How often are they measured?
2. What are the levels and trends in our measurements? How are employee satisfaction and dissatisfaction measures addressed? How well do these compare with competitors or other appropriate comparisons?

7.4 SUPPLIER RESULTS

What are the key supplier performance levels and trends for this organization?   Score: ____ %
How do these compare with performance expectation

Clarifying questions:
1.   What are the key measures for our suppliers?
2.   What are their levels and trends?
3.   How well do they compare with competitors or other appropriate
      comparisons

7.5 ORGANIZATION-SPECIFIC RESULTS

How well does our performance meet or exceed expectations and compare   Score: ____ %
with those of our competitors and other appropriate comparisons?

Clarifying questions:
1.   What are the key measures that we use for our products and services? What are their
      levels and trends? How well do they predict customer satisfaction or dissatisfaction? How
      do we know?
2.   How frequently do we measure product and service levels? What is done with these data
      and information?
3.   For these measures, how well do we compare with competitors or other appropriate
      comparisons?

How well does our performance meet or exceed expectations and compare
with those of our competitors and other appropriate comparisons?

Clarifying questions:

1.   What are the key measures that we use for our products and services?
2.   What are their levels and trends?
3.   How well do they predict customer satisfaction or dissatisfaction?
4.   How do we know?

▉ IT Organizational Survey

Table B.1   IT Organizational Assessment: Survey Form

Items	5 - Strongly agree	4 - Agree	3 - Neutral	2 - Disagree	1 - Strongly disagree
1. IT partners with its customers to understand their needs and mutually identify solutions.					
2. IT has a good reputation with its customers.					
3. Customers find it easy to do business with IT.					
4. IT provides support to help customers resolve their problems in a timely and efficient manner.					
5. IT services meet customer expectations for stability and performance.					
6. IT products and services give the firm a competitive advantage in the marketplace.					
7. IT delivers products and services on time.					
8. IT delivers products and services at a competitive cost.					
9. IT delivers products and services that satisfy functionality and quality requirements.					
10. I can efficiently find information I need using IT's standard communication channels.					
11. Sharing ideas and working together is encouraged across all IT areas.					
12. The people I work with cooperate professionally to get the job done.					
13. Global project teams work together effectively to meet the needs of customers in all regions.					
14. IT effectively communicates important information (*e.g.,* plans, status, changes) to its customers.					
15. IT's internal planning processes drive efficient use of resources and performance to financial targets.					
16. Projects in IT are well planned in terms of resources, responsibilities, and priorities.					

Table B.1 IT Organizational Assessment: Survey Form *(Continued)*

Items	5 - Strongly agree	4 - Agree	3 - Neutral	2 - Disagree	1 - Strongly disagree
17. IT partners with Intel's business groups to define corporate strategies and drive industry leadership.					
18. The work I do supports IT's strategic objectives.					
19. My team effectively uses indicators to measure performance.					
20. I am encouraged to come up with new and better ways of doing things.					
21. T balances risk and opportunity in making business decisions.					
22. I have the freedom to make decisions to get the job done.					
23. I am encouraged to contribute in decisions that define future direction of my work.					
24. New IT employees get the training and development they need to help them quickly contribute to the organization.					
25. IT anticipates and responds quickly to changes in business strategy and customer requirements.					
26. IT quickly adopts and leverages new technology to create solutions.					
27. IT uses repeatable processes and best known methods to promote speed and quality in product and service delivery.					
28. IT continually improves by learning from both successes and failures.					
29. IT responds quickly and effectively to crisis situations.					
30. When I do a good job, my accomplishments are recognized.					
31. My job has the flexibility needed to balance the demands of my work and personal life.					
32. I am encouraged to share my opinions and ideas with management and peers.					
33. As a company to work for, Intel compares favorably to other companies.					

Table B.1   IT Organizational Assessment: Survey Form *(Continued)*

Items	5 - Strongly agree	4 - Agree	3 - Neutral	2 - Disagree	1 - Strongly disagree
34. IT respects employees of different age, racial, sexual, cultural, religious, and ethnic backgrounds.					
35. My pay and benefits are appropriate for the job I do.					
36. The training I have received at Intel has provided the knowledge and skills needed to perform my job well.					
37. IT provides opportunities for professional development that prepare me for the future.					
38. IT and its employees make valuable contributions to our community.					
39. IT's safety program is effective in preventing incidents and raising employee awareness.					
40. IT employees conduct effective meetings.					
41. IT employees understand and perform to our corporate values.					
42. Throughout the year, I receive feedback from my manager that helps me develop my skills and improve my performance.					
43. My manager ensures our group's work is well planned and prioritized.					
44. I understand the criteria used to evaluate my performance.					
45. Promotions within IT are based on job performance, skills and experience.					
46. IT's suppliers are well managed and provide high quality and cost effective products and services.					

P-CMM-lite

Table B.2   P-CMM Assessment Criteria

0	Little evidence of the organization having a consistent way of performing its work.
	Work processes are ad hoc, constantly reinvented and frequently appear chaotic.
	Work is chronically over-committed.
10 - 30%	Organization has established a foundation on which it can deploy common processes across the organization.
	Repeatable processes in place.
	Managers are taking responsibility for their employees.
	(Practices can be repeated.)
40 - 60%	Organization has identified best practices and integrates into a common process.
	Organization identifies, documents, integrates, measures and collects best practices for analysis. The organization is well trained in these practices.
	Common culture becoming well defined.
	There is a person responsible for verifying that practices are conducted according to documented polices and addresses non-compliance.
	Executive management periodically reviews organization and resolves issues.
70 - 90%	Organization has started managing its processes through data and data are used to manage future performance.
	There is a person responsible for verifying that practices are conducted according to documented polices and addresses non-compliance.
	Executive management periodically reviews organization and resolves issues.
	(Variations in performing best practices are reduced.)
90%+	Organization uses its quantitative knowledge to make continuous improvements of its processes; change management is a standard organizational process.
	There is a person responsible to verify practices are conducted according to documented polices and addresses non-compliance.
	Executive management periodically reviews the organization and resolves issues.
	(Practices are continuously improved to enhance their capability.)

■ IT Business Value Maturity Assessment

Table B.3   IT Business Value Maturity Test

	5 - Strongly agree	4 - Agree	3 - Neutral	2 - Disagree	1 - Strongly disagree
A. Managing for IT Business Value					
1. A standard business case template for reviewing proposed investments is in place (including lifetime costs of supporting the solution).					
2. A formal set of proposal valuation criteria that maps to key business variables is deployed.					
3. A standard methodology for managing approved projects is in place (i.e. Program Governance, Project Office).					
4. A methodology that validates, tracks and manages benefits realization is in place (i.e. Investment Governance).					
5. IT project managers and business managers are jointly held accountable for delivering results and business value.					
6. A Total Cost of Ownership (TCO) tracking system is in place.					
7. A formal portfolio management approach with pre-defined investment categories and allocation mix is in place.					
8. A formal investment decision making body/committee with funding authority is in place.					
9. Advanced Investment Techniques are used to analyze and improve IT business value.					

	5 - Strongly agree	4 - Agree	3 - Neutral	2 - Disagree	1 - Strongly disagree
B. Managing the IT Budget					
1. A structured IT cost reduction program is in place.					
2. Financial performance with respect to budgets is predictable and within the variance range.					
3. Systematic cost management and cost reduction systems are in place (e.g. supplier management, service levels models, discretionary, etc.).					
4. An ability to create strategic funding buffers to invest in new IT solutions exists.					
5. IT cost structure is understood and benchmarked against industry best practices.					
6. Capital Expenditure (CapEx) and Operational Expenditure (OpEx) are appropriately matched.					
7. The right balance is achieved between development spending and maintenance spending for your firm.					
8. The IT Organization has a sustainable economic model for its budget.					

Table B.3 IT Business Value Maturity Test *(Continued)*

C. Managing the IT Capability	5 - Strongly agree	4 - Agree	3 - Neutral	2 - Disagree	1 - Strongly disagree
1. Integrated IT organizational capability assessment methodologies are in place (e.g. organizational quality).					
2. Formal customer survey processes are in placed and are acted upon.					
3. Systematic workforce development programs are in place (e.g. training, upskilling, etc.).					
4. A comprehensive organizational competency management system is in place.					
5. A flexible modular architecture which enables speed in developing new applications is in place.					
6. IT customers perceive IT as a strategic partner or capability.					
7. A high level of trust exists between the business and the IT organization.					
8. IT delivers a steady stream of solutions which provide competitive advantage to the firm.					
9. A systematic innovation management and measurement system is in place.					

D. Running IT as a Business	5 - Strongly agree	4 - Agree	3 - Neutral	2 - Disagree	1 - Strongly disagree
1. A high level of Business and IT alignment exists.					
2. IT Governance structure exists and is clearly known across business and IT.					
3. A flexible resource redeployment mechanism to address changing business priorities is in place.					
4. An effective Products and Services cost benchmarking process is in place.					
5. A comprehensive customer segmentation process is in place.					
6. A formal IT customer relationship management system is in place (e.g. feedback, account management, service and support, etc.).					
7. A robust automated asset management system is in place.					
8. A responsive demand and consumption management system is in place.					
9. A comprehensive performance monitoring and management system is in place.					
10. An effective customer billing and chargeback process is in place.					

References

Agarwal, R., and V. Sambamurthy. 2002. "The Innovation Edge: Organization Design Models for the IT Function." Working Paper, University of Maryland, September

Agarwal, R. and V. Sambamurthy. 2002. "Principles and Models for Organizing the IT Function." *MIS Quarterly Executive*, Vol. 1, No 1. March.

Andreesen, M. 2002. "Sidestepping the new IT crisis." *Tech News/ CNET.com*, December.

Austin, Rob (2003). Quoted in Hoffman, T. "Cutter Conference Debates IT Governance Models, Techniques." *Computerworld*, April 30.

Barney, J. B. 1991. "Firm Resources and Sustained Competitive Advantage." *Journal of Management*, 17:1.

Beath, C. and J. Ross. 2001. "Beyond the Business Case: Strategic IT Investment. MIT Sloan, Center for Information Systems Research (CISR).Working Paper #323. October.

Bloor, R. 2002. "Fast ROI." *Bloor Research Report*, June.

Botwinik, S., B. Cameron, E. Boynton, and C. Dawe. 2001. "Making Technology Decisions Count." MA: *Forrester Research*, Inc., September.

Brynjolfsson, E. 2003. "The IT Productivity Gap" *Optimize Magazine*, Issue 21, July.

Brynjolfsson, E. and L. M. Hitt. 2003. Computing Productivity: Firm-level Evidence. MIT Sloan, Center for Information Systems Research (CISR). Working Paper No. 4210-01.

Brynjolfsson, E. and L. Hitt (in press). Computing Productivity: Firm-level Evidence. *Review of Economics and Statistics.*

Busch, D. 1999. Plan 2000 Presentation. Intel Internal Document, September

Cappuccio, D., B. Keyworth, and W. Kirwin. 1996. *Total Cost of Ownership: The Impact of System Management Tools.* Gartner Group.

Carr, N. 2003. "IT Doesn't Matter." *Harvard Business Review.* MA: Harvard Business School Press. May.

Cosgrove, L. 2001. "Measuring IT Alignment." *CIO Magazine*, April.

Christensen, C. M. 1997. *The Innovator's Dilemma: When New Technologies Cause Great Firms to Fail.* MA: Harvard Business School Press.

Christensen, C. M. and M. Raynor. 2003. *The Innovator's Solution: Creating and Sustaining Successful Growth.* MA: Harvard Business School Press.

Curley, M. 1998. "Diffusion Intrabay: Measuring the Business Value of Intel's first Intrabay." MBS Thesis, Graduate School of Business, University College Dublin.

Curley, M. 1999. The Business Value Index: Prioritizing IT Investments. Intel Internal Documents, September.

Curtis, B., B. Hefley, and S. Miller. 2001. *People Capability Maturity Model. (P-CMM) Version 2.0.* CMU/SEI-2001-MM-001. Carnegie Mellon Software Engineering Institute (SEI). Available online at *www.sei.cmu.edu.*

Dedrick, J., V. Gurbaxani, and K. L. Kraemer. 2002. "Information technology and economic performance: A critical review of the empirical evidence." University of California, Irvine, Center for Research in IT and Organizations (CRITO). November.

Dempsey, J., R. E. Dvorak, E. Holen, D. Mark, and W. F. Meehan III. 1997. "Escaping the IT Abyss." *The McKinsey Quarterly*, Number 4.

Drucker, P. 1963. "Managing for Business Effectiveness." *Harvard Business Review*, May-June.

Drucker, P. 1994. "The Theory of the Business." *Harvard Business Review*, September.

Freedman, M. 2002. "Technology Confidence Barometer." NOP World Analyst Report.

Gantz, J. 2003. Personal communication.

Gibson, C. and B. B. Jackson. 1987. *The Information Imperative.* Lexington Books.

Haas, K. 2003. It Business Value Program: Year-End Program Documentation 2002. Internal Intel Document, February.

Hammer, M. 1990. "Reengineering Work: Don't Automate, Obliterate." *Harvard Business Review.* July/August.

Hartman, A. 2002. "Why Tech Falls Short of Expectations." *Optimize Magazine*, Issue #9. July.

Haydamack, C. 2003. IT Business Service Portfolio Management for Plan 2004, Intel Internal Document, September.

Holden, J. 1999. *World Class Selling.* NY: John Wiley and Sons.

Ireland, J. and B. Tucker. 2002. "Enterprise Mobility." Intel white paper, available online at *www.intel.com/business/bss/infrastructure/mobility/enterprise_mobility.htm*.

Jeffery, M. and I. Leliveld. 2003. "IT Portfolio Management Changes and Best Practices." Kellogg School of Management. Available online at *www.kellogg.nwu.edu/faculty/jeffery/htm/publication/ITPM_Study.pdf.*

Jorion, P. 2000. *Value at Risk: The New Benchmark for Managing Financial Risk*. McGraw-Hill.

Jorgenson, D. 2001. "Information Technology and the U.S. Economy." *American Economic Review,* 91:1, 1-32.

Kaplan, R. S. and D. P. Norton. 1996. *The Balanced Scorecard: Translating Strategy into Action.* MA: Harvard Business School Press.

Kenneally, J. and Y. Lichtenstein. 2001. "The Optional Value of IS Projects." University College Dublin, May.

King, Julia. 2003. "Survey shows common IT woes persist." *Computerworld*. June.

Kirkpatrick, T. A. 2002. "Research: CIOs Speak on ROI." *CIO Insight*.

Martin, P. 2003. Presentation at StorageTek Forum.

Matthews, P. 1999. "Bring your applications to Life." *Information Systems Executive Exchange*. Dublin. June.

Mayall, A. 2003. IT Seminar in Dublin. CSC Research Services.

McGrath, R. G. and I. MacMillan. 2000. *The Entrepreneurial Mindset*. MA: Harvard Business School Press.

META Group. 2001. "IT Portfolio Management: Sustaining Proactive Business Alignment." December.

Mooney, J., K. Kraemer, and V. Gurbaxani. 1994. "A Process Oriented Framework for Assessing the Business Value of Information Technology." University of California, Irvine, Center for Research in IT and Organizations (CRITO). April 12.

Moore, G. 1965. "Cramming more components onto integrated circuits." *Electronics*, 38:8. April.

Moore, G. 1991. *Crossing the Chasm: Marketing and Selling High-Tech Products to Mainstream Customers*. HarperBusiness.

Morton, C. 1998. *Beyond World Class*. U.K: Macmillan Press.

Olson, M. and B. Woodul. 2003. "IT Chargeback System." Intel white paper, available online at *intel.com/business/bss/infrastructure/managing/chargeback.htm*.

Owen, S., R. Nannapaneni, M. McKain, and J. Smith. 2003. "Examining IT Business Process at Intel." Intel white paper, available online at *intel.com/business/bss/infrastructure/managing/examine_process.pdf*.

Pope, T. 2001. "ROI in Intel's eBusiness Group." Internal Intel document.

Reese, K. 2003. Intel internal intranet article.

Ross, J. W. 2003. "Creating a Strategic IT Architecture competency: Learning in Stages." MIT Sloan, Center for Information Systems Research (CISR).Working Paper #335.

Ross, J. W. and C. M. Beath. 2001. "Beyond the Business Case: Strategic IT Investment." MIT Sloan, Center for Information Systems Research (CISR).Working Paper #323.

Ross, J. W., C. M. Beath, and D. L. Goodhue. 1996. "Developing Long-Term Competitiveness through Information Technology Assets." Sloan Management Review, Vol. 38, Fall.

Schmidt, M. "Cost of Ownership Analysis (TCO)." White paper by Solution Matrix, Ltd., available online at *www.solutionmatrix.com/tcogo.html.*

Solow, R. 1987. "We'd better watch out." *New York Times*, July 12.

Tallon, P. 2002. "Beyond TCO—Designing Storage Strategies through 'Value at Risk.'" Boston College.

Tallon, P., Kraemer, K., and Gurbaxani, V. 2000. "Executive perspectives on the business value of information technology." *Journal of Management Information Systems,* 16:4.

Tucker, B. 2002. "Linking Productivity Gains to Return on Investment." Intel white paper, available online at *http://intel.com/business/bss/infrastructure/wireless/roi/productivity_gains.htm.*

Violino, B. 1997. "Return on Investment." *Information Week*, June 30.

Weill, P. 1992. "The relationship between IT and firm performance: A study of the valve manufacturing sector." *Information Systems Research* 3:4.

Weill, P. and M. Broadbent. 1998. *Leveraging the New Infrastructure: How Market Leaders Capitalize on Information Technology.* MA: Harvard Business School Press.

Weill, P. and C. Foglia. 2003. Research Briefing. MIT Sloan, Center for Information Systems Research (CISR).

Weill, P., and R. Woodham. 2002. "Don't Just Lead, Govern: Implementing Effective IT Governance." MIT Sloan, Center for Information Systems Research (CISR). Working Paper #326. April.

Working Council for CIOs. 2002. "Responsive IT Portfolio Prioritization." Fall.

Working Council for CFOs. 2003. "Improving the Yield on Information Technology."

Index